ON THIS HOLY ISLAND

ON THIS HOLY ISLAND

A MODERN PILGRIMAGE ACROSS BRITAIN

OLIVER SMITH

PEGASUS BOOKS

NEW YORK LONDON

ON THIS HOLY ISLAND

Pegasus Books, Ltd.
148 West 37th Street, 13th Floor
New York, NY 10018

ISBN: 978-1-63936-841-9

10 9 8 7 6 5 4 3 2 1

Printed in the United States of America
Distributed by Simon & Schuster
www.pegasusbooks.com

CONTENTS

Prologue

I made myself a promise – if I lost my job, I would walk the Camino de Santiago. I pictured the revolving doors of a grey office spinning to reveal silver estuaries and snowy cordilleras. I imagined I would carry my cardboard box of redundancy clutter – my hole punch, my desk lamp – across Galician pine forests, into meadows where my footsteps roused clouds of butterflies. Into walled towns where bells of ancient bronze rang from high towers. I would nap in the shade of a monastery cloister, using my P45 as a pillow.

'Santiago' stood for St James – whose relics were stored in the cathedral of Santiago de Compostela. Of more interest to me was 'Compostela', which, someone had once told me, meant 'field of stars'. I imagined the Camino as a cosmic path – whose constellations would light a way forward.

When I eventually did lose my job, international borders had slammed shut. The ashrams of India, the shamans of Amazonia – all faraway places that promised transcendence were also out of reach. All that was on offer was our own familiar island (and a few lesser islands along its fringes). 'Pilgrimage' here in Britain conjured up images of earnest TV presenters in woolly jumpers striding across muddy fields. By the time I finished writing this book, I understood here, too, one could find paths of transcendence. Ideas of pilgrimage could be powerful. They took wildly diverse forms.

The story of pilgrimage in Great Britain might be explained as a pathway. In prehistory the path is out of sight (though its course might be guessed at). From the first centuries of Christianity, the path began a gentle uphill climb as new saints found their station in the landscape. After the end of the first millennium (when everyone was relieved the world didn't end in the Earth's thousandth year) cathedrals soared, shrines flourished – this was a time when the pilgrim pathways climbed high, and everyone trod the trail. Chaucer wrote a poem about it. It dipped, then dropped off a cliff edge after the Reformation – when pilgrimage was outlawed in the reign of Henry VIII, the shrines were demolished and the paths became overgrown. They never scaled the same giddy heights again. In the nineteenth and twentieth centuries there were small undulations in the path: revivals and rediscoveries. In the twenty-first century the path has braided into a series of trails of diverse meanings, no longer wholly tied to Christianity. Nor, necessarily, even to religion. To make a pilgrimage now was to embark on a journey of meaning that anyone could define on their own terms – it was this new era that interested me.

I did not belong to any religion. Rather, my faith was in the road. I had worked most of my career as a salaried travel writer for a publishing company. The company started in the 1970s when a couple met on a London park bench, decided to drive a Mini Countryman into Asia and write a book about it. It was a time when buses painted with rainbows were trundling along the old Silk Road taking a new generation on their journeys of enlightenment. On the way, passengers slept in the cave churches of Cappadocia, conversed with holy men beside the Ganges, stepped into the mossy temple gardens of Bali. They hired writers who pressed the ejector seat on a sensible life to obey the dip and turn of that open road. These writers became high priests of a new kind of travel: the guidebooks they wrote were called 'bibles' and sold millions, they affirmed there was something transformative (even sacred) in the ritual of travel. Some, apparently, wore kaftans. By the time I arrived there was still a dreamcatcher on an office wall. But the world was changing.

The planet had long been mapped, but the internet now put everywhere under the surveillance of social media. So too travellers themselves had been mapped: their tastes predicted and their journeys steered by algorithm. The last dimension unchartered was an inward one – those journeys of the soul that could not be pinned down by coordinates or measured in miles. I had been fortunate enough to travel all over the world in my career. What interested me now were those places that promised a kind of travel beyond what could be charted on an ink or pixel map.

This book charts ideas of pilgrimage across time and landscape – from a Palaeolithic burial in a sea cave to modern music festivals – via holy wells, holy mountains, and above all holy islands. It profiles pilgrimage places that are pagan, Christian and secular, and some sites other faiths have marked out in the British landscape. I often heard them described as 'thin places' – where the membrane between the mundane and metaphysical was thin. The people you met there were, in some way, 'thin' too: their barriers were down, they were quick to tell their story. Meeting them was what spurred me on. So often, the unfurling of a path went in tandem with the unravelling of a human heart.

Their theories of pilgrimage were diverse: some sought to express devotion to God in footfalls, to accrue a kind of merit like air miles. For some pilgrimage was necessarily a solitary endeavour, though others sought the company of others by their side (both the living and the imagined dead). Pilgrimage could be done in celebration or in grief. It could have a fixed destination, or no destination at all. For some, time in nature and exercising their bodies was enough. Others hoped their journeys would be matched by some symmetry in another dimension. One sunny day, under the spire of Chichester Cathedral, I met a widow who had made pilgrimages to Lindisfarne, Canterbury and Kildare. 'By walking,' she told me, 'I mean to turn my body into a prayer.'

My own theory was that pilgrimage might have pre-dated organized religion – that it rested on an original truth: there were signposts to be heeded on every journey (big and small), to help you navigate in the far greater mileage of a lifetime. This is not a memoir of a troubled soul hoping to be fixed by the road. Nor is it about re-enacting the journeys of the Middle Ages. It is not a definitive catalogue of pilgrimage destinations – but a personal selection of journeys that you might perhaps choose to undertake yourself. It is a very modern pilgrimage: of ancient paths but also of Gore-Tex, of sacred spaces and also of Welcome Breaks and Ginsters pasties along the way. Writing its chapters was like coming up for air in the course of a busy life. It is an effort to understand what sets some places apart, what draws some people to them. It is a portrait of places which are themselves mirrors to the human soul.

And it is also an effort to locate here, in my own country, that longed-for feeling – of escaping into bright morning light, on a path named for the stars.

A Causeway

A Pilgrimage of the Tides

Flood Tide | Ebb Tide | Changing Tide

Causeway – a tidal shelter on the Pilgrims' Way

FLOOD TIDE

I awoke from my nap in a garden shed.

It looked like a brand-new shed – like one you might purchase from B&Q – about 6 feet by 4 feet, with a single window, and a diamond shape marking the apex of a felt roof. Its exterior had been painted a smart off-white that hinted at suburbia. The interior timbers (more unusually) had been done out in racing green. A shed, I know, can be a deeply personal space, with room for a single soul to retreat, potter about and store tools and items for all seasons and contingencies. Somewhere to think and make plans. But this shed was an unusual one. I reached for the stainless-steel bolt. A northerly wind helped carry open the door, to reveal the churning sea outside.

This shed was surrounded on all sides by the sea – perched on four concrete posts that raised it ten feet over the breaking waves. Fourteen wooden steps led down to the waterline (whitewater slopped over the last three). The nearest dry land was visible about half a mile away. This shed hovered alone over the North Sea with the surrealness of a Dalí composition or a Pink Floyd album cover. Many of the people who had been here before me had arrived in a state of panic, and finding myself stranded here brought a beat of fear to my heart. But that anxiety stilled as hours passed, as I looked out of the window, watched the tide unspool around the concrete posts and heard the oystercatchers squawk, the seals bark and rain patter on the roof of that shed out in the sea. High water passed: so did a storm. I saw a single spur of lightning on the horizon and counted: one, two, three, four, five miles. It didn't come again.

Sheds were normally places of clutter. This was one in which you might come to de-clutter your mind. To spend hours trapped in simple rapture at the sea, the sky and all creation. I had snuck into the shed some hours earlier at low tide – to deliberately maroon myself as the sea advanced, and taste some of its strange saltwater solitude. I had been careful no one spotted me entering, in case any rescue attempts were launched – more than anything else, I did not want to be saved.

The shed in the sea had many names: some locals on social media called it 'the idiot hut' on account of those people who ended up using it. Most people knew it as 'the refuge box'. It stood midway across the causeway that linked mainland Britain and Lindisfarne – a three-mile-long island just off the north-eastern shoulder of England. Lindisfarne was also known as Holy Island: it had two names and two selves. For most of the day a thin umbilical cord of tarmac linked it with the rest of Great Britain and a steady stream of cars whooshed back and forth. Twice a day, for five to seven hours, it became a true island: the sea swept over the road and submerged it to a depth of between 1.5 and 4 metres (on a spring tide). In the nineteenth century there had been proposals for a railway to cross the strait. At a recent community meeting one single islander had voiced their support for a road bridge. Everyone else wanted to keep their tidal moat and the fleeting insularity it bestowed.

This was understandable. Six hundred and fifty thousand tourists came to the island every year. Lindisfarne had for centuries been one of Britain's major places of pilgrimage – Christian pilgrims remained part of that flow, along with unconscious pilgrims who solicited other meanings from its nature and history. It was famous as an early beacon of Christianity: a place modern visitors connected with an origin story of England. There were B & Bs, pubs, gift shops. There was also the twice-daily spectacle of the vanishing causeway: an ice cream van regularly served an audience who gathered at the moving waterline on the mainland side, watching the sea close in as it might have done behind Moses.

I could see the ice cream van in the distance that day I marooned myself in the shed. Every so often I saw the driver leave his Mr Whippy machine to slip the clutch and inch his tyres from the flood. Before the melting of the Ice Age, Lindisfarne had itself been a part of Great Britain which, in turn, had been a peninsula of mainland Europe – visitors could see this little island reborn, just as its big neighbour had been seven millennia before. Then the visitors finished their ice creams, took a last glance at the shed in the sea and went home. Most of them did, anyway.

It happened about ten times a year, according to the staff at RNLI Seahouses, the lifeboat station about ten miles away. It was occasionally walkers. But mostly it was cars. If it was high summer, high tide and their pagers went off, they could pretty much guarantee it was a callout from someone stuck on the causeway (such cases accounted for about a third of all launches from RNLI Seahouses). A few groups were susceptible: men in flashy 4×4s showing off, people from inland cities (including someone who thought the tide only came in at night). A Korean corporate executive and some Swiss equestrians had also fallen victim. Some made the mistake of following locals who were experts at timing a safe crossing to the last second. Miscalculation, ignorance and hubris lured people into the deep water.

Over the course of many conversations I had pieced together what generally happened. The trick to a successful crossing was to drive slowly and steadily: to create a bow wave that carved a path through the sea. It seemed laughable when water pooled in the footwell: real fear came when saltwater got into the fuel intake and your engine spluttered to death. At this point you had a decision: whether you should abandon the vehicle while there was still time, open the doors before the pressure from the rising water outside became too much to push against. Panic set in once manuals went soggy in your glove compartment. One woman screamed endlessly – a long continuous note – until she went hoarse. One man instinctively kept his foot jammed on a busted accelerator as his leg disappeared underwater. Electrical systems were quickly compromised: recently there had been the case of a submerged VW whose windscreen wipers started going off, the electric boot mechanism was triggered and luggage floated out to sea. In the words of Linda at AJK Thompson – a local company who specialize in recovering vehicles from this black spot – 'some cars on the causeway suddenly have a mind of their own.' She added they were almost always a write-off.

Someone had once lost their wedding dress in the boot of a drowned car.

Midway on their crossing, motorists found themselves confronted by a force that was almighty and irrevocable. Twenty-first-century cars offered no protection against that ongoing accumulation of water – nor did the reassurance of 650,000 annual visitors to Lindisfarne do anything to mitigate that deluge. They had by then, by unusual means, joined a fraternity of people lost in deep water, witnessing how flimsy a human life seemed against the immense extent of an unravelling sea.

Some climbed onto the roof of their car. Others felt relief as the RNLI arrived in their D-class lifeboat. Many saw a funny-looking shed on stilts at the deepest point of the causeway – just within wading distance – and set out towards it as a last resort. Close by was the ruined priory at Lindisfarne, where medieval pilgrims had gathered: but in its own way, this little garden shed was another building concerned with the salvation of souls on their journey, the fate of pilgrims on the road. It had saved countless lives. No one had drowned on the causeway as long as anyone could remember, which, even the RNLI agreed, seemed almost miraculous.

EBB TIDE

When the tide went out, I left the shed and plodded back to the mainland. That night I found a grassy bank on the shore, and slept under a starry sky. The next morning I set out to walk all the way to Lindisfarne at low tide.

Also setting out that day was Bradley. He had brought three Buddhas with him to Lindisfarne. One sat on the dashboard of his Citroën Picasso (under a dangling air freshener). Another was stuffed in a recess of the passenger door among the CDs. A third he placed in the pocket of his shorts as he left his car on the mainland. I asked if they were Tibetan Buddhas. He said no: they were Buddhas from Poundland.

'I'm not a Buddhist, not really,' he said. 'But maybe I am? I'll take everything. I've got all the loopholes covered!'

Craig Bradley went by the name of Bradley. He was a poet: wavy grey hair fell to his shoulders, and his Yorkshire accent travelled on the wind. He was on a pilgrimage of a kind. It was a few days short of his 59th birthday: to mark the occasion he and his partner, Nicky, had come from Halifax to walk the Pilgrims' Way.

The tarmac causeway had been completed in the 1950s, crossing the strait and taking a wriggly route along the Lindisfarne peninsula known as the Snook. Before that, pedestrians made a beeline three miles across an intertidal zone to the island's only village – moving quickly whenever a portal opened. This original route over the mudflats was the Pilgrims' Way. The word 'pilgrim' comes from the Latin *peregrinus* (*per* meaning 'through', and *ager* meaning 'a field', or 'land'). In this particular case it was ill-fitting: Google Maps showed the Pilgrims' Way striking into the blue. It was a footpath across the sea.

Bradley, Nicky and I passed by the refuge box, unlaced our boots and strode barefoot onto the expanse of squelchy mud. To cross the Pilgrims' Way successfully you needed to seek an alignment – like turning a key in a lock – ensuring hours of daylight coincided with an ebb tide, good weather and good visibility. It was Bradley's fourth attempt: previous efforts had been thwarted by a dodgy ankle and heavy rain. He had recently had bad luck with his health: a transient ischaemic attack, which was a temporary blockage of blood to the brain. This seemed to make the journey more urgent.

'This time I'll swim it if I have to,' he said.

It was a sunlit morning – a few clouds floated distinct against a blue sky, casting islands of shadow onto the mudflats around us. One last notice offered warnings and dissuasions for anyone attempting to walk the route. Soon we were following a line of upright posts, placed apart at distances of about 25 metres, marking the way for anyone lost in sudden fog. At the foot of the posts little pools had formed, brimful with cockles. We pushed on, the mud crusting between our toes. There were other shelters erected in the same spirit as the refuge box on the road – rickety, treehouse-like structures with birdshit and algae on their platforms. But mostly there was wide open space, scuttling crabs and Arctic tern. Our mood was exalted. The dawdling waters of the newly departed tide reflected the clouds above – the mudflats were like an antique mirror, the glass blemished by the casts of lugworms. When the wind blew, you might have imagined yourself a kite, soaring over the clouds underfoot. Bradley was thinking about the generations of pilgrims who walked the path before us, whose footprints were swept clean every few hours. A few strides ahead of him was Nicky: her bright red hair standing out against the endless blues of the causeway. She said you had to constantly look where to put your feet.

'It's like juggling,' she said. 'All you can do is be there, do this. The next post is your goal. Our lives are crowded with all sorts of media. Our heads are full of rubbish. This simplifies everything.'

It was St Aidan who had chosen the island of Lindisfarne as a place for his monastery in AD 635. These tides meant there were hours when monks could go out into the world to spread the word and also hours when they were left alone to pray. Aidan is said to have travelled only on foot, so he would have known the feel of this mud. To cross the mudflats was to align weather, light and tide, but it brought about an inner alignment too: a personal rebalancing. The outgoing tide could be an exhale of breath, carrying with it stress. The incoming tide would submerge the path – a pilgrim could close a door behind them.

Around an hour later we arrived on Lindisfarne, towelling the mud off our feet. We had nearly completed our pilgrimage to the Holy Island. The act of pilgrimage is seen as having the symmetry of a life: with its beginning and its end. Here we were nearing our finishing line: our Jerusalem, our paradise. An end in which we would be reborn.

The main issue on Lindisfarne was parking: the Northumberland County Council car park charged £6 for three hours – but tourists were prone to going rogue and parking in residents' spaces in the village instead. At the Lindisfarne Heritage Centre a local was arguing with a family from Leeds whose Volvo was blocking a cottage driveway. Fifteen islanders had to somehow find space to park on that little street, the local remonstrated – 'fifteen', she said again, but more slowly this time. Lindisfarne struggled under a tidal wave of visitors. Not long ago islanders fought off the intrusion of Larry the Land Train – a neon-green vehicle of the kind seen at theme parks, intended to shuttle visitors between the attractions. For now everyone coped without it: tourists in Berghaus fleeces bumbled about the tiny village, buying souvenir tea towels from the gift shops. We found the priory: it cost £9.50 to enter (English Heritage members went free). Bradley, Nicky and I went to a café instead. We ordered coffees and sausage rolls.

'There's too many people,' said Bradley, wiping something off his spectacles. 'Too much tat for sale.'

The Buddha never came out of his pocket. Tourism was prone to destroying the things it celebrated: that much was nothing new. The solitude had been fragile for St Aidan and his successor as bishop, St Cuthbert. Those early British saints emulated the first Christian hermits of the Egyptian desert in craving silence: remote places where they could hear God's voice more clearly. When the hubbub of Lindisfarne, its priory and its pilgrims got too much for them, they retreated sometimes to the island of Inner Farne (which is roughly the size of eight football pitches), eight miles away, and at other times to the offshore islet now named St Cuthbert's Island (which has a patch of turf slightly smaller than a bowling green). On Inner Farne, Cuthbert enclosed himself in a cell surrounded by high walls so he might only see the sky. There his solitude would be more pristine. It was a retreat from a retreat. A structure for a single soul. But Inner Farne was closed to visitors now because of avian flu. St Cuthbert's Island was itself already full of tourists.

Bradley, Nicky and I talked about the peace of the mudflats: we wondered if our pilgrimage was more about the journey than the destination. This was the kind of crappy truism you found on motivational posters, but that day on Lindisfarne it seemed appropriate. We left the café. And soon after I left the paradise of Lindisfarne and walked alone back onto the purgatory of the Pilgrims' Way. Out in the distance was the structure known as the refuge box or the idiot hut – another structure ideal for a single soul, which at that moment in time felt more holy than anywhere on the Holy Island.

CHANGING TIDE

The refuge box – in its current form – was actually brand new, installed in April 2023. It turned out that it was not an off-the-shelf garden shed but had been built to order by Lindsay Miller, a joiner at Northumberland County Council. A previous incarnation had been there for decades but had become rotten – the last straw came when Storm Arwen shucked a plank off the side in November 2021. Lindsay built an identical one from scratch in the council depot in Berwick upon Tweed. It took him three weeks: he used four coats of marine paint, expected the thing would last about 50 years (give or take). It was an honour to build it, he told me. The new refuge box was transported and installed one Friday evening by Peter Blewitt, a contractor from Morpeth. (It was important to him too: he persuaded the council to delay the job until he was back from his holidays.)

'I just imagined the people inside, waiting to be rescued,' he told me on the phone. He had family on the island.

Peter sawed off the bolts and took the old one home on the back of his lorry. His dad now uses it as a shed to grow tomatoes. It was late when I found myself once again in Lindsay's new shed, watching the stilts submerge and the darkening sea begin its slow crawl to shore. As the water rose, the mirror lost its blemishes and blots, its surface becoming more perfect as the sandbanks submerged. Pilgrimage is a contract between a traveller and a landscape – an equation whose sum might be counted in another realm. Such an otherworld seemed near that day, amid the endless reflections of the causeway and the fathoms of that ever-deepening sea.

The shed itself was featureless – or almost featureless. In the floor was a hole the size of a large coin – ostensibly there to drain water but also a peephole to the waters below. I crouched on the floor, pressed my eyes to the hole, looked down into the writhing liquid, black as oil. On the wall was an old BT telephone – with no dial or buttons – that would connect you only to emergency services. It made me think of the saint in his lonely cell a few miles away, waiting to hear just one voice.

The last evening light departed. The faint lamps of boats inched out, departing the Firth of Forth. To the west, the streak of a late Edinburgh express lit up the East Coast Mainline, the silhouettes of the Cheviot foothills rising beyond it. To the east was the island of Lindisfarne, its visitors gone, looking more beautiful now, the night wind skimming the dunes and the marram grass. All around it now was the soft song of the sea, which held the island again in its temporary embrace. Looking out from the shed, low tide felt like a lifetime ago. It was hard to believe it had ever been any other way.

Only just visible across the water was the church of St Mary the Virgin. The Reverend Canon Dr Sarah Hills was the vicar here: she later explained to me that the ebb and flow of the tide went in tandem with the ebb and flow of prayer in her island parish. She also said that there was also something significant about timing a journey over the foreshore.

'In making that pilgrimage across the sands, you've allowed yourself to become vulnerable,' she told me. 'There is something about the vastness of the sands around you. The knowledge that the sea, when it comes, will come very quickly – and you can do nothing about it. Creation can get you. The thing about Christianity is: if we're in control, it doesn't work. If we try to box in God, that's not how it ought to be.'

Lindisfarne's monks turned the tide from paganism to Christianity in northern Britain. But now, almost a millennium and a half later, the tide had turned again – with dwindling congregations in churches, a diminishing pattern of services, the steady retreat of Christian worship across Britain. We were only a few generations into this ebb tide. It was not clear what low water would look like, or if this tide would ever turn again in the future. When any tide retreats there is an absence, but also a presence – a ghost of what was there before, lingering in rock pools, in glistening mud and sand. In channels that tell of its path of retreat, which might also be a path of advance.

And for reasons not easily explained, more people of no explicit faith – like Bradley and Nicky – made their pilgrimages to Lindisfarne, were lured here by its geography. The island's lessons were many and profound. Its tidal rhythms invited associations with heaven and earth, of two places sometimes linked but somehow separate from each other. High tide saw Lindisfarne become its own true landmass: the creation of that island seemed to stand for an entire world coming into being. And, whatever your belief in creation or an afterlife, there was wisdom to be found on that causeway, on whose course – like a human life – you had a finite amount of time.

Hours later I readied myself for my final departure from the shed. A reflected shooting star sparked in a puddle. There were no more lights out on the horizon now: no more ships at sea. I had chosen Lindisfarne as a starting point for a series of pilgrimages around Great Britain for a reason. Though people generally considered the causeway to be a gateway to Lindisfarne, coming from the east (as seafarers often had) this was a gateway to the British mainland. The shed in the sea was a watchtower for this kingdom, standing guard beside its tidal moat.

Ahead of me lay this great sleeping island – black and vast, of drawn curtains and dimmed streetlights, lone truckers on the dual carriageways, lone foxes in moonlit fields. Up close it might have been prosaic. From the perspective of the causeway it had a new sheen of mystery. Out of sight, rolling farmland rose to Pennine moorlands, which – much farther still – fell away before a second, wilder sea.

Somewhere far away on this western shore of Britain was another place guarded by tides: a place that might have lured pilgrims before Cuthbert or Aidan stood on Lindisfarne. Indeed, before Lindisfarne or Great Britain were islands themselves.

2

A Cave

A Palaeolithic Pilgrimage

Peninsula Country | The Reverend and His Quests |
The Climb In | The Red Lady of Paviland |
Palaeolithic Pilgrimage | At Bedtime | An Imagined Journey |
The Druid's Vigil | The Next Flood

Cave – the entrance to Paviland Cave

PENINSULA COUNTRY

At the north-western edge of Europe a series of peninsulas fray out into the Atlantic. When I was a kid, I had a laminated map of the continent Blu-Tacked to the wall beside my bed. After bedtime, visible from the glow of the landing light, these peninsulas seemed to resemble a series of human hands, each straining out into the dark ink of the ocean. The southernmost was Brittany – this one looked like an open palm. The long arm of Cornwall ended in a tight, angry claw, which might have scattered the crumbs of the Scilly Isles. Then came the chubby hand of St David's Head and, last, the Llŷn peninsula, which looked like an index finger pointed in accusation across the Irish Sea.

There were more of these arms in Scotland and Ireland – but they were too convoluted, too intricate to tell apart. I have since been to some of these peninsulas, driven the narrowing country lanes to their dead ends, felt my cheeks redden as the winds make landfall on their cliffs. The peninsulas are, the old stories go, the nooks of the continent into which the Celts were chased. Some names – Finisterre, Land's End – recall the days when they were the limits of the known world.

There was another hand I had not counted among them – shorter than its cousins but nonetheless following the same trajectory, lurching westward into the sea. The Gower peninsula branched off from Swansea and made a feeble stab into the Bristol Channel. Like all the others, it ended with a few islands, like fingerprints left in the sea. At the far end was a car park by a beach where retired people often parked their cars and drank tea from a thermos. One winter's day I entered that car park as my destination in Google Maps.

Sudden snow fell as I drove along the M4: the flurries thatching the roadside woods with whiteness. After Leigh Delamere the snow relented, and in its place came a thick, curdling fog which swallowed the towers of the Severn Bridge. At the Gower peninsula the fog had withdrawn a little, revealing that the sea too was white – the waves furious with surf, surging over rocks where temporary waterfalls tumbled, drained and replenished by the rush and retreat of seawater. At a car park I unloaded my backpack and everything I would need for the night. I squinted at my map. It was a short walk along the coastal path to the cave. When the weather was nice, you could look across from the Gower to see the cliffs of Devon or Pembrokeshire. For now, under its lingering blanket of fog, this place might also have been one of the ends of the earth.

The coastal path meandered through patches of gorse and farmers' fields, and eventually reached a four-way crossroads. A wooden sign provided distances in three directions:

Rhossili 4 miles
Port Eynon 3¼ miles
Pilton Green ¾ miles

The fourth path was unmarked. A vague trail followed a drystone wall down a steep gully towards the sea. Travel in this direction was not encouraged. If you checked the internet, you'd know this was a route only passable once a month for a few hours – and only then at the very lowest tides. Passage along this path was dependent on the whim of the sea. Down there, in that dead-end gully, at a dead end of the Gower (which was, if you looked at it sideways, a kind of dead end of Europe), was a place implicated in a story of beginnings, and somewhere that may have been Britain's first holy place.

THE REVEREND AND HIS QUESTS

I hadn't planned it that way, but it was 199 years since the Reverend William Buckland had stood at this crossroads. It would have been a neater coincidence if it had been 200 years ago, but nothing seemed especially neat and tidy about the life of the Reverend. I thought back to a Victorian cartoon I had seen of him: a man in a flowing black cloak and a professor's cap, entering a cave with a burning torch clutched in his right hand. By the light of the torch, this cave revealed itself to be long and labyrinthine. His torch caught the attention of various exotic creatures inside:

pterodactyls, bears, hyenas and a deer that happened to be looking the wrong way.

Reverend Buckland was a devout Christian and the first Reader of Geology at Oxford University – he spent his days scurrying through the subterranean world of Great Britain in search of geological confirmation of the scriptures. Born just the other side of the Bristol Channel, beside the smugglers' coves of south Devon, he was taught from a young age to read the hand of God in the natural world: to understand that everything – from a daisy petal to the beat of a blackbird's wing – was designed in the workshops of heaven above. He was part of a generation for whom natural science was not in competition with religion, as it is seen today, but rather a means of understanding the almighty's intentions, by scrutinizing the finer details of his creation.

At the dawn of the nineteenth century the scientific consensus was that the universe began around 23 October, 4004 BC, at 9 a.m. – just after breakfast time. Two millennia later, it was surmised, came the biblical flood, when it rained for 40 days and 40 nights and the 600-year-old Noah sailed high above the world in his ark made of cypress. God had pressed Ctrl Alt Delete on his creation: everything was rebooting as it was meant to. It was at this point, speculated Buckland and his contemporaries, that the planet took shape: that continents drifted, landscapes were sculpted by the flood waters and everything was neatly arranged for the day the ramp went thud and the animals trotted, scampered and slithered onto dry land.

Buckland's mission was to find evidence of Noah's flood in the soggy island of Great Britain (a place where rain for 40 days and 40 nights was not exactly unusual, and certainly not by the seaside in Wales). In the Lickey Hills, Worcestershire, he found pebbles whose arrangement suggested an ancient deluge. Later, excavating Kirkdale Cave in north Yorkshire, he found the bones of hyenas, elephants, hippos and rhinos – he initially surmised that the flood waters had washed these creatures up from the tropical regions of the world to a cavern in God's Own County.

Buckland himself was something of a Noah figure. In his rooms at Christ Church, Oxford (and later in London), he kept a menagerie of animals: pet hedgehogs, rats, a cobra, a crocodile and a turtle that (on separate occasions) took up residence in the college fountain – plus a donkey that his children rode around his drawing rooms. Most famous of all was a pet bear named after an obscure Old Testament king, which wandered around the Oxford cloisters frightening students.

On top of his personal zoo, Buckland's understanding of the natural world was marked by a tendency to put things in his mouth and eat them. As well as licking various rocks to investigate their composition, he had a fondness for unusual meats (including tiger) and served mice on toast to his guests. A legend went that, later in life, he ate the heart of King Louis XIV, after it was rescued from France by English travellers. Maybe the heart that quickened pacing the corridors of Versailles met its end digesting in Buckland's stomach. It seemed unlikely. For some he was an eccentric genius, famous for theatrical lectures wielding animal skulls, sometimes delivered on horseback. Not all were impressed. A young man named Charles Darwin labelled him 'a vulgar and almost coarse man ... like a buffoon'.[1]

Although sensational stories swirled around Buckland, few doubted he was a pioneer: he was among the first to delve into those yawning chasms whose contents would later rewrite human history. The gentle tapping of his geologist's hammer helped set in motion seismic shifts in our understanding of the world – though Buckland himself would not live to see the dust settle.

By December 1822 Buckland had entered into correspondence with the Talbot family of Penrice Castle, south Wales, who had stumbled upon a cavern near their home beside the Bristol Channel. This cavern, it was explained, was almost inaccessible, necessitating a dangerous climb down a sea cliff to gain access. Only a few farmers seemed to know about it. There, a party of amateurs had unearthed mysterious bones. Buckland promptly ordered Mary Talbot to seal it off, to 'have the mouth closed up to prevent destruction' – to silence the cave, to ensure its secrets were not disclosed.[2] Not long afterwards he was standing at that crossroads, about to trace the events of Genesis in the depths of Paviland Cave.

THE CLIMB IN

The seawater came barrelling down the gully in a blizzard of foam. A stiff offshore wind was holding up the tips of waves that day – the low tide approach to Paviland Cave I had originally planned to take was impassable. There was another way to get inside. To be sure I could gain access, I'd called on the services of Andrew Price, a bushcraft instructor based on the Gower who regularly visited Paviland Cave (which, on certain maps, is referred to as 'Goat's Hole'). He arrived at the crossroads with a climbing rope slung over his shoulder, a Swedish army stove and a few tins of Sainsbury's chicken curry in a green backpack. He was in early middle age, handsome, wearing a fleece adorned with a picture of Cernunnos, the horned Celtic god associated with wildness, woodlands and the hunt.

'I think of myself as a kind of pagan, in a way,' Andrew said. 'That's probably because I spend most of my time living out in the woods.'

Reaching for his phone, Andrew showed me a picture of himself posing with antlers on his head, pretending to be Cernunnos. Andrew used to work as a TV presenter, hosting shows on ITV Wales about the great outdoors. Now he worked full-time as a survival expert – he taught everything from spoon whittling to making rafts, offering courses in his own woodland nearby.

He seemed to be a bit of a 'prepper' – a specialist in being ready for the end times. He had started digging a bunker after seeing the nuclear war drama *Threads* as a boy. Later, when he lived in London, he planned an escape route out of the capital in case of unrest arising from the millennium bug, caching supplies in Essex. He ordered a supply of iodine tablets some years ago in case of a nuclear attack. With Vladimir Putin threatening nuclear war the weekend before we met, Andrew had stocked up on supplies for his family. He announced, in all seriousness, that if a nuclear winter was coming, Paviland Cave would be a good place to hide out. You could catch fish, live off wild cabbage that grew on the cliffs – the cave itself was dry. No one would bother you there. He didn't advertise guided trips to the cave on his website because it was a niche activity, and the access could be a bit scary. He didn't want just anyone showing up.

From the crossroads we followed the drystone wall halfway to the sea, then climbed an eroded footpath along a steep grassy ledge – shimmying on all fours where the grass was sodden and slippery. A kittiwake glided over the waves below us. The foghorn of a ship boomed from somewhere out in the white oblivion. Soon the path came to a dead end at the foot of a limestone wall. From here, Andrew explained, we would have to climb up the sheer rock face which teetered high over the Bristol Channel. Then we would shuffle along a narrow ledge to the cave. It was, at a guess, a 20-metre drop into the sea below. Whatever Armageddon happened in the wider world, any slip would probably spell our own personal end times.

'It looks worse than it actually is,' said Andrew, uncoiling his rope. 'Once you're on the wall, try not to look down too much. It's only a few simple moves.'

Andrew clambered up and, a minute later, beckoned me to follow. I started climbing slowly. One hand. One foot. A deep breath. Another hand, another foot, another breath. Rain fell as clouds of spray rose from the rocks – droplets from above and below danced their disorientating dance as I clung on. Looking for the next foothold, I half-spied the sea seething below my shoelaces. A rogue wave exploded like a bomb, bringing an icicle-jab of fear to my heart. I concentrated on the limestone at my fingertips – finding reassurance in its miniature landscape of canyons and crevices, in the tiny rock pools marooned up the cliff. Eventually I reached another, much wider ledge. I steadied myself as we shimmied around a corner.

And there was the cave.

THE RED LADY OF PAVILAND

Paviland Cave had its mouth open to the sea, as if it hoped to ingest all the winds gusting in off the Atlantic. The opening was shaped like a keyhole – Andrew said the shape reminded him a bit of a prehistoric arrowhead. Buttresses of rock formed a few alcoves inside, and the strata of rock meandered in marbled formations about the ceiling. There were threads of fishing rope on the floor, and someone ('some vandal', said Andrew) had recently carved some Viking runes into the wall. Other than that, there was no sign of human activity. Andrew put down his rucksack and started boiling water for tea.

'Given the history of this place, you'd expect it to feel a bit sinister,' he said, tending the stove. 'But I've never felt that. I've always felt that it was a comforting place to be. Like a church, almost.'

The cave was about the dimensions of a small chapel: a rockpool at its mouth might have been a baptismal font. Barring a few drips, it was just as dry as Andrew had promised. Most of all, it was loud: the mesmeric music of the sea echoed endlessly – sound waves breaking against the walls, murmuring in more distant niches. This soundtrack changed all the time. Mostly it was like the white noise of motorway traffic or the static of an AM radio. Andrew said he had slept here once before and woken up convinced he was hearing human voices. There was no one there: it was just the waves.

Andrew pointed to the ceiling, and a blocked chimney that tapered out of sight. It was through this hole that Buckland made his theatrical entrance in 1823 – a diagram shows the Reverend abseiling down the cliff edge and descending by ladder on to the floor. He quickly found those strange bones the Talbots had mentioned to him – some of which had already been unearthed – hyena, rhinoceros and extinct animals that might have cast his mind back to his finds in Yorkshire the previous year.

But six inches deep in the mud at the back of the cave he found something else: a humerus, a radius, left arm ulna, a left leg and left foot, part of a right foot, a pelvis, some ribs. There were human remains in the midst of the prehistoric animals – someone whose bones had been deliberately coloured red with ochre. Two limestone blocks may have been deliberately placed at the head and foot of the body. There were periwinkle shells where a pocket might once have been.

In his book *Reliquiae Diluvianae* ('Relics of the Flood') Buckland coldly describes his findings as 'Portion of Female Skeleton, clearly postdiluvian'.[3] Buckland asserted his belief the skeleton dated back two millennia or so – the redness of the bones may have been a clue she was a Celtic prostitute linked to an ancient camp that once existed on the cliffs nearby. Another time, he suggested, she may have been a Welsh witch in her cavernous lair: a mutton bone found nearby was her conjuring tool. She became popularly known as the 'Red Lady of Paviland' – whatever she was, she was definitely ancient. Buckland joked that she was a Welsh Eve, and that the Welsh would soon be claiming descent from Adam.

But his jokes masked a serious problem. The presence of a human body ritually buried in the midst of ancient, exotic creatures made no sense: it challenged the chronology of human history, that mankind had arrived in Britain in comparatively recent times, well after prehistoric creatures, and well after the biblical flood. I imagined Buckland on the short winter day he found those red bones – hunched on the floor, perhaps a cloak draped about his shoulders, teeth chattering in the chill, the sounds of the winter sea echoing in the cave. Fervent Christian though he was, was there a briefest sense of vertigo, a possibility he was gazing deep into a vortex of time, touching someone who walked in the nothingness before the *In the beginning*? Perhaps.

In any case, Buckland took the bones of the Red Lady in his carriage back along bumpy turnpike roads back to Oxford. He didn't know it, but in dispatching the Red Lady to the university collections he was sending her off on another journey into deep time. As science advanced, the date of her origins retreated further and further into prehistory. It eventually became clear she was the first fossil human skeleton uncovered by a scientist. She was among the oldest ritual burials found anywhere in Western Europe, and one of the first humans to imprint their footsteps on Great Britain. And, moreover, she was also a he.

By early evening, the winter sun was straining through the clouds. A few gulls yabbered above the cave mouth. Andrew set about making dinner. The climb up the cliff had brought us to the edge of the world. At one point a lonely bar of mobile phone reception drifted into range to pay us a visit – perhaps from a mast across the sea in Devon. Then it disappeared again. Out in the gloaming, the waves were tall and clean: not the surfy chaos of the mid-afternoon but gunmetal grey, marching in neat military formations towards land. A few lights blinked in the distance – tankers heading to Port Talbot or Portishead maybe.

'Go in a straight line in that direction,' said Andrew, pointing out to sea with a spoon, 'And you'll eventually hit Brazil.'

A new sound had joined the cacophony in the cave. Below Paviland Cave was a second submerged cavern, where giant boulders were being picked up and thrown about by the incoming tide, making a sound like a door slamming shut. If you lay down, you could feel the rock quaking. Andrew said the innards of Paviland Cave made him think of being a baby in the womb.

Andrew, it turned out, was a regular visitor to caves across the Gower. This peninsula was one of Wales's foremost holiday spots: above ground were campsites, holiday cottages, country lanes jammed with weekend tourists. On the fringes was a coastline Swiss-cheesed by a subterranean world where few ventured and where Andrew and others could slip off the map. Not far away was a walled-up cave associated with eighteenth-century smugglers. Close to the crossroads was another small cavern – Foxhole Cave – where a man had come to take his life a couple of years before. Andrew was guiding a TV crew to Paviland Cave when the group saw a pair of boots and walked by, assuming the owner was taking a nap. Later they saw the body. Andrew pointed to a platform of pebbles midway along the cave and suggested I sleep there.

'That's where the Red Lady was found. It's all been excavated of course. You'll be sleeping below where the body would have been buried.'

PALAEOLITHIC PILGRIMAGE

By the turn of the century Buckland's deluge hypothesis had been discredited, while the evolutionary theories of his critic Charles Darwin had become more widely accepted. The Red Lady remained the subject of academic interest all the same. By the early twentieth century he was correctly identified as a young male and was proudly paraded by some as a highly evolved prehistoric ancestor – a useful prop to justify the supremacy of the British, whose empire encircled the globe at the time. As the years dragged on, he was flung further into the past – the advent of radiocarbon dating in the 1960s suggested he had lived 18,000 years ago. But the last word seemed to lie with a project undertaken at the turn of the millennium, led by Professor Stephen Aldhouse-Green of the University of Wales, Newport.

The summary of its findings lay in a volume titled *Paviland Cave and the 'Red Lady': A Definitive Report* (2000) – a giant black volume, its cover embossed with three golden bones. It included chapters from experts in myriad different fields: geologists, anthropologists, archaeologists. It was full of impenetrable scatter graphs and jargon – but behind it all lay a startling conclusion, almost as befuddling as the initial discovery was to Buckland all those years ago.

The Red Lady was identified as being in his twenties, and dated to 26,000 BC – a full 16,000 years before the last ice age had ended: a time when Great Britain was smothered in glaciers and largely uninhabitable to *Homo sapiens* (and most other things with a heartbeat). The Red Lady could only have been in Britain during one of the brief so-called 'interstadial events' – episodes in the ice age when the climate had been a little milder (still chilly, never quite T-shirt and shorts weather). Even during those interludes, the report's message was that Britain would have represented a frontier of the known world. At their maximum extent, it was suggested glaciers would have rumbled and creaked only a few miles from the mouth of Paviland Cave: a kingdom of ice extended all the way to the pole.

Great Britain would have been linked to the continent, and – with so much water trapped in the ice – the sea levels would have been some 80 metres lower than the present day. The cave would have looked out not at the sea but across a broad valley where mammoth and woolly rhinoceros probably grazed and lions and hyenas prowled, and where a river – the ancestor of the modern Severn – meandered in the far distance. Seen from the land, Paviland was no sea cave but rather a crevice in the top of a mountain range that rose sharply from the plains. This northern land, Aldhouse-Green suggested with a flourish, might have been a wilderness comparable in its remoteness to the Empty Quarter travelled by the explorer Wilfred Thesiger in his book *Arabian Sands*. The mountains might have been a cold boundary for humankind – an Ultima Thule, The Wall from *Game of Thrones*. A threshold beyond which no one returned to tell the tale.

The few souls who came up here then may have been pioneers, distant from communities in the rest of Europe. It was possible that hunter–gatherers came from France to hunt mammoth in the years before the temperature dipped. One thing was evident: the Red Lady was not easily regarded as a direct forebear of modern Brits but was instead seen as someone who had rather happened to stand on what was now British soil before the ice emptied the land of living things. He was a faraway figure we might only glimpse across an immense expanse of time and ice.

For the most part, the book acknowledged the extreme limitations of the available evidence in drawing conclusions. Yet Chapter 11 saw Aldhouse-Green take a different approach, dabbling in speculation. He suggested the amount of ritual deposits found with the Red Lady – the pocket full of seashells and the red ochre itself – suggested an elaborate burial ceremony, and someone who was regarded as important in some way by their peers. He began to draw on instances of other bodies smothered in ochre across the continents. There was one story from the Kalahari desert of Namibia, where British special forces had undertaken training exercises during the Second World War, when conditions were so extreme that a few soldiers had died. After the war, officers returned to locate the bones of their comrades, finding they had been buried and ritually painted with ochre by the local San people – the Kalahari Bushmen said to practise one of the oldest continuously surviving cultures on earth.

Aldhouse-Green drew on contemporary practice in the Andaman Islands – an archipelago in the Indian Ocean – where the bodies of the deceased are daubed with ochre to make them seem more alive. He cited studies of perceptions of the colour red across the world, red being the brightest colour the human eye can perceive and almost universally regarded as representing blood, life, happiness, health, resurrection.

But most striking of all was Aldhouse-Green's inference that Paviland Cave might have served as a holy place for a period of over six thousand years. A range of deposits – not just the bones of the Red Lady – suggested humans made consistent journeys here through the cold times. They might have trudged through blizzards and drifts, passed under the shadow of advancing glaciers, and suffered frostbite. Those journeys seemed to speak of a purpose for the cave beyond a place of shelter, or a base from which to go hunting. Then, as now, it was almost inaccessible – albeit for different reasons. With that inaccessibility came an aura of mystery. There was the faintest whisper of pilgrimage.

'The cave was very much on the edge of the world,' Aldhouse-Green's widow, Miranda, told me. 'And the whole idea of pilgrimage is the journey itself. It's not just the point where you want to get to – but the whole effort is part of the pilgrimage. And you become – as you're walking – a sacred place. You actually become a holy site.'

Stephen Aldhouse-Green passed away from Parkinson's in 2016. His work had overlapped with that of his wife, herself an Emeritus Professor of Archaeology at Cardiff University. Miranda remembered days when Stephen was studying the cave: he swam to Paviland Cave when he hadn't the time to wait for low tide.

'I think one of the magical elements of Stephen's thinking is that he allowed emotion to enrich the interpretation – without being over-emotional. Because the care and the love that was visited upon that young man's body says it all. It's by no means inappropriate to bring out the emotional thinking of the people who took him that day, on that arduous journey to the cave.'

There was another dimension to the Red Lady that the Aldhouse-Greens had together considered. In 2004 Stephen and Miranda co-authored another book, *The Quest for the Shaman: Shape-Shifters, Sorcerers and Spirit-Healers of Ancient Europe*. The word 'Shaman' has its roots in Siberia, from the Tungusic word *saman*. Put simply, shamans are people who claim to interact with the spirits through altered states of mind, to journey to other worlds to petition in the interests of their community.

Shamanism isn't a religion as we understand it in Britain, but rather a term that has been applied to different cultures worldwide: anthropologists have drawn on similarities between contemporary shamans practising everywhere from Siberia to South America, sometimes in hunter–gatherer contexts. The use of the term isn't without controversy: some say it's reductive to group together cultures on opposite sides of the world. Others might say it's patronizing to consider the belief systems of ancient Europe through the prism of ones that are still alive.

But the Aldhouse-Greens, like others, pointed to the idea that shamanism relies on underlying tendencies in all *Homo sapiens* – that dancing, drumming, fasting, meditation, drug-taking and sensory deprivation, particularly in places like dark caves, stimulate the brain to experience visions. The shaman who could master such intense visions would go on a journey, swimming or flying into other dimensions. An upper world of the spirits. A lower world of the dead. Here he or she could communicate with ancestors, deities or other beings. To ask for changes in the weather. To get a better understanding of the movements of the herds.

The remote north of Siberia – the homeland of the *saman* – has a climate somewhat analogous to the Gower peninsula of 28,000 years ago. Could Paviland Cave then be a shamanic site? Was there a possibility that the Red Lady himself could be a shaman – were his bones left to watch over the mammoth herds by the Severn for the benefit of his descendants? What rituals might have been performed here we would never know. But these were *Homo sapiens*, beholden to some of the same impulses as ourselves. Chapels and temples are still set in high places: shrines often exist in caves. Kinds of sensory deprivation have continued in various forms in religions the world over as a way of nudging closer to the divine. It all seemed plausible.

'There's an awful lot of symbolism hedging around shamans,' Miranda told me. 'And one is the kind of mystery, the seclusion and the remoteness of the sites where they practise. One of the strong points about the choice of this cave is its inaccessibility. Cave situations are so important, because now they're both safe and dangerous. They're sanctuaries, but also – you don't know what's lurking in the dark.'

AT BEDTIME

After dark we burrowed deep into our sleeping bags – me in the spot where, some thirty thousand years before, some people had heaped the soil atop their friend, Andrew a little further back. The mouth of the cave framed a black sky. My eyes calibrated to the gloom. I soon saw subtle ripples of light playing on the ceiling above – the night sky reflecting on waves breaking ever closer to our beds.

'It just doesn't take much to imagine really,' said Andrew. 'The shape of the cave hasn't changed in thirty thousand years. The view outside has, of course. But the cave would have been much as it is now.'

Andrew subscribed to the Aldhouse-Green shaman hypothesis: the idea that the cave was used as a portal into another realm. He had other theories too. The remains of the Red Lady did not include a skull – Andrew thought that the nomads who came here might have carried it away with them, as a relic of their companion.

Other theories suggested a storm could have stolen the skull from the cave: quite possibly the great Bristol Channel flood of January 1607, which submerged the Somerset levels, made an almost-island of Glastonbury Tor and smashed up the bridges along the Severn. It claimed some two thousand lives in England and Wales. Some climbed church steeples or clung to treetops to survive. There was speculation it was a tsunami – though now the consensus seemed to be that it was a storm surge.

'There happened such an overflowing of waters,' wrote one contemporary observer, William Jones of Usk,

> the like never in the memory of man hath ever been seen ... The sudden terror struck such an amazed fear into the hearts of all the inhabitants of those parts ... deeming it altogether to be a second deluge: or an universal punishment by water ...
>
> Huge and mighty hills of water, tumbling one over another, in such sort as if the greatest mountains in the world had overwhelmed the low valleys or marshy grounds. Sometimes it so dazzled the eyes of many of the spectators, that they imagined it had been some fog or mist, coming with great swiftness towards them: and with such a smoke, as if mountains were all on fire ...
>
> ... if it had not been for the merciful promise of God, at the last dissolution of the world by water, by the sign of the rainbow, which is still shown to us: we might have verily believed this time had been the very hour of Christ's coming.[4]

Perhaps that same cataract had crashed into the sanctuary of Paviland Cave that January day, disturbing the soil, fetching the skull with its watery fingers, carrying it into the oblivion of the Atlantic. Perhaps the head still lurked somewhere on the seabed beyond the cave, beyond the reach of the trawlers' nets, somewhere in Lundy, Fastnet, Sole. Perhaps.

'I think we can speculate all we want,' said Andrew. 'And I like to speculate. I like to imagine standing down on the plain below, looking up at the cliffs and the cave. And I do think this was a place of pilgrimage.'

We said goodnight. Beyond the cave mouth, the lights of a descending plane shone over the sea. I waited until I heard Andrew snoring. Then I tried to meditate – to use the heavy darkness and hypnotic echoes all around to shift my mind to a new focus, like adjusting the aperture of a camera.

Six years before, I had been by Lake Guatavita – a highland lake in the green Cordillera Oriental of Colombia, believed by some to be the origin of the legend of El Dorado. This lake was sacred to the Muisca people: one of the pre-Columbian civilizations of South America, whose holy men sailed its waters on a raft, sinking exquisite golden objects as offerings to the deities in the fathoms. Later, conquistadors and Western entrepreneurs tried to drain the lake – to plunder its riches and to dispatch them to the courts of Europe. For one reason or another, they never found the treasure they sought. But the legend of El Dorado still resonates about Lake Guatavita. A contingent of Muisca descendants clung on, affirming the sanctity of the muddy-brown lake and what lies beneath its surface.

One September day I met a quiet Muisca shaman called Marco, sporting starched white robes and a mane of black hair. We walked a lap of the lake, then he took me to a ravine nearby where – among a tangle of tree roots – there was a hobbit-sized door hardly big enough for an adult to crawl through. Behind the door was a cave a little bigger than a coffin. Within this pitch-black recess, Marco explained, he had exiled himself for some time, visited only by people who came to post him some food. That retreat into darkness was to purify himself, he said. To enhance his vision. Like the gold down in the depths of the lake, Marco's underworld held truths that would wither and vanish in the full glare of daylight.

And this – more clumsily – was what I was hoping for from my meditation in the cave. On some level, I wanted to journey deeper, further into the cave – beyond the cold, hard fact of its rock. On the stroke of 11 p.m. my Casio watch started beeping under my backpack. I scrambled around for my torch to locate it and shut it up. By that point it was too late. Under the beam of electric light the spell of the darkness was broken: I was back in the cave with a bellyful of chicken curry and a man I had found on the internet snoring nearby. All I could picture were ordinary humans, who – 28,000 years before – had deemed this a good place to leave their friend, maybe because its gloom approximated the nothingness from which all humans had come, and to which their friend was returning. A nothingness as unknowable to me as it might have been to them.

I thought of those people striving to imagine a future without their friend, with the same futility with which I was trying to imagine their past. I envisaged blank faces at the opposite ends of time. And feeling like the whole endeavour had been a bit daft, I fell asleep.

AN IMAGINED JOURNEY

A landscape, late afternoon, a Tuesday. The smell of summer meadows. Insects thrum about a sea of wildflowers. The River Severn – not the wide-open leagues of the Bristol Channel but a rushing river, a Scottish Highland kind of river, just about shallow enough for you to ford. The feeling of pebbles under your heel. The current so cold your legs tingle afterwards. Salmon are leaping out of glass-clear waters: the boundary of Gloucestershire and Glamorgan runs midstream. Dotted about the river plain are woolly mammoths – lumbering slowly and determinedly, stopping in the copses to snap branches off the birches and scratch their arses on tree trunks. The sounds of grunts and footfalls and the buzz of insects. They're big furry vegetarians. Don't bother them and they won't bother you.

Somewhere near Ilfracombe – the cliffs that rise to the south of the plain. Four or five people in brown coats. Normally, this is the high place they come to watch the herds move. But they're not watching the herds: they're forming a circle around a young man who is leaving the middle world. Someone says this is not a good place to stop, up on the cold, northern edge of everything. Now the sun is setting in the sea to the west, setting icebergs glittering like diamonds. The mammoths below cast lengthening shadows across the plain. Wildflowers lose their lustre in the departing light. With dusk everything changes: it's so cold you can see your breath, and then so dark you can't see anything at all. Piled under coats in the gloom is the young man: his lips are hard, and someone is holding him tight enough to feel the vanishing heartbeat within his chest.

Dawn on Wednesday: the sun rising over Exmoor. Morning: the heft of the man on shoulders. The pilgrims descending, crossing the plain, fording the river. Walk for a bit, rest for a bit, toilet break, start again. The body is awkward to carry: insects are biting, but you can't wave them off because you've got your hands full. Best look where you are putting your feet. Though sometimes they look up to see the mountains – the cliffs on the northern edge of the plain, a boundary past which no one has trodden.

Days later: sunset at the cave mouth. Frost on the rocks. The painting of the body: redness dabbed on the young man's skin so he looks like a baby fresh from the womb. It will soak into the bones. A bag of seashells from days by the seaside – from the walks along the beaches in Brittany. People gather around to perform the ceremony – squeezing hands in support. The holy man picks up the drum. Hours later, heartbeats slowing, the young man is lowered into the grave prepared for him.

A week or so later: the group heading south, crossing the cliffs at Ilfracombe, towards safety. Someone looks over their shoulder for a last time at the northern mountains, trying to work out where the cave is, perhaps hoping for a sign that a young man has been entrusted to safety. Indeed, he will be safe for thousands upon thousands of summers and winters. Safe through the advance and retreat of ice, the retreat and advance of the seawater. Some cliffs will crumble under the action of billions of waves and tides; some bones will crumble too – but others remain intact, the redness of life on them undimmed in the cave. But the sea is coming. The storm surges reach into the cavern, threatening to wash away the bones, until the remains are only inches from the surface.

Then one day comes the tapping of a Victorian hammer above. Someone is working away, humming a tune. After 28,000 years of darkness, there is the bright, clear light of a winter day. A figure in a gown. The redness of the ochre touches the redness of an outstretched human tongue ...

I woke up only once in the night, to go for a pee on the ledge outside the cave. It was low tide then. The crashing boulders under Paviland Cave were quiet. Some of the drowned world where those ice age pilgrims might have trodden had temporarily emerged, barnacled and strewn with seaweed, shining weakly in the darkness. Then I returned to my bed and dozed off again, as the tide turned once more – its watery blanket drawing back towards the land.

THE DRUID'S VIGIL

Now imagine another gathering on the Gower, 28,000 years later, give or take a few thousand. It is dusk on the autumn equinox of AD 2006: a solitary figure is bedding down for the night in Paviland Cave. He is a Druid – a smudgy photo of that night shows a man with wispy grey hair wearing a sleeveless top. He has few possessions apart from a plastic bottle of mineral water. Some stray rays of sunshine are finding their way into the cave.

A little further inland are four figures making camp at the Pitton Cross Caravan Park – they are all magicians. They are burning incense to liven the evening air. Before them is an altar adorned with a replica of Venus of Willendorf – a female figurine with giant breasts and a dipped head, found by the Danube in Austria and believed to date to 25,000 BC. To the Red Lady, it could have been as distant in time as an iPhone would be to the masons of Stonehenge. Never mind, it represented an effort to reach into the past – plus I've checked and you can buy a Venus of Willendorf off Amazon for about £30. One of the magicians is a middle-aged man, bald with piercing blue eyes. He starts beating a drum, and – in tandem with the metre – recites a poem composed for the occasion.

> Here we gather, in the gloom,
> our little space like to the cave
> wherein the Druid fasts and prays,
> Paviland, the Goat's Hole cave
> wherein the Druid fasts and prays
> for restoration, seeking balance.
> As we approach the Equinox,
> the seasons give a quarter turn,
> the nights are getting longer now,
> the Indian summer turning cool
> but in the cave so cold and dark,
> still the Druid keeps his watch.

This poet was Kaitŵm.625, though most people found it easier to call him The Kite. I found him because he was the administrator of a Facebook group – the Swansea Pagan Moot – which, he explained, was a monthly gathering of pagans (some might say 'neo-pagans'). The Moot was – he explained without irony – 'a broad church'.

'The pagan world is not unified,' The Kite told me some weeks before I came to the cave. 'People come at it as individuals. Everyone takes their own path. So as a result we can talk to each other without getting into fights and even play together nicely.' In 2006, a Druid in the Moot named Cyt Ap Nydden (otherwise known as Chris Warwick, a former engineer from Birmingham) was pontificating about the rights of dead people.

'Obviously, the practice has always been to find a grave, dig it up, make an exhibition,' The Kite explained. 'Which is what happened to the Red Lady as he is now known – when he was taken to Oxford. From a pagan point of view that's grave robbing.

Cyt went on about this and said: "I'm going to do a vigil." He said, "I'm going to Paviland Cave, and spend the night there, and be with the space and learn what I can from it." I thought: yes that's the perfect thing to do.'

The Kite and three other chaos magicians from the Moot volunteered to help – Swansea sits at the eastern edge of the Gower, so it's less than a half hour drive to Paviland. They found a campsite nearby which had hot showers.

'We were the crew – we were the backup. We spent the evening basically in a tent doing magical stuff. Just getting that kind of vibe to support what Cyt was already doing. The poem demanded to be written.'

The Kite sent me his poem by email. It was long – it stretched to a thousand words. I found it sad and moving. It began with feverish visions of the seas, of living creatures turning to fossils which in turn became rock, and out of which was formed the cave. Paviland Cave he called the 'Chapel of the Ancient Dead'. I imagined The Kite reciting the poem in the tent in his Swansea accent – the fly sheet flapping in the autumn breeze.

> Six and twenty thousand years
> ago, between the Ice Age cold,
> humans sheltered in the cave,
> one of them alive no more,
> brought inside by those who cared,
> as they consigned him to the earth.

Into the poem, some twenty lines later, walked Buckland:

> Nigh on two hundred years ago,
> humans visited the cave,
> found the bones, found the horns,
> found the body's open grave
> and in the name of higher learning
> took what they could find of it.
> They were not like ones who cared,

coming to the hall of stone.
Without a thought they took the man,
laid among the ancient dead,
took him as their property,
dealt with him as they saw fit.
What they took they kept but some,
threw away the ancient dead,
stole away the mammoth skull,
robbed the sanctuary of
the chapel of the ancient dead.

The morning after the vigil, with the turn of the tide, the backup team met the Druid Cyt, who said he had picked up positive energies in the empty grave. They took him for a well-earned breakfast. Cyt didn't want to speak to me – perhaps it was a private matter between him and the Red Lady. But The Kite told me he himself still felt strongly about the Red Lady, though well over a decade had passed since the vigil.

'I feel something more needs to be done than having him stuck in a drawer in Oxford,' he told me. 'We wanted to be the people who say that our ancestors aren't just some dead people who contributed our DNA. These are the people who've stood where we stand now, they are responsible for us being here.'

'The Red Lady was felt for and cared about by the people around him. You're building a picture there – not of a bunch of Stone Age savages dragging their hands. But of a living, vibrant community, as sharp and clever as we are. They made their mark. And maybe that's what I'd like to see: that these sites are treated as places that our ancestors marked. That remind us who and what we are for a very long time.'

Cyt, The Kite said, wanted the bones to be returned to the cave where they were originally buried. The Kite wasn't convinced this would work – he worried it would be dug up and 'on eBay within a fortnight'. What was needed was a change in society.

'It's our lack of a sense of history that has got us into the trouble that we are now in. If you realize what has happened in the past, you realize global warming could happen again. Now the ice is melting in our gin and tonic. That's why it's still important. That's why it still matters.'

THE NEXT FLOOD

Morning came to the cave. Sunbeams streaked from the mouth of the Severn estuary. Andrew got up and started making instant coffee from a sachet. As we ate breakfast, the outline of Devon emerged – the rise of Exmoor, Lundy Island, the cliffs around Ilfracombe and Morte Point, the shore vanishing to Cornwall. We packed our backpacks, left the cave, shimmied along the ledge and clambered down the cliff. Back at the crossroads, our phones jingled and chirruped with notifications, welcoming us back to the world. We trudged in silence across the fields towards my car.

I hadn't picked up on the positive energies Cyt the Druid had felt in Paviland Cave. I felt no presence: the cave was, after all, an empty tomb. But the threads of stories from within that cave – the way they had interwoven – moved me.

A few weeks later a curator at the Oxford University Museum of Natural History replied to my request to see the bones. I met her in the museum reception area: she was wearing a mask printed with prehistoric mammals. She led me up a little staircase, past paintings of Vesuvius towering over Naples. We entered a library and there, in a nondescript wooden drawer with a sticky marked 'PAVILAND BONES', were the bones of the Red Lady. They were redder than I expected – the redness like dried blood. They had recently been carbon-dated yet again, and had retreated further still, to a point up to 34,000 years ago. The curator explained they were stored in a secret location within the museum, ready to be evacuated in the event of fire or another Act of God.

The suggestion of Palaeolithic pilgrimage to Paviland was scoffed at by some academics in a 2011 *Guardian* article. They instead suggest the cave could have just been a convenient place for a burial, and that it was probably not a place of pagan pilgrimage – that people today saw what they wanted to see. Indeed, the reddening of those bones 34,000 years ago was an act whose meaning would forever remain uncertain.[5]

Nonetheless a sense of memorial had endured. That burial had been continually reconsecrated: by Cyt's vigil, by The Kite's poetry, by the vandal that carved the runes into the cave. The red bones still furrowed the brows of academics. If the intention of the painters was that their friend would not be forgotten, the magic of that ritual had worked. Pilgrims still sometimes came to Paviland, in search of origins, just as Buckland once had. In the years after visiting Paviland Cave, Buckland continued to lead an illustrious career in geology and later became the Dean of Westminster. In old age he lost his sanity; he died in a mental asylum in Clapham just as the architecture of biblical time was crumbling.

On the drive back from Oxford I switched on the car radio. It was full of news of impending doom. A new UN climate report warned the planet was sleepwalking into environmental disaster, with sea levels on a trajectory to drown coastal cities from London to Lagos. The cave had contained someone present in Britain the far side of the last climate apocalypse. Who might step inside after the next deluge?

Then again, it might not come to that. A panel of experts were debating whether Vladimir Putin would decide to unleash strategic nuclear bombs if his regime fell – citing Louis XV's famous expression of nihilism and contempt for all that followed him: 'après moi, le déluge.' Which translates as: 'after me, the flood.'

3

A Ridge

A Neolithic Pilgrimage

The First Road | Lost Boys | Keeper of the Horse |
Robin Hood Messiah | Inside the Circle | A Night in the
Long Barrow | At All Cannings

Ridge – All Cannings Long Barrow

THE FIRST ROAD

Midway along the M4 (between the Welcome Break at Membury and the exit for Swindon) is a bridge.

The bridge marked 120-1 is a simple nondescript concrete and steel span – one a driver in a moving car might only consider for about ten seconds before their vehicle passes under it. It can be seen for a further ten seconds in the rear-view mirror – but by that point the chances are that Bridge 120-1 has already been forgotten. It is not tagged or graffitied. It is too remote to be a loitering place for bored teenagers. If you happened to glance closely at a car satnav you might just see a name for the road it bears on its back: the Ridgeway.

The M4 does not offer a slipway or a means to connect to the Ridgeway, although the Ridgeway was its predecessor of a sort: once the great thoroughfare leading out of the Thames Valley and out into the west of Great Britain. At some point in the 1960s, bulldozers ploughed through a chunk of the sacred path of the Ridgeway, shunting its compacted earth into the banks that buttress the hard shoulder. The builders offered this measly bridge at the intersection by way of apology. As a pedestrian, you have to step over the crash barrier to cross it.

I stood for a while on Bridge 120-1, watching the sunlight catching the windscreens and wing mirrors. Each lorry came with its own whiplash rush of air. The terrible power of the motorway thundered under my boots. By that point I had started to understand that the Ridgeway was also a current of energy. In practical terms it was a long-distance footpath – indeed one of the UK's 15 National Trails. But people experienced it also as an idea – a westering pull, an impulse to strike into the interior of Great Britain, which was a direction that, in the minds of some, also led into the past.

I left the bridge behind, and pushed on further, to where the tarmac road turned into another form – a long ribbon of chalk that wound through green Wiltshire fields.

The Ridgeway 'has a fair claim to be the oldest road in Europe', wrote the journalist J. R. L. Anderson in 1975 'for men and women... walked it long before Britain was an island, before the onset of the last ice age'. On a few occasions the path has also been described as a route of pagan pilgrimage. Walking the Ridgeway, you find that 'Britain's Otherworld is close at hand' – according to a walking guide from the British Pilgrimage Trust. Legends lurk along the route: myth and magic mist its many miles.

But when all this fantastical fog clears, cold, hard facts about this long path into England's West Country are oddly difficult to come by. Beyond practical walking guides and a few photography books, I could find few books devoted to the Ridgeway. Where it is mentioned, it makes only brief appearances – ghosting in and out of the pages, meandering off into the distance. It was 'a track of the primitive peoples', according to the nineteenth-century nature writer Richard Jefferies, 'that has maintained its existence through the strange changes of the times'.

It's been suggested the Ridgeway could have been trammelled since the Neolithic or perhaps the Bronze Age – the *New York Times* put the figure at five thousand years ago.[1] But in truth there is little material evidence of a road to analyse or carbon-date. For the Ridgeway has been engraved into the English landscape by thousands of years of plodding feet. Twenty-first-century mountain bike tyres, the hooves of medieval cattle going to market, the sandals of Roman legionaries – all have cumulatively left an imprint, or perhaps a scar.

And perhaps so did the Stone Age feet that first blazed a trail. The route would have been of use to a prehistoric traveller – the Ridgeway follows a spine of hills from whose summits you could scan for approaching brigands or scour for new pastures. At a time where wildwoods had yet to be wholly cleared, you could walk up on the escarpment, looking down on the treetops, safe from predators (wolves and bears were not necessarily extinct). The solid ground of the ridge made for easy movement whenever the plains below turned to bog and mire.

The Ridgeway may possibly be England's oldest road – and it may also mark a crossroads in prehistory. The Neolithic saw a new kind of society being formed: from around 4,000 BC the hunter-gatherers of the Palaeolithic and Mesolithic were being replaced by farmers. The roving life of the Red Lady was ending, as permanent (or at least semi-permanent) homes were being established. The part of England through which the route passes was among the first to be cleared and intensively farmed. It was tempting to imagine Neolithic farmers in procession along the Ridgeway: making the first ever homecomings on this first road of Great Britain. But, as I came to learn, it is also possible that the origins of the path were older, and that the Ridgeway could even have been pioneered by herds of animals making seasonal migrations, long before the footfalls of *Homo sapiens* followed in their wake. Whichever way you considered it, the origins of the Ridgeway trailed off over the horizon of time and vanished out of sight.

Even in the twenty-first century the physical path can be elusive – braiding, forking – continuously being gobbled up by a B-road before soon being spat out again, emerging as a nettle-flanked footpath on the far side. The confusion extends to what actually counts as 'the Ridgeway'. It is itself a constituent part of the Greater Ridgeway, which runs 362 miles from the Dorset coast to Norfolk, cutting a diagonal swathe across England, linking the Channel to the North Sea. The Wessex Ridgeway is the southernmost component of this Greater Ridgeway – beginning in Lyme Regis, ending in Wiltshire. The Ridgeway National Trail is its 85-mile central section, picking up the thread in Wiltshire and continuing through Oxfordshire, Berkshire and Buckinghamshire – at which point the Icknield Way and the Peddars Way complete the Greater Ridgeway on its long march to the Wash. Here and there are other 'Ridgeways' which, though they carry walkers along the hills, do not carry the definite article.

But *the* Ridgeway – in the eyes of those who care most about it – seems to apply only to the section I set out to walk: specifically the western part of the Ridgeway National Trail, running 40 miles from the River Thames. Here the route, once locally known as 'The Rudge', travels a chalk escarpment strewn with a succession of prehistoric sites from the Stone Age to the Iron

Age: megaliths, earthworks, symbols of uncertain meaning. Their proximity to the path cannot easily be dismissed as a coincidence. They hang like beads from the necklace-thread of the Ridgeway, or like prehistoric Stations of the Cross. Some believe such an accumulation of ritual sites must surely charge the Ridgeway with a deeper resonance. Perhaps this was indeed Great Britain's first holy road.

A long day's walk west of the Thames comes the hill figure of the Uffington White Horse – believed by some to be a Bronze Age deity. Soon after follows the Neolithic long barrow of Wayland's Smithy, named after a Saxon god of metalworking. South of the M4, the path crests a series of Iron Age hill forts: grassy observatories vaulted high over the Wiltshire farmland. But its end destination – indeed the Santiago de Compostela of this ancient Camino – is the ritual landscape around Avebury. The path terminates close to the largest prehistoric stone circle in the world – a place which – five thousand years since its first stones were hauled into position – still provokes profound responses from those who enter within its orbit. One popular interpretation of Avebury's stone circles is as a seasonal gathering place for farmers – in this context, the Ridgeway may have been a pilgrimage route for Neolithic Britons travelling to pray at the stones for good harvests. Or perhaps it was the other way around – perhaps sacred sites sprung up to serve what was already a busy thoroughfare.

'Perhaps' is the mantra you hear when researching or talking about the Ridgeway. Perhaps, possibly, maybe, who knows? – words that plodded in rhythmic succession like footsteps, before tapering off into a silence: often a defeated one. The path was a mystery: the places along it were mysteries within this mystery. Nonetheless I came to think of the Ridgeway as a path that somehow wound deep into an English heartland. Perhaps I could make sense of it by walking it. I would see these ancient sites not as part of an idle, hands-in-pockets potter from a National Trust car park but rather watch them slowly arise from the landscape, revealing themselves from the brow of a hill, as they may have appeared to a Neolithic pilgrim.

I wanted to find people for whom the Ridgeway still had a spiritual resonance today. Before leaving, I sought the help of a second Druid (and the first one who actually picked up the phone). Philip Carr-Gomm is a leading figure in the Order of Bards, Ovates and Druids (OBOD), a leading organization in modern British Druidry. He patiently explained that today's Druids are not direct descendants of the priests who are recorded at the time of the Roman conquest of Britain, but rather a movement that gained momentum in the twentieth century, taking inspiration from accounts of their nature-worshipping forebears. Veneration of ancestors and communion with the environment define the modern Druid path. Decades ago it might have seemed to some like tree-hugging silliness. In an era of accelerating climate breakdown, it seemed more prescient.

I had contacted him because the OBOD website was unambiguous: 'the Ridgeway … brought pilgrims from the East to the sacred complex of Avebury.' Philip, however, believed the Ridgeway might be just one survivor from a network of paths that led from all directions into the Neolithic sites of Wessex (which included not just Avebury but also neighbouring Stonehenge).

'Imagine a starfish shape,' he told me. 'You've got the South Downs, North Downs, the Marlborough Hills and the Ridgeway all converging on Avebury and Stonehenge. I suspect that all these hills had trackways in ancient times to reach these extraordinary ritual sites.'

In lying at the centre of these hills, Avebury – and by association the Ridgeway – may have had a sanctity that was predestined by the geography of southern England. Walking the Ridgeway could be akin to entering into a vortex, slowly gravitating to the island's sacred centre. Perhaps. In any case, Philip would put me in touch with people who might know more. I contacted another order of Druids who were based in Avebury, who also returned my emails. It was a busy time of year, they said. 'Samhain' was the season of death and renewal. They were conducting ceremonies in service of the recently bereaved. But they would try their best to fit me in.

LOST BOYS

Low clouds scudded across the Berkshire Downs the day I set out, lathering the world in dampness. I stepped off a train at Goring station, crossed the Thames to reach the village of Streatley and followed sombre black signs that pointed to the Ridgeway. From here the path ran for 40 miles to Avebury. Those signs pointed me along a country lane flanked by gated mansions, a fancy golf course and drifts of decaying leaves. A poster announced the Goring Gap Players would soon be performing a Noël Coward play. Other signs offered only threats to passers-by: 'Private Property'; 'CCTV in use'; 'Trespassers will be prosecuted.' The purr of an electric gate was my cue to step into the verge and let a spotless Range Rover thrash past.

By lunchtime, the bad weather had eased off. Gaps began to open in the clouds: sunshine lanced through apertures of blue sky, setting faraway fields aflame with sharp autumn light. I trudged onwards, to where the Ridgeway rode the crest of the escarpment.

To my right, the lip of the ridge fell away into thin air – out of which rose a panorama of England: a decommissioned power station, science parks, housing estates – places of industry and life. The uplands of the Ridgeway, by contrast, were mostly empty. Beeches stood sentry on the path, huddled together in solidarity against the winds that ranged and rummaged about those downs. Sometimes those winds changed direction to usher up new sounds from the world below: the boom of an articulated lorry on the A-road, the peel of church bells from a Norman tower. But mostly they sounded much as Richard Jefferies had described a century before: 'a faint sound as of a sea heard in a dream – a sibilant sish sish … dying away and coming again as a fresh wave'.

Jefferies grew up beside the Ridgeway in Wiltshire. In a passage from his book *Wild Life in a Southern County*, he describes a path distinct from all the many others that criss-crossed the hills, a thoroughfare no farmer dared encroach upon with his plough (nor did Jefferies, perhaps for a similar superstition, mention it by name). The scent of wild thyme hung heavy along Jefferies's Ridgeway: shepherds played wooden whistles under the trees and carved their names into the bark. Mostly it was a highway without people. 'Mile after mile, and still no sign of human life – everywhere silence, solitude. ... Hill after hill and plain after plain.'[2]

For me at least, this solitude endured. A few dog walkers pottered along the path near car parks. But I saw no other long-distance hikers between Goring and Uffington. Between the River Thames and the final approach towards Avebury, the Ridgeway – quite remarkably for a long-distance path – passes almost no villages, shops, pubs. Only a few hamlets intersperse the route. It has the feel of a path that does not want to stop and chat, a path hurrying onward to elsewhere. For long periods its spell is unbroken by the interruptions of the modern world. You forget you are in southern England – in a crowded corner in one of the most densely settled parts of the continent. Only occasionally do you remember you are under the flight path to Heathrow – whenever you hear the key change of a jet engine, throttling away unseen in the clouds. Though climbing the Ridgeway is faintly akin to taking off from Heathrow. You rise higher, the fields below become distant. You are at once in their midst – and yet separated from them, as you track a lonely course aloft.

I passed the junction with the A34 around lunchtime, and started feeling peckish. My guidebook noted that to find food or shelter on the path you need to climb down the escarpment, into civilization. Like a river, the guidebook noted there were specific 'entry' and 'exit' points onto the Ridgeway. Like a river, it generally sought the path of least resistance. And, just like a river, the Ridgeway could shape-shift: sometimes it broadened into a wide lane, and sometimes it contracted into a narrow opening where you had to part thorns to pass. Its default form was a thoroughfare of strange width: too narrow for a vehicle track, too wide for a walker. I found myself caught in its slipstream and I forgot I was hungry. So I carried on.

The firm chalk surface of the Ridgeway may have been helpful to Neolithic pilgrims making journeys to Avebury. But even to a walker today it has a useful quality – not tough on the knees like tarmac or concrete, nor does it ever descend into mud. Apart from a few sloping sections (chalk can get slippery as a waterslide in the rain) you are able to take your eyes away from the path. You can trust in its evenness and rigidity: your gaze is liberated to roam the horizon. You might even tilt your head upward as you walk.

By mid-afternoon, torrential showers were falling across Oxfordshire: pillars of rain inching along the landscape, three or four in even succession, like the columns of an immense temple. Eventually a stiff wind swept the sky clear, these columns fell: the temple collapsed into the rubble of ash-grey clouds. Within a few minutes rainbows arched out of the chaos. It felt like a scene staged for the benefit of the Ridgeway, whose slope fell away as steeply as the gods of a theatre. At its highest point the path reaches little over 250 metres. But it also possesses a sense of elevation that would not register on an altimeter.

'It was as free as the blue paths in the snowy heavens,' wrote Edward Thomas, walking it a century ago. 'It looked down upon everything but the clouds, and not seldom on them in the early morning or in rain.'

Thomas was another writer who trod the Ridgeway, detouring up here as part of his book *The Icknield Way*, published in 1913. For him it was a place of intense visions: one moment he describes the path as being like the battlements of a castle, another its summits are islands, floating over the world below: 'I never wished to descend,' he wrote.[3]

Both Thomas and Jefferies left the world too young – both, in fact, died amid chalk landscapes like those of the Ridgeway. Thomas was shot in the chest, aged 39, in the fields of Arras, soon after arriving at the Western Front during the First World War. Jefferies succumbed to tuberculosis at the age of 38 in Goring-by-Sea, under the contours of the South Downs. But there was also a third, tragedy-struck writer who wandered this sacred path.

Kenneth Grahame is famous as the author of *The Wind in the Willows*, an allegory of riverbank animals which presents an Arcadian vision of England where happy creatures live in harmony with each other and the land. It is a cosy, conservative, countryside text. Reading it, you would never guess the writer was neither

English nor a happy man. Grahame was born in Edinburgh in 1859: his mother died of scarlet fever when he was almost five, and his alcoholic father, unable to look after his four children, sent them to live with their grandmother at Cookham Dean, in Berkshire. It was here, on the banks of the Thames, that Grahame found a balm for childhood trauma: pressing his eye low to the waterline, he imagined the insects as sea monsters, and dreamt up stories and characters to populate that reedy, riverine world. Later, as a young man, inspiration came to him walking the blustery tops of the Ridgeway, which began its journey not far from the riverbank. Roving this mystical road could provoke 'a certain supernal, a deific, state of mind', he wrote in his collection *Pagan Papers*. It was a threshold to the past. He imagined Saxons, Vikings and Romans passing by on the ancient thoroughfare: 'by your side the hurrying feet of the dead raise a ghostly dust.'

Grahame was part of a group of writers known to critics as the 'neo-pagans': their 'paganism' was less about reawakening pre-Christian worship and more a recoil from modernity and industry, about seeking solace in the natural world. Perhaps the most famous pagan God in modern English literature gatecrashes the central chapter of *The Wind in the Willows*.

'The Piper at the Gates of Dawn' begins with Ratty holding a crisis meeting with his friend Otter one hot, uneasy midsummer night. Otter's son Portly has been lost for days: his father fears he may have drowned by the weir (he has not yet learned to swim). There follows an interlude of ethereal beauty, in which Mole and Rat cast a rowing boat on the midnight river to search for Portly, before being lured by celestial music to a river island.

> 'This is the place of my song-dream, the place the music played to me,' whispered the Rat, as if in a trance. 'Here, in this holy place, here if anywhere, surely we shall find Him!'[4]

On the island Mole and Ratty encounter Pan – horned God of wild places – who has kept young Portly safe, the animal dozing as if he had 'fallen happily asleep in [his] nurse's arms'. For Grahame it was perhaps less risky to insert a pagan god into a book about animals than one about people. The chapter is a haunting and incongruous intrusion into a children's book. But maybe it hinted at Grahame's days roaming the landscapes of the Thames Valley and the Berkshire Downs, looking for something sacred in its secret nooks.

Later – after a successful career as a writer and (somewhat surprisingly) as Secretary of the Bank of England – Grahame's life was bookended by more sadness. He reluctantly married his wife, Elspeth, having not had the heart to tell her he had changed his mind. Their only son, Alastair (nicknamed Mouse), was born blind in one eye. Neglected by a troubled mother and a workaholic father, Mouse committed suicide on the railway lines at Oxford's Port Meadow, not far from the banks of the Thames, and was buried on his 20th birthday. In the wake of this tragedy, the story of a heartbroken otter keeping vigil for his lost son might be read in a different light.

The bereaved Grahame went on a tour of Italy, before returning to England and a cottage beside the Thames at Pangbourne – a village just south of Goring. He wrote little after the passing of his son. His marriage remained an unhappy one. Upon retirement, he had renewed his walks along the Ridgeway – a lonely figure dressed in an Inverness cape, once again wandering its wide-open spaces, perhaps hoping to outstride his grief.

'Out on that almost trackless expanse of billowy Downs such a track is in some sort humanly companionable,' he had written of the Ridgeway in *Pagan Papers*. 'It really seems to lead you by the hand.'[5]

KEEPER OF THE HORSE

I had timed my walk badly that first day. The weather was as warm as September – but the sun stuck to its usual November timetable, and by half-past five I was trudging through the darkness, my end destination still miles away. The amber glow of Wantage receded behind my back. The B-roads buzzed with commuters heading home. A white van idled in a lay-by beside the Ridgeway, something sinister in its presence. At certain intersections the white trail of the

Ridgeway was a graveyard for white goods: a fly-tipped freezer, the drum of a washing machine stuffed with KFC boxes. But swiftly the Ridgeway slunk away from such places, shuffling again into the dark fields of its habit.

As the day had worn on, I had come to like the Ridgeway, come to admire its shyness, its misanthropic tendencies. I liked it most at night. By six o'clock the surrounding fields were fretted with shadows. Crows cawed as they departed the copses. A full moon had launched into the sky somewhere near Didcot, casting a spectral blue light over the land. The chalk path shone with a silvery intensity in the moonglow – like a thin thread of daylight that had clung on past its bedtime. Switching off my head torch, I followed this luminous path as it wound past the Iron Age hill fort at Segsbury Camp. Down in the hollows, all that could be seen of the world was this trail – a milky way winding through the dark void. The sharp point of my walking stick left dots of freshly churned-up chalk – shining behind me, like the pebbles left by Hansel and Gretel.

By eight o'clock rain began to fall again along the Ridgeway. I had planned to end that first day meeting my friend Al at the village of Woolstone. We would have a big pub dinner, sleep in his camper van and he would join me the next day on the path. I picked up the pace. The moon disappeared behind a cloud. The path frayed into little wisps of chalk, and somehow I got lost. I knew I had to descend. I wandered hopefully over a field, vaulted over a five-bar gate into a cowpat. I was stumbling blindly downhill, wondering how I might get to Woolstone, when I looked over my shoulder and saw the horse rearing up behind me.

It is on rainy nights just like these, Andrew Foley told me, that he wakes up in the small hours, parts the curtains and worries about the horse. Heavy downpours can create channels of water that wash off the chalk, leaving smears, muddying its proud white coat. Even in good weather you can get blemishes, he said: shrews and voles dig tiny holes into its back. But more often than not Andrew arrives in the morning and finds that everything is OK. The horse is a robust animal. Officially Andrew is the National Trust Area Ranger for this part of Oxfordshire. But for a decade he has been the closest thing the Uffington White Horse has to a custodian and overseer: the stablehand for this ancient and possibly sacred steed beside the Ridgeway.

'It'll be my legacy to keep the horse going,' he told me. 'It's given me a life purpose, if you like. Some people have a religious connection to the horse. To them, I'm like a church warden, tending to the graveyard.'

Andrew's house is adorned with pictures of the Uffington White Horse: his nine-year-old daughter Emily has a White Horse T-shirt and a White Horse brooch, and Andrew hopes one day she will take over from him as the horse's guardian. Since Emily was 'aged zero' she has been present at every year's chalking – the annual event in which weeds are cleared from the horse, and people armed with hammers smash up new chalk to renew its equine figure. They're often National Trust volunteers, but anyone can turn up and join in. Recently the chalking was done as corporate team-building for staff at BT. By the end of the process the horse is once again a brilliant white. It is, in a sense, reborn.

'Different parts of the horse require different management,' said Andrew, 'On the head and the ears, the chalk is nice and smooth. On areas of steeper inclines, chalk is spread in a rubble – which deters sheep from walking on it.'

Along much of the Ridgeway the simple act of stripping back turf reveals the bony white matter below – making these hills, in one sense, a vast undulating canvas. Not so long ago, children of the Downs amused themselves by writing their names (and ruder stuff too) into the earth. Further along the Ridgeway are the spindly legs of the Hackpen White Horse (cut in 1838, perhaps to mark the coronation of Queen Victoria). A little way further off the track lie the inquisitive pricked ears of the Alton Barnes White Horse (a commission handed in 1812 to a journeyman painter named John Thorne, who secretly hired a subcontractor, ran off with all the money and was later hanged for his many crimes). Six other white horses preside over the hills of neighbouring Wiltshire – most of them eighteenth- or nineteenth-century creations. But by far the oldest – the stud that sired them, or the mare that gave birth to them all – is Oxfordshire's Uffington White Horse, cantering along a 30 degree slope, and measuring 110 metres long.

Where the other horses are obvious silhouettes, the Uffington White Horse looks like it might have been conceived by a prehistoric Picasso: it is formed by a series of wisps, a hint of muscle and movement in its limbs. It is 'close to something half-glimpsed or apprehended in the dark of a dream', according to Paul Newman, the author of a book on hill figures evocatively titled *Lost Gods of Albion*.[6] And so too this mysterious 'god' has featured in the dreams of those looking for a foundation story for England. In the seventeenth century, Reverend Francis Wise announced it was first cut by Saxons to commemorate King Alfred's victory over the Vikings – he pronounced it would 'vye with the Pyramids for duration, and perhaps exist, when those shall be no more'. In the twentieth century some suggested it was not a horse but a dragon – specifically the one slain by St George, or perhaps a manifestation of the Gallic horse-god Epona – Celtic symbol of divine femininity. There were other vague hypotheses involving Woden and King Arthur. The theories changed. The idea of the horse as a cryptic symbol of nationhood endured.

In the past, as now, the horse had to be continuously re-chalked to retain its appearance. Victorian accounts describe a big, boozy festival to mark the so-called 'scouring' of its chalk, coinciding with cheese-rolling contests, pipe-smoking marathons, pig chases and the chance to retrieve a silver bullet from a sackful of flour (using only your mouth). By the 1920s these festivities were over and things had taken a turn for the worse: passengers passing by on the Great Western Railway were grumbling that the horse had been neglected and couldn't be seen for the weeds. By the 1940s it had been covered up entirely, lest it be a useful point of navigation for German bombers.

By the 1990s the horse was shining once again, and archaeologists attempted to date its origins by using a method called optically stimulated luminescence – measuring when buried soils were last exposed to sunlight. Drilling into the horse's nose, they discovered the Uffington White Horse was probably Bronze Age in origin – carved between 1400 and 600 BC. It was older than had been presumed possible. Few imagined that the horse could have been continuously chalked and repaired over such a period of time. That it had been cared for as though it were a living thing.

Interpretations of the horse now centre on Bronze Age Britain as a place of societal upheaval: its hills overfarmed, people setting out in search of new pastures. Horses were becoming widespread in this mobile age, both as instruments of warfare and as a means of herding animals. Perhaps, amid the chaos, a white horse was cut into the hill as a mark of permanent ownership. Andrew had other theories about who was meant to see the horse.

'The horse is not easily seen from a distance,' he told me. 'It's not easily seen from close up, either. If you were trying to make that kind of statement to people down below, then you probably want something like the HOLLYWOOD sign. But the horse, in its entirety, is pointing towards the sky.'

As the person who has probably spent more time than anyone with the horse, Andrew had mulled over its possible meanings.

'There's a theory I'm more comfortable with. Going back to the beginning of civilization, there is the symbolism of a horse pulling a chariot, in which the sun god sits. This makes sense to us, because our horse faces west. So on particular days – like on the winter solstice, when the sun is lower in the sky – you could look up from Dragon Hill and see this belief manifested in physical form: the chalk figure carrying the sun.

'I'm not particularly religious myself. But if I had to, then I would probably go with the worship of this sun-horse. It's more realistic to me than some guy with a white beard looking down on us. People would have worshipped the sun because they knew that without the sun we're finished. And now humanity is waking up to the fact that – if we don't sort all this out soon – we're going to turn this planet into Mars in very short order.'

Andrew invited me to the chalking of the horse next year. It sounded, in a strange way, like an act of hope.

Investigations have revealed that the Uffington White Horse probably shrank over centuries of chalkings. Its neck has thinned since the 1980s. It has also inched slightly up the hillside. Like a real horse, there were shifts in its posture: subtle flexes of its limbs across the millennia. But it was still there. Dynasties, empires, faiths had fluctuated – but the horse stayed in its paddock beside the Ridgeway, in communion with the Oxfordshire sky. It was a symbol of life and movement – the perfect companion for a pilgrim's road. Who knew how many other sacred symbols had faded from the chalk hills, once people had lost the will to look after them?

In *Lost Gods of Albion*, Paul Newman wrote that 'that in order to survive [hill figures] require regular and coordinated action', adding that 'if a community falls apart, so does the god'.[7] For mysterious reasons, a community had sustained this god of the Ridgeway over three millennia, had repeated the ritual of chalking – even after its members no longer understood the horse's identity, its power or whether it was a deity at all. To walk the path was another way of renewing an ancient mark on the chalk hills: polishing the ground with footfalls. People did this too for reasons they could not easily articulate. Or perhaps fully understand.

ROBIN HOOD MESSIAH

I met Al in the White Horse pub in Woolstone. You couldn't see the horse from this part of the vale, but a version of it appeared alongside the specials on the blackboard inside – sketched out in chalk. Al had parked his van in the car park: on board were supplies for the next section of our hike – dehydrated food, a tarp for camping out and his Portuguese water dog, Laska (Al had fashioned her a portable dog bed from a yoga mat and a blue IKEA bag). We sat in a corner and ordered fish and chips.

Al and I had become close friends walking together in Scotland and Wales: he had gone on to qualify as International Mountain Leader in Chamonix. He had some time in his schedule and agreed to walk with me to Avebury. He was, he said apologetically, not an ordinary pilgrim. Then again, this was not an ordinary pilgrimage.

We woke early the next day, brushed our teeth in the car park, found somewhere discreet to park the van for a few days – then climbed the hill to be caught once again in the westward flow of the Ridgeway. We passed the White Horse. We skirted Dragon Hill – a flattened hillock possibly used for Iron Age rituals, mentioned by Andrew as the observatory from which believers might have watched the Uffington White Horse carry the sun god across the sky. In the daylight it looked eerily familiar.

Only some time later did I realize that Dragon Hill featured in the video for Kate Bush's 1985 single 'Cloudbusting'. The video, inspired by the life of Austrian psychoanalyst Wilhelm Reich, stars Donald Sutherland as the scientist who has invented a cloudbusting machine, a yank of whose levers can control the weather. Kate Bush plays his young son Peter. The video begins with the pair hauling the home-made contraption up onto the Ridgeway – the young boy in awe as it summons rainstorms, births billowing clouds and then wipes the sky clean so the sun can blaze through. It ends with the father being led away by men in black coats – for the crime of possessing this dangerous technology. The closing sequence shows Kate Bush as another lost boy, fatherless on the Ridgeway.

Back on the path, dawn rays arrowed through the gaps in hedgerows, while the world below remained in shadows, still feeling the chill of the departed night. A strong wind had blown through the small hours as we slept in Al's van: the leaf litter left leopard-print-like markings on the white road before us. We pushed on for over a mile, until the Ridgeway arrived at the Neolithic long barrow of Wayland's Smithy. Here the mood darkened.

Wayland's Smithy is often lumped in with the wider Uffington ancient landscape – along with the horse, Dragon Hill and the Iron Age fortress of Uffington Castle. The latter three are places defined by a sense of space: open to the sky and scoured by Wessex winds. Wayland's Smithy is the exception. It feels withdrawn from the world, surrounded by a wall of beeches. And, being a Neolithic chambered long barrow, it is millennia older than its neighbours. People were first buried in a timber tomb around 3600 BC: excavations revealed the remains of adults and children. It lies directly beside the Ridgeway – its creation may coincide with the path's own origins. Even sensible, level-headed people have remarked it is a place where no walker wants to linger too long. We put down our packs, drank a cup of tea and listened to the wind raking the autumn leaves.

Anyone visiting Wayland's Smithy late one summer night in 2019 would have beheld a curious sight: a dozen or so cloaked figures in a circle, each carrying a burning torch aloft. Surviving pictures of the night are vague. Smoke drifts among treetops: the glow of the flames illuminates the standing stones at the barrow's southern end. Newspapers reported that swastikas were later found carved into the trees. Details are scarce, but it seems likely that a prophecy was recounted that night beside the tomb:

> In the days of the Lion, spawned of the Devil's brood, the Hooded Man shall come to the forest. There he will meet … Lord of the Trees, to be his son and do his bidding. The Powers of Light and Darkness shall be strong within him. And the guilty shall tremble.[8]

The group was Woden's Folk, a far-right organization which had been using Wayland's Smithy as a focus for their rituals since the late 1980s. Its followers were self-proclaimed believers in Woden – the Anglo-Saxon equivalent of the Norse god Odin, the father of the gods. Woden's Folk was formed by ex-National Front members who formed a breakaway sect of nationalists that had branched into mysticism. Central to the group's creed is the emergence of a 'Folk Führer' – a 'hero' to save England's Aryan people from extinction and rescue the racial 'purity' of the nation. Newspapers reported on 'neo-Nazi' goings-on at the ancient site. The National Trust said patrols would be stepped up.

Amid all those reports a detail went unnoticed. A blogger quietly pointed out the prophecy of the hooded man – the central theology of Woden's Folk, proclaimed on its website – wasn't particularly ancient. It was, in fact, lifted directly from the ITV show *Robin of*

Sherwood, a programme later starring Jason Connery (son of Sean) in the title role, which ran for three seasons from 1984 to 1986. It all seemed tragicomic – a myth for England, sourced from a Saturday teatime TV show that ran between the wrestling and the local news, and competed with *Brookside* on Channel 4. In 2022 an academic had tried to make sense of it all.

'Fascism is a somewhat unanchored ideology, not tethered to any foundational text or thinker,' according to Clive Henry of Northampton University, writing for the Centre for Analysis of the Radical Right. 'Some ... have pointed to themes of an endangered national community [in fascism] that require total rebirth, and these themes are readily found in popular culture narratives – even BBC [*sic*] family television programmes.'[9]

On his blog, a member of Woden's Folk made his riposte to his detractors.

> Firstly, yes this does come from the TV series *Robin of Sherwood* and was no doubt made up for the series. But that does not invalidate this as a prophecy, but we can only recognize it as such through the knowledge of what its hidden meaning is. ... The *Robin of Sherwood* series ... was a kind of 'trigger' for the heralding of the coming Avatar whose appearance will be made here in England. There is no doubt that the writer and the director and everyone else concerned did not do this consciously.

The blog's author seemed to believe the creators of the TV show were divinely inspired. He continued to post YouTube clips of *Robin of Sherwood* on his blog – the merry men sporting mullets, the synthesizer music of Irish folk group Clannad playing in the background. It was, by all accounts, a very popular programme back in the 1980s.

But what did any of this have to do with Wayland's Smithy? Wayland was a figure of Anglo-Saxon legend: a master smith (possibly a god) who was imprisoned by a king before killing his sons and taking flight by means of magic. *Sword of Wayland* was the name of the Woden's Folk magazine (and, perhaps not coincidentally, the name of series 2, episode 5, of *Robin of Sherwood*). Beyond the name, Wayland had associations with the real-life Oxfordshire long barrow: folklore goes that a horse that stopped for the night here would have a new set of horseshoes by morning (provided its owner left a sixpence, made themselves absent and never glanced over their shoulder to see the phantom smith at work).

Only one thing was clear. The figures of Wayland and Woden had absolutely nothing to do with the long barrow in its first form. The Anglo-Saxons – the English of whose 'purity' Woden's Folk cast themselves as guardians – arrived in Great Britain in the fifth century AD, about four thousand years after the mound was created. The Anglo-Saxon idea of 'Wayland's Smithy' would have attached itself to the site thereafter and was – in the greater scheme of things – almost as recent an imposition as the torch-wielding fascists and their Robin Hood messiah.

Wayland's Smithy was a Neolithic tomb and, as with many ancient sites along the Ridgeway, little could be said with certainty about its function or purpose. It was a ripe place for fantasies to flourish. I had walked the Ridgeway hoping to get a sense of prehistoric pilgrimage, but I could only ever seem to glimpse it through the prism of the more recent past, coloured by the prejudices, priorities and peculiarities of others.

I picked up my bag. We still had a long way to go before sunset.

INSIDE THE CIRCLE

The last stretch of the Ridgeway was the most beautiful. Soon after Wayland's Smithy, the path crossed the M4 on that concrete bridge. Then it swept upwards to the Iron Age hill fort at Liddington, and another later at Barbury – where, close by, a lone standing stone was adorned with a plaque dedicated to Richard Jefferies (1848–1887), engraved with words from his autobiography, *Story of My Heart* (1883):

IT IS ETERNITY NOW. I AM IN THE MIDST OF IT. IT IS ABOUT ME IN THE SUNSHINE.

Jefferies often wrote about the ocean-like vastness of the downs. It is a quality that others have identified in this landscape, where – with the absence of hedgerows or other obstructions to the wandering eye – the contours of the hills appear to dip and heave like swells. The flapping and flailing of crops could be surf cresting the waves. There is, of course, a deeper truth in these observations. The chalk of these downs was created millions of years ago, when plankton settled upon the seabed and became compacted into a brittle white mass.

The liquid tendencies of the land showed in the ancient earthworks too. At the Iron Age hill forts concentric rings of ditches and ramparts rippled outwards – as if a stone had been dropped into water from a great height, and the immediate aftermath frozen in time. Sometimes the Ridgeway itself seemed like a tsunami of chalk rearing over the world. We, the walkers on this aerial path, were riding its lip in the last instant before it broke and collapsed under its own weight.

You can see these earthworks from on high by watching the YouTube channel OpenMindedWonderer, which features drone videos about the prehistoric sites along the Ridgeway and other places. The channel is run by Cara Coles, an anaesthetic practitioner and advanced life-support provider from Devizes. She walked the entire Wessex Ridgeway from Avebury in 2019, and has since walked part of the Ridgeway in Wiltshire.

'I couldn't pinpoint as to why my walk was a pilgrimage,' Cara had told me over the phone. 'But it was. There was just an undying urge to walk it. There's a different feel to the Ridgeway to other paths. I don't know whether or not it's psychological, but I feel a sense of peace on it. A loss of mind.'

We continued along the Ridgeway for some hours, following a wrinkle in the brow of the hill. As on many pilgrimage routes, navigating was instinctive. We did not need to check the map. Such a well-defined path was an affirmation: we knew we were not lost. We had fallen into it as easily as a needle falls into the groove of a vinyl record. On the final leg into Avebury, the Ridgeway muddled through farmers' fields and country lanes, and then regained its foothold on a long, straight ridge where somebody was flying a kite. We stopped for lunch while Laska, the dog, chased a squirrel.

Eventually, Avebury appeared in the distance: standing stones, thatched cottages, the spire of the church of St James, the patron saint of pilgrims. The official Ridgeway National Trail terminated, rather anti-climactically, at a car park on the A4 just outside the village. Here the Ridgeway was one strand of a dense network of paths and roads that webbed through the countryside to converge on Avebury. We walked into town, smearing chalk on the tarmac as we went.

———

Fate had brought Marcus to Avebury.

Marcus was putting up fencing at the Equinox festival in Grimsby (he got a free festival ticket in return). Here he made new friends. One of them threw a 20-sided dice – the dice determined that everyone would get in a van and travel seven hours across the country to see the autumn equinox at Stonehenge. There the new friends did mushrooms. They watched the dawn. Marcus remembers walking barefoot into the inner sanctum of the stones, feeling dewdrops falling on his head from the megaliths. Then a security guard escorted him away.

Later that morning – still without sleep – the new friends drove 24 miles up the road to that other great stone circle at Avebury. At some point someone handed Marcus a wooden staff. He was already wearing a white hoodie. That morning, entirely by accident, he had adopted the attire of a Druid. Then he met a real Druid: Alix. He had a pack of Earth Warrior cards: she picked the Rainbow Jaguar, which – for reasons lost to my notebook – was a moment of significance. All of that was about two months ago. I was ending my pilgrimage in Avebury, but here, among the ancient stones, Marcus was only just starting out on his path into Druidry.

'I'm really owning this,' he told me. 'Giving back to the earth is what I want to do, the way they used to do it – back in the day. I'm so excited. I'm struggling to hold it all in.'

I met Marcus and Alix in the National Trust café in Avebury – I ordered him a chai latte; she didn't want anything. Marcus was in his early thirties, still wearing a white hoodie: he talked quickly, veering off at sudden tangents, and smoked roll-ups. Before becoming a Druid, he had been a busker and a skateboarder, he said. At Stonehenge and Avebury he had an epiphany. He was now staying with Alix in her house a few miles away, earning money doing odd painting and decorating jobs. And all the while learning from her about the Druid path, and how these ancient stones fitted into it.

'Three times in my life I've jumped into the unknown,' he said. 'This time I'm doing it properly.'

One other time, he said, was during the Covid lockdowns – when he left a four-year relationship in Spain (and a dog) to make sure his family in England were safe from the jabs. It was all about choice, he said. Even so, he missed the dog.

Alix, meanwhile, was older, and authoritative. I had contacted her by email – her signature marked her as a 'Scribe/Peace Druidess' belonging to the Druid Order of Avebury. In her hat were the feathers of a kite, a pheasant, a cormorant and two barn owls. With great kindness she agreed to show me around the landscape so I could see it through the eyes of a neo-pagan pilgrim. The Ridgeway, she believed, was a southbound pilgrimage route to Avebury used by Neolithic tribes during the winter solstice – a means of escape from the worst of the midwinter cold. We arranged to meet but had to push our appointment back a bit, because someone was coming to unblock Alix's sink.

Stonehenge may be the most famous ancient monument in Britain. But, in the words of the seventeenth-century antiquarian John Aubrey, Avebury did 'as much excel Stonehenge, as a Cathedral doth a parish church'.[10] It is part of a landscape formed by thousands of years of humans shifting about earth and heaving around rock. Around Avebury lie causewayed enclosures, mounds, avenues and other vague forms and patterns which – from aerial photos – look like almighty fingerprints impressed upon the earth. But the central focus is the Neolithic stone circle, whose origins

stretch back almost five thousand years, and which measures almost
a mile in circumference. It is ringed by an outer ditch and bank
which would have taken a million man-hours to excavate. It is seen
as a defining landmark of a new farming culture, when surplus
food meant people had time to turn their minds to greater matters,
to take their eyes away from the soil and up to the heavens. They
built the biggest prehistoric stone circle in the world (according to
the National Trust).

There were originally thought to be over 98 stones in Avebury's
outer circle, some weighing as much as 40 tonnes. Many were later
seen as heathen relics, destroyed in fits of rage by pious Christians,
cannily recycled as building materials or shifted about like chess
pieces in subsequent years. Nonetheless Avebury still remains a
discernible circle – dating to a time when circles seemed to be the
dominant holy symbol of the British Isles. There are other so-called
'superhenges', but what makes Avebury unique is the village that
sprung up at the centre of that circle. Little cottages, a gift shop and
a car park are all enclosed by the ancient stones: an A-road pierces
the henge, and a cricket pitch, a church and a daycare nursery rub
up against it. Close to the geometrical centre of the circle is a pub,
the Red Lion. Whatever the original religious function of Avebury
may have been millennia ago, the stones have – quite by accident
– come to enclose a slice of everything that is holy about England.

Pilgrimages of various kinds continue to be made here – mostly
by car, on coach tours, on the number 49 bus from Swindon. Alix
was responsible for coordinating the annual pilgrimages made by
travellers (which she said divided into off-grid travellers, pagan
travellers and music/ketamine travellers, who aren't doing the
others any favours). Even among stone-hearted atheists, the stones
of Avebury induce a strong reaction. Some experience a temporal
vertigo being in the presence of rock first heaved into position
almost five thousand years ago. When it all got too much, you
could always go to the pub.

Alix and Marcus would take me on a clockwise perambulation
around the outer stones so I might understand the power of the
temple. The size of Avebury meant that, to appreciate it fully, you

had to go for a hike. Willingly or not, it turned every visitor into a pilgrim.

'We know that ancient Druids would travel,' said Alix. 'When you travel, you are allowing new insight to enter into your head. We are taking in thirty thousand pieces of information every second. What is it you learned on your journey? What did you see?'

That day we saw a red kite circling in the distance. Trees swaying in the breeze. Bored grandparents in Barbour jackets pushing a pram along the muddy pathway. A British Gas van speeding along the A-road, into the circle and out the other side. I asked Alix and Marcus what they were feeling as we crossed the threshold into the circle. Alix was feeling a stirring in her chakras and her solar plexus; Marcus felt energy flowing up his legs into his jaw. The stones, Alix said, contained quartz – the same material found in watches, radios and satellites and the communicators from *Star Trek*. They stored vibrations, frequencies, past emotions. Some stones, she said, were best not touched because of the millennia of trauma stored within them.

Like Wayland's Smithy and the Uffington White Horse – indeed, like the Ridgeway and most prehistoric sites along it – no historian could explain with full confidence the function of Avebury's stone circle. They could only speculate on the basis of thin archaeological evidence. It seemed very likely it was a space set apart from the rest of the world, for within Avebury's innermost circles excavations had found almost no trace of human activity. Perhaps it was somewhere set aside for holy beings. Or perhaps the stones were the holy beings themselves.

The form of the circle may have represented the sun, the moon, the turn of the seasons, the passage of the year, a never-ending line that meant infinity – some of the above, all of the above – perhaps none of them at all. No one knew for sure. Many interpretations of the circle seemed to go around in circles.

Alix had plenty of explanations. She believed each of the 98 stones stood for the different tribes that gathered here. She understood that energy lines coursed through the ancient temple, supplying its power, and also that the outer bank of the henge was once exposed chalk – so that it could be seen by pilgrims arriving from the surrounding hills like the White Horse. Alix had once, out of the corner of an eye, seen a white chalky light rotating around the henge. She came here with other Druids to conduct ceremonies in flowing robes, in sunshine and in hail. It was heartening to see these ancient stones still had meaning to someone. But I couldn't help but feel that every precise explanation of Avebury unrobed it of some of its mystery.

Avebury has been associated with Druids since antiquarians made the first investigations in the seventeenth century, proclaiming it to be a Celtic temple. Modern historians now understand that any link between the Druid priests known to exist at the time of the Roman invasion of Britain and Neolithic Avebury is fanciful – a temporal gap of almost three millennia separates them. Indeed the Druids mentioned by Julius Caesar and others are closer in time to the present day than they were to the builders of Avebury. Alix was undeterred. She was open-eyed that her version of Druidry was a modern reinvention of something ancient. To her it didn't matter.

'We all have a calling: a "knowing"', she said. 'We always had it within us anyway – it's in our genetics. The first people who came to Avebury were coming to feel love with their fellow man and with the planet. Now we are on the edge of another awakening.'

Halfway around the stone circle we stopped under a copse of four copper beeches. People had tied ribbons to the branches and roots in memory of the departed. There were other memorials: poppies for a fallen soldier, marmalade in memory of Queen Elizabeth II and – in a little hollow of the beech trees – the figure of Jar Jar Binks from the *Star Wars* prequel *Episode I: The Phantom Menace*.

Samhain was the time of the dead: a 'thin' time of year, Alix explained, when the boundary between this world and other worlds was less defined. A few days before I had arrived, the Druids had been conducting ceremonies for the departed along the Avenue – a Neolithic thoroughfare which led south-east, away from the main stone circle, to a second called the Sanctuary. Marcus had joined the procession, carrying an apple in memory of his grandma and grandpa. They were both nice people, he said, from County

Durham. They had been pen pals as kids. His grandma played the organ in the church. Halfway down the avenue he had seen – out of the corner of an eye – what he thought was an old woman walking beside him, under a white cloak. But when he looked closer it was one of the standing stones.

He placed his apple on a wicker basket, which was then cast out onto the River Kennet. He said he hoped one day the apple seeds would grow into a tree downstream. Everyone paid their respects. Marcus said he was also thinking about his dog in Spain.

A NIGHT IN THE LONG BARROW

I said goodbye to Marcus and Alix. My friend Al and his dog Laska returned from an evening ramble. Our pilgrimage to Avebury ended with a burger and a pint (and a bowl of dog biscuits) in the Red Lion. The van was still back in Woolstone, which meant we needed somewhere to sleep that night.

'You lads could sleep inside the long barrow. Lots of people do.'

Ted Walker was sitting on the next table. He had driven here from Newbury for his evening reiki class, and was having a pint before the session started. The landscape of Avebury was, of course, ancient, but its oldest components were the long barrows – tombs like Wayland's Smithy, which pre-dated the formation of the stone circles by many centuries. Long barrows spanned the Atlantic coast of Europe, from Scandinavia in the north to Spain in the south. Collectively they were the oldest tradition of stone structure in the world. They were certainly tombs, and perhaps shrines for ancestor worship. From above, the particular kind of long barrows around Avebury looked like the earth had been heaped in the shape of a teardrop.

There was one with a chamber big enough to sleep inside: Ted had slept there himself three years ago. He was a natural cynic, but he woke up at 2 a.m. feeling that he was being pushed on the shoulder.

'I said out loud to whatever it was: "You can push me, but you can't get me out of here!"'

Then he went back to sleep. He looked pleased to have fought off the invisible force. He was an open-minded person, he said as he put on his coat. There had to be more to life than us all turning to dust at the end of it.

Walking through fields once again: moonlight quivering in the River Kennet, moon shadows creeping out from the megaliths, like black ink spilled across the autumn fields. A few cars sped along the A4, the beams of their headlights flushing the underbelly of clouds, before disappearing over the hills and allowing the night to reclaim the road. Ahead of us rose the prehistoric silhouette of Silbury Hill, the largest artificial prehistoric mound in Europe. Alix had said lightning struck here once a year, to inject nitrates into the soil and fertilize the earth. Over the road was Farmer Mark's pumpkin patch, where the fields were full of plump pumpkins. Farmer Mark's was closed now, but in the daytime you could have tea and cake there. There were tractor rides for kids.

We eventually found the long barrow Ted had mentioned – a bump in the earth at the centre of a large field. Giant sarsen stones guarded a black opening in the soil. We hesitated and then – dropping our heads – stepped down a long passageway, into the murk of the five-millennia-old tomb. We moved slowly. Inside, the beams of our head torches illuminated the clefts in the rock, and a sequence of tiny rooms. Offerings had been placed on natural shelves: apples, incense, crystals (one with the price tag still on). We switched off our head torches and listened to the drip drip drip of water. The tomb felt entirely different from the cave on the Gower: its darkness was thicker, its sounds more intimate and uneasy. There was a smell of soil and rotting. In the warmth of the pub we had talked ourselves into sleeping here. Now we were too proud to talk our way out of it. We unrolled our sleeping bags and Laska's dog basket. We each had a sip of whisky from a hip flask. Roughly an hour before midnight, still unable to sleep, Al suggested we meditate.

He looked for his usual meditation podcast. Soon an American voice was telling us to feel the force of gravity beneath us. The voice explained the entire world was mediated by our own perceptions. That silken voice was comforting down in the damp of the Long Barrow. The electric light of the phone offered a toehold of familiarity in the gloom.

'Allow your thoughts to centre on every breath.'

Laska the dog began to shuffle uneasily.

'Perceive the flow of your own experiences.'

Laska turned to the entrance of the barrow and began to emit a low, angry growl.

'Feel the raw sensations ... the galaxy of sensations.'

Al still had his eyes closed, but his dog was becoming more and more agitated, barking at someone, or something, at the entrance of the tomb.

'Return your attention to your breath.'

The dog was still barking, straining at its lead. Suddenly – dimly discernible against the night sky – there was movement near the entrance to the tomb. We both froze, as it came nearer. Fear daggered through me as it manifested itself as a human figure.

'Evening gents, how're you doing?'

The figure turned out to be Daniel Elliot, an account manager for a telecommunications firm, from Purton (near Swindon). He had had a rough day at work, he said, and decided to go for a walk before bedtime. A voice in his head had told him to come to the long barrow. He sat down for a chat. It turned out he was a regular walker on the Ridgeway.

'There's a feeling of something bigger on the Ridgeway. Perhaps it's the resonance of all the years gone by.'

A few years ago, Daniel explained he started going to lectures on what he called 'non-mainstream' subjects. Then he had started dowsing – using metal rods to detect energies in the earth – and set about investigating the stones around Avebury. He sometimes felt like he was on the fringe of piecing it all together. Most recently, Daniel had seen a big muscular biker – a Hell's Angel-type figure clad in leather – step inside a stone circle. The biker faced the sunset, fell to his knees and pulled out a can of beer, ritually pouring the golden liquid down into the Earth, as tears streamed from his eyes.

'I wanted to say to him: "What do you know? What do you know about this place that the information boards aren't telling us?!?"'

I drifted in and out of a shallow sleep, occasionally rolling over to feel the cold stones pressing against my forehead. There was the uneasy fidgeting of the dog against my back. I half-dreamed about the things that Daniel had said before he left us and went home.

At 3 a.m. a noise woke me up. Close by – on the opposite side of the tomb to Al and Laska – was a sound I could not place: like a piece of paper being ripped. That sound came again from the blackness: some kind of rupture, quieter this time.

Instinctively, I didn't want to see where it had come from. I pulled my sleeping bag over my head and switched on my head torch. It was something I had imagined. It came again ten minutes later. Now, fully awake, my blood went cold. I lay inside the sleeping bag for an hour or more, trying to distract myself by reading and re-reading the little label about washing machine settings, trying not to think about what we might have disturbed. I must have finally fallen asleep around five. At breakfast time there was nothing to suggest what might have caused the strange sound in the long barrow. And so my journey along the Ridgeway ended as it began – with unanswered questions.

Al had to rush back to Avebury early, to catch a bus to Swindon and somehow reach his van. A grey, grudging dawn lit the puddles at the entrance to the tomb as we packed our bags. In the half-light outside was an information board we hadn't noticed the night before, explaining that three dozen people had been buried here, five millennia before.

Samhain was a season of the dead. And more than anything else, walking the Ridgeway stirred thoughts about mortality. The dead writers. The temple of the dead at Avebury. And the long-dead who had buried their own dead in the barrows like Wayland's Smithy – and also the tomb in which I had slept so uneasily, disturbed by something that perhaps was not living. I had walked the Ridgeway half-hoping to understand the intentions of ancient pilgrims from the many chalk markings and stone monuments along the trail – I had wondered if, when you panned back, the Ridgeway might form a kind of sentence to be read from on high, a story woven from its many strands. But it did not seem so simple. Every stop on the path had its own kind of cryptic silence, or almost silence. The rush of the wind at the White Horse and on the hilltop paths. The white noise of traffic passing at Avebury stone circle. The drip drip drip of the tomb in which I had just slept.

This long barrow – and many others like it – were the first markers of human settlement in Britain after an eternity of wandering. Some of the first roofs to be erected under these skies. Perhaps the accumulation of soil here embodied the earliest expressions of home – the first ideas of belonging. Perhaps the people interred within it were guardians of the farmland – the dead who kept watch over the fields from that original home of the long barrow, up on the hill. Could there ever be a way of knowing?

AT ALL CANNINGS

There was one very last place I wanted to visit. If you follow the trajectory of the original Ridgeway six miles south of Avebury, you eventually crest the summit of Tan Hill – a green, whaleback ridge (just a metre short of being the tallest point of Wiltshire). At the top, the Vale of Pewsey unfurls to the south: red-brick villages, barns, the glint of a wandering canal. It would be a scene of the utmost serenity – were it not for the artillery of the British Army, then busy training Ukrainian soldiers on Salisbury Plain. The ground shook beneath my boots as I left Al behind and stepped into the morning mists of Tan Hill.

It was along this same route – the farmer Tim Daw remembered – that another lone hiker had walked from Avebury one autumn a few years before. He was dressed much as I was – woollen socks, walking boots, anorak. Descending Tan Hill, this pilgrim would have seen the outline of All Cannings long barrow on the plains to the south. It looked much like the many other long barrows that dotted the landscape around Avebury: another teardrop-shaped mound in the earth, a roof tufted with grass. Tim Daw watched the hiker approach, greeted him and explained that, unfortunately, he couldn't go in the tomb today: it was closed. Someone was being interred, and they were having a service. Then the pilgrim held up the urn he was carrying – the ashes of his brother, who he had taken for one last walk in the hills.

'I wasn't really prepared for dealing with bereaved people,' said Tim. 'I hadn't really thought that part of it through. But I've had lovely conversations with people who are terminally ill. Knowing where their ashes are going has given them ... some peace.'

I had arranged to meet Tim outside the All Cannings long barrow – he was softly spoken, middle-aged, wearing a Carhartt jacket and a New York Yankees beanie hat. Tim was first and foremost a farmer – he worked a few arable fields. But a lifelong interest in archaeology had led him to work for English Heritage at Stonehenge for some years. It was here that he conceived of a new addition to the Wessex landscape: a brand new Neolithic long barrow, or perhaps a 'Novolithic' one, that would occupy a corner of his farmland. He would sell 340 niches to anyone who wanted their ashes entombed in the Wiltshire earth (at £1,000 each). The money would fund the construction of a mound inspired by five-millennia-old equivalents at Wayland's Smithy and, of course, the famous West Kennet Long Barrow near Avebury. Ground was broken at the winter solstice in 2013. Construction was undertaken by stonemasons who travelled down from Anglesey every week, speaking to each other in Welsh and using only construction techniques familiar to Neolithic builders. 'We're not using concrete,' they had told Tim. 'Because concrete doesn't last long enough.' The All Cannings Long Barrow opened on the autumn equinox in 2014. The niches quickly sold out.

Tim unlocked the iron gates and showed me into a gloomy passageway – eerily similar to the one I had half-slept in the previous night, down to the dripping water. The walls were lined with different kinds of rock – flint from the fields near Stonehenge. A slab of blue dolerite from the hills of south Wales, sparkling like stars in the night sky whenever it got damp.

We then branched off into a series of antechambers, lined with shelves. These niches – I would guess 50 centimetres square – in turn contained urns of all sizes. The ashes of Sylvia and John were kept in ceramic tea and coffee pots made in a pottery class in the 1970s. Other urns were adorned with Christian crosses, Wicca pentangles, pyramids. Beside them were objects that somehow represented a life lived. A decanter. A ceramic penguin. A pair of reading glasses and a dog collar. Yellow photographs were spotted with mould. Little memorials offered the last words: *Peter Butler: Quantity Surveyor, Stamp Collector, All Round Top Bloke.* Some niches were waiting for owners who were still living – but who had already placed objects in anticipation of their own passing. These were the things that people had wanted to survive of them – to be exhumed and decoded by archaeologists in another five millennia.

Tim explained that the All Cannings Long Barrow was registered as a pagan place of worship (partly for business rates). There were plenty of pagans and Druids inside. He himself followed no particular religious path.

'We're very keen to make it for people of no faith, or any faiths,' he said. 'I'm probably like a lot of people for whom there's a feeling that the established churches don't speak for us. But we also don't want to live in a soulless world. The underlying belief that I've got is that – well – that it's a wonderful world. We come inside the long barrow and we celebrate people who've done wonderful things. To "give" thanks, shouldn't be a transitive verb: you don't have to give thanks to some great God. You can just be thankful.'

I spent an hour inside the tomb – Tim showing me the niches, the many urns, the work of the Welsh stonemasons. He showed me one niche upon which a butterfly had landed the moment someone was being interred within it – another in which his own remains would one day be laid. This would be his final home. His idea had caught on. New Novolithic burial mounds were now popping up across the UK. In coming to All Cannings I had branched off the Ridgeway – had detoured too from the ancient world. And yet here I felt far closer to understanding the path I had walked from Goring.

'I've lived here all my life,' said Tim. 'And I feel very settled in this landscape. I know its lumps and bumps. I've seen its changes over the years. It's only when you're settled in a place that you want to build something to mark it, and say: "I'm going to stay here permanently." I think that's probably why, as a farmer, I was drawn to the idea of building a long barrow.'

As we left, Tim pointed to a stone at the back of the passageway – it could be a seat, or an altar – it could be whatever you wanted it to be. In any case the passageway was aligned so that the winter solstice sunrise lit this stone – a feature like some other ancient long barrows and stone circles – perhaps even like the White Horse carrying the sun god. On 21 December, when the northern hemisphere was farthest from the sun, precious rays of light entered into the darkness and dampness of the tomb at All Cannings – the beams bringing with them the promise of summer, and fresh hope. People had wanted to be buried in All Cannings to connect their remains with the ancient past, under a roof which would preserve them into the distant future – to position themselves in a greater context of time. Similarly Tim had wanted to place his corner of this Wiltshire field in the greater context of the universe.

'The idea is that by aligning with the sunrise you're connecting it to something bigger. There's nothing much bigger than the sun. You're putting the stake in the ground. You're saying, "This is built like this for a reason." We're monumentalizing people's lives. We're saying Gran was worth remembering. She was someone special.'

We stepped outside, briefly dazzled by the daylight. The ground still rumbled with explosions on Salisbury Plain. This was where my journey ended. The Ridgeway had unquestionably changed with the passage of time. The stones of its monuments had been rearranged, the long barrows had been deconstructed by archaeologists (and put back together again), the chalk figures re-sketched, the path itself diverted and tarmacked over – bisected by busy roads, encroached on by new buildings. In this upended landscape it took a great lunge of imagination to visualize the Ridgeway as a place of prehistoric pilgrimage. But in those hours when the vapour trails of Heathrow-bound planes dissolved, the sky at least was unchanged since prehistory: this sky which had been my companion since walking on the escarpment. The clouds flew by. The moon and sun rose and set. And once a year the sun passed the passageway at the All Cannings Long Barrow. For Tim and his customers, these were the points with which to orientate ourselves in this life – and into the next – as sailors did out at sea.

As the iron gates of the tomb clanged shut, Tim pointed to his own design – a sole concession to symbology, two intersecting lines welded onto the bars.

'It's based on DNA – DNA is the ultimate life force, for which our bodies are just temporary receptacles. But it could also be two paths that cross. I suppose the idea is that we're all on journeys. We come together. We pass away. Something carries on.'

4

An Island

A Celtic Christian Pilgrimage

The Size of the Boat | Pilgrimage | Islanders | Work Week |
Another Boat | The Bay at the Back of the Ocean |
Hill of the Angels | Reading Again | At Martyr's Bay

Island – Inside Iona Abbey

THE SIZE OF THE BOAT

St Columba was a man who performed many miracles.

Like Christ, he turned water into wine, helped fill the nets of fishermen and raised the dead from their slumber. Like Moses, he spoke to angels and could summon water from a rock. Columba could see into the past and the future (and was always especially knowledgeable about what was going on in Ireland). He could open locked doors by making a sign of the cross. He fought demons: some attacked him with iron darts in the wilderness; another one hid inside a milk pail. He slayed a serpent that some have identified as the Loch Ness monster. It was believed, in later years, that invoking Columba's name could cure indigestion and toothache. It was said he could control the weather.

He did all these miraculous things. And yet St Columba's best-known act was the sea journey he made from Ireland to Scotland – sailing the edge of the Atlantic in a coracle of wicker and cowhide. The size of this boat remains a matter of conjecture for artists in particular. A painting beside the nave of Iona Abbey shows Columba in a craft you'd guess to be eight feet long – the sort of boat you might hire by the hour on a boating lake, perhaps for a picnic. Within it, a dark-eyed saint holds a book of psalms aloft into a tempest, as his disciples heave at their oars. On a windowsill by the abbey altar is a model of something more substantial: a skiff or a little sloop maybe, in which Columba and his followers might have braved the squalls with greater confidence. Others envisaged even smaller boats. In the corridors of Iona Abbey, near the spot where staying guests deposit their used laundry, is a painting of a vessel roughly the dimensions of a bathtub, with 12 seasick disciples stacked in a pyramid at the stern (Columba was depicted haloed at the bow). Of all the paintings I saw, the one that resonated with me most was a 2012 commission I found online by American artist Daniel Mitsui. It showed a boat about the size of a washing-up bowl, on which the saint had travelled alone through the Atlantic swells. Bearded and blue-eyed, Columba stands steadfast and upright in his tiny coracle, no fear of the powerful waves that fissured at his feet.

Some things about Columba are clearer than others. It is believed he was born to a noble family in Ireland in 521 and studied at some of the first Christian monasteries to emerge along the Atlantic seaboard of Europe. He was tall, had a loud and mellifluous voice that projected to faraway hills and – despite his Christian mercy – was prone to fits of sudden rage. Some historians have speculated that Columba might have been crowned King of Ireland had he lived out his days in his homeland. But in 563, when he was in the throes of middle age (just as Jesus and Mohammed were when their lives changed), Columba made a decision to sail to Scotland. Possibly it was because of a quarrel with another holy man. Perhaps it was because he had got in trouble for copying a manuscript without permission.

Or perhaps it was because he wanted to immerse himself in a life of *peregrinato* – the spirit of sacred, directionless wandering embodied by those early Irish saints. He may have been a bit like three monks recorded in the Anglo-Saxon Chronicle who landed on the coast of Cornwall in an oarless boat and who said they were content to be steered by Christ. Another term associated with Columba is the 'white martyrdom': a form of suffering without blood. In this case it was a self-imposed banishment from your homeland, and a separation from everything you hold dear. To travel further was a way to become nearer to God. To make a journey into the unknown was to step beyond the self and propel the soul forward. For whatever reason, Columba set out to sea. In the words of one poet, Beccán mac Luigdech, Columba 'crucified … his body on the grey waves'.

> In scores of curraghs [coracles] with an army of wretches he
>   crossed the long-haired sea
> He crossed the wave-strewn wild region
> Foam-flecked, seal-filled
> Savage, bounding, seething, white-tipped, pleasing, doleful.[1]

Columba decided he would settle in a place where his native Ireland was out of sight. From Donegal he travelled across the Mull of

Kintyre. Squinting on the shore at Southend, he could perhaps still make out his homeland on the horizon – and so he cast off once again, sailing northward until he hit a pebbly bay on Iona: a tiny crumb of an island off the Isle of Mull.

Here Columba established a monastery made of wood, wattle and daub in a model of Jerusalem. A community of monks joined him, farming the fertile strip of land at the island's centre, fishing the Atlantic and the Sound of Iona, hunting the seal colonies and copying the gospels by candlelight. Iona represented a lasting foothold for Christianity in the pagan wilderness of northern Britain. From here the news of Christ began to spread up the glens. Soon Iona was the brightest star in a nebula of daughter houses that stretched across Scotland. The island was a place set apart from the world – not by political, administrative or notional boundaries but by the sea that enshrined it. The island was a place where the world could be remade in microcosm. The island was the seed of a radical new idea.

Iona was home to a unique religious tradition that had crystallized at this westernmost cusp of Eurasia. Celtic Christianity came to be synonymous with solitude, and oneness with nature. Legends went that birds perched in the hair of the monks as they wrote, and nested in their skulls once they had passed. Columba often wandered the island's wild interior. He once nursed a sickly crane back to health over three days. His very name meant 'dove'. In May 597 the elderly Columba was visited by a white horse that shed tears into his breast. It was a sign. The next day the saint died: a pillar of fire blazed in the sky. The ferry to Mull didn't run for a few days (ferry disruption still happens today).

Thereafter the island's sacred solitude seems to have been short-lived. Pilgrims came to Iona. Forty-eight Scottish, eight Norwegian and four Irish kings were buried in the island's holy soil – funeral armadas sailed here via Loch Linnhe, Loch Feochan and Loch Spelve (among them were Macbeth and Duncan, who, someone said, can still be heard quarrelling in their graves). Iona became a hub of learning, literature and art. Trees barely grew on this gale-whipped isle, but stone crosses did. Accounts say some 360 Celtic crosses towered here: a forest of sculpted stone, garlanded with lichens. These crosses were among the first to establish the now familiar design – vertical and horizontal lines intersecting over a circle – which has been interpreted as representing the sun, or the moon or perhaps the earth (maybe it was just a circle).

In the eighth century the Vikings raided Iona. The monastery's power began to wane. Almost all the crosses were smashed to smithereens once the Reformation reached the Hebrides, at which point the monks fled, and pilgrims came no longer. The Benedictine abbey that was the inheritor of Columba's monastic tradition was ruined, parts of it recycled in local buildings. Iona had burned brightly throughout the so-called Dark Ages. Its sacred light had been extinguished by the time of the Scottish Enlightenment. By the late eighteenth century a minister only visited Iona four times a year, on the ferry.

Only later did Iona become a place of pilgrimage for Victorian travel writers craving an echo of Columba's miracles. In the sixth century it had been a model from which the world to the east might take heed. But for those now arriving from that direction Iona came to be regarded as an otherworld that had been preserved by the western seas: a place apart, where time ticked along at a different speed, and where Celtic Christianity intermingled with magic and an undercurrent of paganism. Some writers confidently asserted the island had been a place of sun worship, moon worship and Druidry – others said locals still cast oats into the sea, in hope that a sea god would bring seaweed to fertilize their crops, and did not pass by the old monastery alone after nightfall. 'Seeing is believing,' wrote William Maxwell in *Iona and the Ionians* (1857): 'all of [the islanders] have stories "by the hundred" of personal encounters and rencounters with the supernatural.'[2] A potato famine and emigration to America saw the population of Iona dwindle to a hundred. As its original inhabitants left, the fantasies of others continued to creep in.

And they still do. Iona is an island imagined from afar in complex and contradictory ways. Bookshelves creak with volumes on Iona: explorations of early Christianity, and more dubious texts describing a place populated with fairies, Druids, ghosts (and even visited by Jesus Christ and Mary Magdalene). More than anywhere I travelled for this book, Iona seemed a place that prompted wild infatuations – dreams drifted northwards, to settle on this little Scottish island. Its sonorous and beautiful name has travelled far – the three vowel sounds put me in mind of the changing notes of an ocean wind, snagging only on the hard rock of the letter N. The name *Iona* was recently bestowed on a P&O cruise ship with capacity for 5,206 people and a gross tonnage of 184,089, with four swimming pools and an onboard bar conceived by Gary Barlow. Yet no boat ever seemed so remarkable to me as that small coracle that brought St Columba across the sea from Ireland.

But what also drew me to the island were those thoughts of the saint in his craft, traversing the ranges and ridges of a stormy sea – crossing through the canyons that cleaved between the waves, cresting the summits of snowy-white surf, feeling the quake of the North Atlantic under the thin cowhide hull.

Then, as now, it could be a long journey to get to Iona.

PILGRIMAGE

It was still dark when my alarm clock went off in London. Outside, foxes were rummaging about the wheelie bins. Cats stalked the amber pools cast by streetlights. It was too early for the tube, too late to find a taxi easily. Also waiting for the night bus were a couple returning home from a party and some cleaners bound for City offices. This bus stop was where some people's days ended and others' began, though neither group looked at the other: they just watched their breath plume in the chilly air. At Stoke Newington a drunkard in a leather jacket lurched on board and demanded the driver take him home. The driver parked up the N73 and put on his hazards.

'But I can't take you home if you can't remember where you live, can I, mate?'

Snow was falling outside the northbound train from King's Cross – the flakes fleeting past carriages, feathering the windowsills. Then the snow turned heavier: heaping by the lineside, turning the fields and fenlands the same pale blue as a before-dawn sky. The train ran slowly. The turbines at the Biggleswade wind farm were dead still. Near Peterborough a frightened rabbit bolted, blotting a field with its footsteps. The snow was heaviest near Grantham. Close by, Isaac Newton's apple tree would have seen its fruitless branches burdened by this late winter flurry. Once or twice in Nottinghamshire the train slowed and cut its engine, and for a minute passengers could press their noses to the cold pane and watch gravity bring flakes down on that muted morning world – a moment when the memory of past winters seemed to be stirred. Then the engine whirred up again, and we were on our way. Schools were deciding whether or not to close.

Further north the sun came up and the snow thinned out. York Minster had a few patches. Durham Cathedral a light dusting. The Angel of the North spread out snowless arms. We crossed the border. I stopped for a Costa coffee in Edinburgh.

A smaller, slower train hauled out of Glasgow Queen Street on that grey afternoon. One of the American tourists at the table opposite me said *Condé Nast Traveler* had described the West Highland line as 'one of the most beautiful railway rides in the world'. They stared blankly at the retail estates at Dumbarton and the perimeter around the Royal Navy's nuclear submarine base at Faslane. They cooed as we passed the frozen edges of Loch Lomond and Loch Awe, and counted a 12-pointed stag near Tyndrum. Highland air snuck through the gaps of that old, arthritic train and brought with it the mood of the mountains outside.

Eleven hours and 14 minutes after leaving King's Cross my ticket expired at the port of Oban. The doors opened, and the smell of the harbour hit high in the nostrils: seaweed, engine oil, fish entrails. Most of the passengers headed straight to the next-door Wetherspoon's, where people sat among heaps of luggage, killing time between the Glasgow trains and the ferries to the islands. The Wetherspoon's was called The Corryvreckan – named after a sea channel not far to the south, between the islands of Scarba and Jura. Here the Atlantic flood tide squeezes into a narrow cleft, where it is obstructed by an underwater pyramid of basalt. The whirlpool formed here is one of the most powerful in the world. The Corryvreckan today is regarded as unnavigable by many seafarers, though apparently the medieval bishop Cólman mac Beognai had other ideas. Columba had a vision of the bishop as he sailed through the maelstrom while making his pilgrimage to Iona.

> St Columba was in his mother church, he suddenly smiled and called out: 'Cólman mac Beognai has set sail to come here, and is now in great danger in the surging tides of the whirlpool of Corryvreckan. Sitting in the prow, he lifts up his hands to heaven and blesses the turbulent, terrible seas. Yet the Lord terrifies him in this way, not so that the ship in which he sits should be overwhelmed and wrecked by the waves, but rather to rouse him to pray more fervently that he may sail through the peril and reach us here.'[3]

At the bar in the Wetherspoon's, a man in a SuperDry hoodie asked me what I was doing in Oban. I explained I was on a pilgrimage to the holy island of Iona. It was a long journey up from London – two days, three trains, two ferries and also a bus – a complex trip in which one missed connection risked domino-ing into the next. I could take a flight to Australia in the time it would take for me to get there, I said. But the effort of getting there was part of it. I was going to the island to work as a volunteer – to help the religious community there prepare the abbey for the season ahead. And in the process I wanted to get to know this mysterious place. Had he ever been there?

'No,' said SuperDry, sounding weary. He took a sip of lager. 'I've just come up to Oban for the weekend with my da. We've come here to get absolutely smashed.'

A few figures on the deck of the evening ferry to Craignure, puffing into cupped hands. Above us, a captain's chin, lit neon-green by the electronic displays at the bridge. The sea below dark – its surface suddenly silvered by the sweeping beam of the Lismore lighthouse, the water like mercury for one illuminated instant – and then returning to darkness again. Lesser beams sparked on the horizon, and car alarms were going off somewhere below deck. Drivers were always forgetting to put the handbrake on, a man in a hi-vis jacket said to no one in particular, however many fucking times you told them.

Craignure was the main ferry port for Mull (island population around 2,500) – which was itself a stepping stone to the far smaller Isle of Iona. There was not a huge deal to see in Craignure, apart from a Spar shop, a fire station and a pub which was about to call time. The police station seemed to double up as a family home, and had a trampoline on its front lawn. The last bus from Craignure for the Iona ferry had left hours before, so I pitched my tent at a seaside campsite, ate cold pasta from Tesco and dozed off to the hoots of owls hunting the waters of the Sound.

A deep sleep. A steely dawn, which reeled a mackerel sky out of the west. A bus driver on the pavement mainlining fags. On you go, son. The journey across Mull was an hour-long bus ride along a single-track road, during which signs of humanity thinned out. A primary school seemed to have just six pupils, of varying sizes, in the playground. There were conifer plantations – some neat and regimented, some scythed down to stumps. Pebbledash houses clung on amid the immensity of moorland, mountain and salt marsh. The final half-hour the bus ran along the Ross of Mull – the narrow peninsula that juts out like a pointing finger towards Iona. By the roadside were upright stones, said by some to be markers to guide Christian pilgrims on this weather-beaten road to the holy island. Others conjectured that the monoliths had prehistoric origins, suggesting a more ancient sanctity to this route.

At the end of the Ross of Mull was the tiny harbour of Fionnphort, from which you could see all of Iona for the first time: three miles long, barely a mile and a half wide, still not a great deal more than a hundred residents. The northern and southern ends of the island were defined by bulbous hills – in between was a plain, in which stood the only village: Baile Mór, meaning 'big village'. The abbey which rose at the edge of Baile Mór was still the biggest structure on Iona. The view from Fionnphort pier was the classic summer postcard of Iona, now rendered in the greys of winter. I went to board the ferry.

A ferry across the Sound had existed since the days of St Columba – it used to be summoned by setting alight to clumps of heather. Today it was a rusty 1992-built ship that had crashed on its first day in service, but enjoyed better luck since. This mile-wide strait looked easy to navigate, but people had died crossing it, and the pilots were some of the bravest in Scotland, someone told me. Sometimes when the swell got up and the storms blew in, Iona could be cut off for five days or more.

Ten minutes later, the ramp thumped down on Iona's pier. Lobster pots were stacked up on the quays, beside python coils of ropes. A woman in high heels hobbled past me carrying a bouquet of flowers, probably purchased in Oban and already wilted from the journey. Everything on the island was shut. Cuddly Angus cattle toys sat on the unlit shelves of the gift shops. A sign said the Columba Hotel was closed for the winter, and you should check social media for updates. The one thing that was open were the public toilets. Someone had written 'Fuck The Police' in one of the men's cubicles. The nearest police station was well over an hour away. I wondered if they meant the policeman with the trampoline in his garden at Craignure.

I followed the island's solitary, single-track tarmac road, and it began to drizzle. By the road were the Celtic crosses that had survived the Reformation – some were replicas or surviving in jigsaw pieces. A car pulled up next to me, a man wound down the window and asked in a Canadian accent if I would like a ride. Five minutes later, in the warmth of the Abbey, I was given a key.

'You're in Room 13. I don't know what you've done to deserve that.'

ISLANDERS

In 1904 tentative restoration efforts began on the ruins of Iona Abbey – among the tourists paying a visit was a nine-year-old from a well-off Glasgow family, named George MacLeod. Exactly one decade later MacLeod fought in the First World War, whose horrors lead him (exactly one decade on from that) to become a Church of Scotland minister. Seeing Britain in the aftermath of the First World War led him to conclude the church was estranged from the everyday struggles of ordinary people. MacLeod was a paradoxical figure. The son of a baronet and a vicar. A pacifist and a socialist. A man who visited a parishioner dying of cancer carrying a bottle of champagne for consolation.

He saw it as his mission to apply his Christian faith to matters of social justice, and his thoughts wandered back to his boyhood island. In 1938, when he was the same age as Columba when he set out in his coracle (42), MacLeod founded the Iona Community, with the aim of both restoring the largely ruined Benedictine abbey and also restoring its spiritual life. He would bring in unemployed tradesmen from inner-city Glasgow to do the graft. He would welcome people from afar into the new Community's healing embrace. The relationship with the existing islanders wasn't always easy (there were disputes about boundary walls), but progress was made. New roofs were fitted to medieval buildings. In 1957 electricity came to Iona: MacLeod organized the illumination of a Celtic cross. A kind of light was rekindled.

Today the Iona Community endures as an ecumenical organization unaligned with any denomination, sitting at the most progressive wing of Christianity. It offers stays in the abbey – with warm, cosy guest rooms arranged around medieval cloisters and a daily programme of prayer, work, conversation and thought. Around 50 people gather in the refectory three times a day – staff, long-term volunteers and guests – to eat mostly vegetarian meals. Flying over them are the banners of Black Lives Matter and the Progress Pride Flag, representing the LGBTQ+ community. In the cloisters is a sign saying 'Refugees Welcome', while in the nave of the church are displays about nuclear disarmament. It presents a different vision of Christianity from the one to which many are accustomed. And yet it was not the first time this island in the sea had been a place for a radically different kind of faith.

The people I met there represented a spectrum of belief: there were committed Christians and also folks who were curious. Some had just graduated, others had been made redundant, a few recently retired – many were in a weightless stage of their lives, and had come to ground themselves on the rocky island. Many were (or had been) islanders themselves.

Ken was the softly spoken Canadian librarian who had offered me a lift: he had previously been a teacher on Baffin Island, which straddles the Arctic Circle. It was a challenging place to live, he said. When the kids did cross-country runs, parents went out in their ATVs armed with rifles to make sure no one got eaten by polar bears.

Jonathan had grown up on the Isle of Wight, in a more innocent age when people didn't lock their front doors. Then one day someone walked in and stole the family's cooker. He liked to holiday often on remote islands: Lundy, Fair Isle, Lewis, Harris. He had also lived in Mauritania – where he had played rugby in the stony desert and taught the air traffic controllers to speak English.

Tracey was in charge of housekeeping. She had grown up on the Isle of Sheppey in the Thames estuary: she described herself as a mermaid, because she was only settled when she was surrounded by water (which she said was a metaphor for the ebb and flow of life). She had a hamsa hanging on her bracelet, symbolizing the chakras. She had taught yoga in a Category-B prison on Sheppey, to murderers and paedophiles. She described their minds being full of guilt, and their bodies begging for release.

Ian was a chaplain for the NHS in Lancashire. He had spent time on Lindisfarne and had called one of his sons Aidan. He spoke at length when I asked him questions for my book. In life, he told me, you did not know which way the winds would blow or the tides would flow. The sea was full of that potential. He also had a friend at BBC Radio Lancashire who rang him up sometimes to ask him the complicated questions about life.

Then at breakfast one day I sat next to Paul, a sculptor and visual artist. He was about 30, with distant blue eyes and a bushy explorer's beard. He had grown up amid the islands and peninsulas of Zeeland, a region of reclaimed land in the west of the Netherlands. Geography was strange there, he said: you had to 'look after' islands and build defences to make sure they did not disappear into the sea. Sometimes you could take land from the water. At other times you had to give it back. There were about a hundred drowned villages off the coast of Zeeland, he said. He had become especially interested in the North Sea flood of 1953, when a storm surge overwhelmed the Dutch defences in the small hours of a Sunday morning, killing two thousand people, some asleep in their beds. He was working on a sculpture which commemorated this deluge. He spoke quietly, with long pauses.

'I feel it in my body when I am by the sea,' he told me through a mouthful of toast. 'I feel the tide. Everything changes – and also in a way, nothing changes.'

I asked him why he had come to Iona. Not so long ago he had come out of a bad relationship, he said, and had now entered a period of searching. Last October he had walked the Camino in Spain – it was a time of year when it was still warm enough to wear shorts. He felt something powerful when he arrived in the holy city of Santiago and stood in the presence of the relics of St James. But he felt something even more powerful when he decided to carry on with his pilgrimage to Cape Finisterre – to the lighthouse-strewn cape at the north-western tip of Iberia, which – like Iona – stood at what was once the edge of the known world.

WORK WEEK

Days at the abbey fell into an easy pattern. I woke at seven, to the din of seabirds on the slate roof outside, and the peal of the bell across the cloisters, summoning members of the Community to breakfast. After bowls of porridge, toast and jam, we organized ourselves into teams and sub-teams to do tasks around the abbey and its outbuildings: cooking, cleaning, moving furniture and driving vans full of rubbish to the nearest tip (which was a five-hour round trip away, the far side of Mull).

My teammate for the week was Lakshmi, in her twenties, from Durham. Her dad was from Wallonia, Belgium, and her mother came from French-speaking Pondicherry in India: she was named after a Hindu goddess but was raised a Roman Catholic. She had recently quit her job at a tech start-up after suffering burnout, and had also just recovered from long Covid. She wanted to start a religious community one day, and had come to Iona for inspiration.

We started out on window-cleaning, and then were moved on to gardening: gathering seaweed from the shore, laying out a quilt of it on the raspberry bushes in the Community garden. The island was beautiful in the sharp winter light. Geese flew over in V formations. Winds ruffled the meadows around the abbey, and daffodils grew where Columba's hut had supposedly stood. We were planting crocuses when a sudden snow shower blew in from Skye. A tissue-thin coating of whiteness lay on the land. It was enough for everyone to adjourn to the common room, where cups of tea were presented, and a few people laboured over a jigsaw of Piccadilly Circus until the weather improved.

Over tea, Lakshmi told me she didn't feel anything especially stirring treading the holy ground of Iona: she first had to 'wear down' a place with her prayer before it felt familiar enough to be meaningful. But she made sure she set out on an hour's walk every day – part ritual and perhaps part pilgrimage – to be alone with God. She walked to quiet parts of the island to be alone, though she did not need to travel far. For her, as for Columba, solitude was a facilitator.

'Entering a place of solitude means I can be my purest self. No one is looking at me. I can dance when I want to. I can stare at things. I can be free.'

For her, the noise of the world was always in English, but her conversations with God were in her family's native French. Not long ago she had heard a voice: 'confiance en moi' – *trust in me* – and more recently a mysticism had entered into her faith. Her partner, Demarius, was experiencing visions. Her friend Tim started speaking in tongues. Most notably, her father had experienced a sudden showering of love and grace in his bedroom in Durham one morning. He wanted to lie flat on the ground, to take it all in, but there wasn't enough room. He had emerged from the experience a gentler man, and had lost what Lakshmi described as 'a ton of weight'. He was a lecturer in what Lakshmi called mathsy-physicsy stuff.

'Speaking in tongues, angels, prophetic prayer – those aren't things I grew up with, and would have been sceptical about,' she told me. 'But now I see things happening time and time again: things aligning. My dad now doesn't believe in God. He knows.'

Perhaps in another environment I too would have been sceptical about these claims. But over a week on the island, Lakshmi came across as balanced and open-minded. We ate flapjacks as the snow continued to fall outside.

Days concluded with a 7 p.m. dinner followed by a 9 p.m. service in the abbey, where the model of Columba's boat was just visible in the shadows left of the altar. Growing from the ancient walls were clumps of sea spleenwort, a fern native to Iona whose seeds had somehow found their way into the mortar during restoration. Just enough light found its way through the windows and just enough moisture hung in the air for the plant to thrive. It provided a faint echo of the old ruined abbey and those years when Columba's story had been half-forgotten. It had been left to flourish by the Community as a redoubt of nature in an age of climate breakdown.

The living quarters were warm, but the church itself was always chilly: the medieval stones enclosed a coldness that felt ancient and cherished, and many of the congregation wore bobble hats. Twice during evening services a storm blew outside – the wind harassed the iron handles on the doors, fluting through the gaps in the stonework. The panes shook in their Gothic arches, pressed and released by sudden gusts from the Sound. Long ago, I read, the wind had blown so strongly it had picked up chickens from Iona and deposited them a mile away on Mull, their feet still dry. At certain times – when the flames of candles shrank in the draft, and the only light was from Fire Escape signs – there was a sense that something was trying to get inside the building. On other nights, when it was quieter, a steady white noise persisted: the sounds of the wind and waves outside coalesced into a single note, similar to a seashell pressed to the ear.

It was in the abbey that my thoughts turned to Fiona, a publisher and writer I had got into conversation with on Twitter some months earlier. Fiona was writing a book about the modern life of standing stones – we had been in touch to discuss the idea of the Ridgeway as a route of Neolithic pilgrimage. She had first walked the chalk path to Avebury some 20 years before with Stephen, the man who later became her husband. They had only recently met at the time: it could easily have gone horribly wrong, but fortunately they were 'attuned' to each other. Fiona wasn't religious, but she believed there was a 'divinity you could access' along the Ridgeway.

You could find it too on Iona, a place she had been to three times in her life, drawn by stories of witches and of Columba. The first time she had stayed at the youth hostel. She loved the white sands, the way the sea changed from turquoise to black, the sense that anything might happen.

Her last visit was in Easter 2022, when she and Stephen came to Iona to get married. They followed the standing stones along the Ross of Mull, on what was, Fiona said, 'a bit of a pilgrimage'. They stayed in the Argyll Hotel. Stephen by that point had been diagnosed with terminal cancer and was having chemotherapy. The night before the wedding, Fiona came to a service in the abbey. It was beautiful and candlelit.

'All the time I was hoping and praying that something would happen to cure him,' she told me. 'That was partly why I wanted to go there. Because I had quite strong faith in the power of Iona to effect transformation upon him. I thought if there was anywhere it could happen, it was there.'

The morning of the wedding, Fiona went on a run to a sacred well in the island's northern hills. Stephen looked well on the bright, blustery afternoon of the ceremony, held on the island's north coast. They had as their guests their two children, the registrar and her neighbours as witnesses. Stephen had packed his wetsuit – but did not feel up to joining his family splashing about in the sea afterwards. The next day he was in hospital in Oban on an antibiotic drip. He passed away a few months before I left for Iona. One day Fiona wanted to make a fourth trip, to scatter his ashes. In return for borrowing some of her books about Iona, she asked me to pick up a pebble from her favourite beach.

Those nights in the abbey the Community sometimes prayed for certain people, whose names were written on folded paper. They prayed too for a few particular nations of the world. Later I realized that the countries being prayed for were on rotation – and that with each new service we were slowly working our way around the planet, like a ship making its never-ending circumnavigation. One night we prayed for Belize, Guatemala and Honduras, the next for Nicaragua, Costa Rica and Panama. Sermons were often political. One touched on the topical issue of refugees in small boats crossing the English Channel. It was clear the Iona Community still claimed their inheritance from a man who had arrived on this island long ago, in a very small boat.

ANOTHER BOAT

A week before I arrived on Iona, a bored teenager had shuffled into a backroom of a warehouse to retrieve order number 2141225313. Half an hour later, I opened the shoebox-sized package on my living room floor. It weighed about two kilos. Out of it came the smell of canvas, and a leaflet showing a handsome French man sporting sunglasses, paddling his packraft on a sunlit lake. There were a slew of caveats. Do not overinflate. Do not use alone. Do not exceed max weight. And do not use on the sea.

I had wondered if I could purchase a coracle for my trip to Iona. But a coracle would be too big for the luggage rack of a train – so I instead settled on a packraft: a tiny inflatable craft whose defining feature was its portability. Packrafts are single-passenger boats that have evolved for expeditions: for short hops across rivers and lakes, swiftly deployed on backcountry hikes through Norwegian fjords or Alaskan estuaries. They look like the sort of inflatables kids muck about with in swimming pools or on bank holiday beaches but are smaller, more robust and come in serious, military colour schemes. I heard them described as 'wearable boats'. I had wanted to see the island as Columba and his disciples might have once beheld it, from the deck of a little craft, while putting myself at the mercy of the Atlantic. I had stashed the packraft and a collapsing paddle in my backpack, with the intention of making a circumnavigation of the island in sections over my week with the Community. There were different kinds of pilgrimage on Iona: the long journey to the island; a journey to the many holy places dotted about its little landmass. Mine would be a third, saltwater pilgrimage: to consider it from all angles. To fully grasp its island-ness.

On the one hand, the project was dumb. The currents around Iona were deadly, and the conditions changed in a heartbeat. A year earlier I had undertaken a kayaking course close by on the Ross of Mull, and saw a fellow paddler thrust onto a rocky cliff by a rogue wave. She capsized and made a fortunate escape by clambering onto a boulder as her crewless boat sailed away. She was shaken enough not to get in a kayak again. Two years before that a lone kayaker had drowned at the southern end of the Sound.

On the other hand, I would be careful: checking the weather, monitoring the wind direction and tides, remaining close to the shore, enlisting someone staying with the Community to check on my progress. Tom came along to watch my maiden voyage. He was originally from a village outside Avebury but had come to Scotland to study geology, and later got a job as a soft fruit farmer, because he wanted to work with 'something tangible'. After our working day was done, he and I inflated the raft on a beach at Baile Mòr. The farting noise of an inflating raft sounded pathetic amid the weathered fishing boats solemnly guarding the shore. Soon I cast off onto the Sound, strands of seaweed tickling the underside of the packraft as it slipped from the shallows.

The water was as translucent as newly blown glass, the sand on the seabed the same white as the snowy summits of Jura, that were now visible across the strait. When the wind died down, all I could hear was the sloshing cadences of my paddle in the water. The droplets beaded from every withdrawn blade. They glistened in the winter sunlight as they fell, ending as a galaxy of expanding circles in the Sound. I paddled northward to the abbey, whose tower rose over the rockpools. It was somewhere near here – according to Columba's biographer Adomnan – that the saint came daily to stand in the shivering cold sea and recite 150 psalms before dawn. The wind exposed the outline of Columba's ribs.

I drifted further from the shore – the sea still calm and clear. I paused my stroke, lay back against the stern and let the packraft go adrift. For a few minutes I allowed myself to be rocked by the cradle of the waves, listening to the music of the skylarks high in the blue dome of the sky. A few months earlier I had paddled the length of the River Spey through the Scottish Highlands. Also in my canoe had been Josephine, a teaching assistant from Leeds. She decided to set out on the expedition after divorcing from her husband of 27 years. She had recently purchased her own flat by a canal – and a kayak. She believed there was something transcendent about being afloat.

'I step off the riverbank – where all the rest of life happens – and then I'm away from it all,' she told me. 'I've felt bouts of anxiety and depression: they are like a leech that sucks life out of you. But on the water I have a total release.'

I wondered what it was about surrendering to the currents and the winds: what peace there was allowing yourself to be captained by a greater power. When I sat up again, I remembered I was off Iona: specifically, heading towards its northern tip at Eilean Annraidh, and a place where the currents were said to be especially powerful. And so I turned south again. I landed the packraft on the beach at Baile Mòr, and Tom had a go instead. Later the wind stiffened, ribs of waves rose out of the evening sea and we lugged the packraft to the abbey dry room.

Close by, in a large chamber off the cloisters, a coracle lay propped against the wall. It was a vessel as long and wide as my armspan, and had been made to a Welsh design by a member of the Iona Community and brought here in 2017. Beside it was some information on A4 paper:

In one regard you can think of a coracle as a fragile island of peace and security on stormy waves in a troubled world. Islands offer safety, limits, edges, refuge and solitude, but a coracle also has a purpose – a movement 'towards …'

The text went on to explain the core structure of the Welsh coracle: three central struts as its backbone, ash laths to give it shape, calico as an outer shell and black bitumen as waterproofing. A seat had been placed at its centre. The coracle was, the A4 sheet claimed, a metaphor for a spiritual life:

> God might be the struts and laths, the Holy Spirit being the calico and waterproofing. And all the time Jesus sits on the seat beside us … taking our oar when we tire and encouraging us through his calm voice that conquered storms (it still does).

What lessons might be learned from my packraft, I wondered, which was a bit of rubbery canvas and a lot of inflated air. That night at dinner I sat next to Marianne Pedersen, a minister from Copenhagen. She was volunteering at the Iona Community shop, which sold fridge magnets, woolly hats, scarves and books on Celtic Christianity. I told her about my paddle along the coast. She said she was sure the presence of the sea must have had an effect on Columba and his disciples.

'You can look out at the horizon here, and know that the next stop is Canada,' she said. 'In those early days of the abbey, they did not know that Canada was even there: they were looking at something that was unending. I think the sea might be an image of God. Like God, it is not controllable.'

THE BAY AT THE BACK OF THE OCEAN

The week went on, and the weather got worse. The Sound became mussed with white water, while the western coast was beset by wind: wave trains scudding over rocks, the spray soaking the sheep that munched unflinchingly along the shore. I saw that my plan to circumnavigate the island in my tiny packraft would be stupid. One evening I tried to launch at Columba's Bay – its name in Gaelic meant the 'Bay of the Coracle' – where the saint had allegedly first landed on a pebbly beach. It proved impossible. Another time – on the north shore – I lost my grip on the packraft and only just stopped the boat from flying away in the wind.

A window of opportunity came at the Bay at the Back of the Ocean – the most beautiful name for the most beautiful beach on Iona. It formed the central arch of Iona's western coast, a storm beach wide open to the Atlantic where, in the words of one community member, 'you could feel the entire Gulf Stream blowing down your neck'. The sea was heavy here, but a barrier of rocks sheltered a patch of water from the full ire of the breakers. I paddled out alone here early one evening. For a while I fought with the phases of the waves – making no progress, expending just enough energy to maintain equilibrium with a wind that was willing me back to shore. During a lull I unexpectedly broke free – entering deeper, rougher waters. Soon I was balancing the boat on teetering waves, plunging my paddle deeper to eke stability out of a chaotic sea. Then, about 50 metres further ahead, I spotted a seal, poking its head out of the water like a periscope. It was an island of grace in the churning water. It looked at me with its sad black eyes.

As it disappeared, I felt a rush of water down my back, trousers and underpants. An exploding wave had flooded the packraft, and with the sudden coldness came a single word: Canada. Only twice before had I ever been truly afraid for my life, and both times was on water of one kind or another. Once I was climbing a glacier in Norway, which was melting in the afternoon sun. A second time I was caught in a riptide while surfing on the Cornish coast and did the opposite of what you were meant to do: I fought the current, rather than exiting at a right angle. A lifeguard had set off a siren, but with help from a friend I found my own way back to shore. Ever since, I had been engaged in a long process of reconciliation with the sea. Buying this packraft had been part of that.

Now, in the Bay at the Back of the Ocean, I fixed my eyes on dry land, which was about 500 metres away. I spun the weighty, sodden packraft around and – feeling my paddle begin to buckle under the strain of the water – heaved myself landwards, with my back to the tumult. Five minutes later I was on the sand, trying to catch my breath, tipping water out of the hull and letting the air slip from the packraft valve. I hadn't gone very far out. I felt embarrassed. I remembered the seal.

Seals were recurring figures in Hebridean folklore. In some accounts the pagans Columba failed to convert to Christianity were condemned to live as seals. In others, seals were the descendants of Pharaoh's pursuing army, drowned as the sea closed in behind the Israelites. The divide between human and seal seemed to be a thin one. To my north was the hill of Dun Mhanannain, which, according to the author Fiona Macleod, was the home of a pagan god of the sea, Manaun: 'His body was made of a green wave. His hair was of wrack and tangle, glistening with spray; his robe was of windy foam; his feet, of white sand.'[4]

Manaun, Macleod wrote, had fallen in love with a 'woman of the south'. He captured her, and brought her north to Iona at a time when Vikings ruled the Hebrides. She was happy when she arrived in September, the so-called 'month of peace'. By November she longed to return to her southern home, unable to survive in this cold northern climate. The god of the sea transformed his lover into a seal. She swam the oceans by night, and by day Manaun called her to the shore, where she changed once again into a woman, sleeping beside him on this lonely sheep-munched hillock beside the bay and the island's golf course. This was one of many tales compiled by Fiona Macleod in her 1900 book, simply titled *Iona*. Its opening lines had a feverish and dreamlike quality:

> Iona is the Mecca of the Gael. ... To tell the story of Iona is to go back to God, and to end in God ... There is, too, an Iona that is more than Gaelic, that is more than a place rainbow-lit with the seven desires of the world, the Iona that, if we will it so, is a mirror of your heart and of mine.[5]

Macleod was a shadowy figure who claimed to have been born on Iona: her book explored the holy geography of the island. Though little heard of today, her books sold well and brought her fame in the first years of the twentieth century. Many authors had waxed lyrical about Iona – Wordsworth and Samuel Johnson among them. What marked out Fiona Macleod were the claims that took Iona's sanctity to a whole new level. Centuries after Columba, she seemed to be revealing a whole new collection of island myths in time for the new millennium.

Macleod believed Iona would be a kind of Bethlehem where a second Messiah would one day be born (except this time it would be a woman). She speculated that Iona might once have formed the central part of the Garden of Eden. She also touched on her youth on this enchanted island, in which she learned from elderly fishermen about various prophecies, and had her dreams shepherded by Columba, waking afterwards to the cries of curlews. Reading her book, it was hard to imagine a nondescript day had ever gone by on Iona, that anyone could go to the shops or walk the dog or put out the bins without some profound message from the heavens interrupting their daily business. According to her, the entire landscape was layered in meaning. Her island teemed with prophecy and portals.

I dusted the sand off my packraft and, with the light dwindling and my body feeling cold, left the Bay at the Back of the Ocean. I trudged east towards the warmth of my room at the abbey, which was a little over a mile away. Just beyond the golf course, where a rough track met a five-bar gate, lay the gentle green rise of Sithean Mòr, the so-called 'fairy hill'. Its other name was the Hill of the Angels, for it was here that Columba supposedly conversed with God's messengers. There was not much to see. A telephone line ran over it. Some farm buildings with corrugated iron roofs flanked its southern slopes.

Fiona Macleod, of course, had her own story about Sithean Mòr, which was recounted in *Iona*. It was here that a fisherman that she knew dozed off one evening. When he awoke, a figure stood before him: a fairy with thistledown hair, holding a wand of hazel in his hand. This fairy made the fisherman an offer:

you can have the sovereignty of the world. Ay, and more than that: you shall have the sun like a golden jewel in the hollow of your right hand, and all the stars as pearls in your left, and have the moon as a white shining opal above your brows, with all knowledge behind the sun, within the moon, and beyond the stars.[6]

It was a good offer. The fisherman was distracted by the hazel wand.

'What is that for? …'
'It is to open a door that is in the air.'

The fairy disappeared. The fisherman apparently came around, wondering if it was all a dream. He later told Fiona Macleod his story. In summer Sithean Mòr bloomed with wild flowers, but it was grey when I passed it that winter evening. Most people didn't give it a second glance. Three decades after Macleod published *Iona*, Sithean Mòr featured in newspapers across the country.

HILL OF THE ANGELS

One autumn day in 1929, islanders would have sighted a strange pilgrim arriving on the dock – a tall, intense woman from London wearing home-made clothes and silver jewellery, her black hair tamed into two thick plaits. She was the latest in a long line of spiritual searchers to come to Iona. She carried with her enough luggage for an indefinite stay: she had, by some accounts, brought her own furniture.

Marie Emily Fornario (referred to by some as Norah Marionetta Fornario) was born in Cairo in 1897 to an Italian father and an English mother, and was known as 'Netta'. Her mother died when she was an infant, and so – estranged from her own father – Netta was put in the custody of her maternal grandfather, a wealthy tea merchant in south London. Not needing to worry about money, she grew up instead devoting her time to spiritual affairs. She joined a section of London society that immersed itself in mysticism and magic after the trauma of the First World War, becoming a member of the occult society the Alpha et Omega temple. In the words of her former landlady she had often been to the 'far beyond' and had 'come back to life after spending time in another world'. In her early thirties, Netta felt an urge to depart for Iona. She felt that Christianity had gone astray by following the rule of Rome, rather than the example of Columba. She had apparently also visited Iona in a previous life.

It was allegedly Netta's intention to go to Iona to make contact with the 'green ray elementals': fairies that were perhaps the same ones described by Fiona Macleod (whose writing she had loved).

Netta ended up lodging with a family at Traigh Mhor, a crofter's cottage now available as self-catering accommodation, south of Baile Mòr. Here she lived as a night owl, taking nocturnal walks to secluded parts of the island, writing by the light of two oil lamps. She never drew the curtains in her bedroom, because she wanted to see the faces of people in the passing clouds. As September turned to November the temperature dropped: something changed within her. Netta became agitated, speaking in tongues, giving the impression someone or something was trying to attack her.

On 17 November 1929 Netta Fornario rose earlier than her habit, her hair no longer plaited but left loose and dishevelled. That morning she was hysterical – speaking about a rudderless boat sailing in the sky – insistent that she must leave Iona immediately. Perhaps she felt homesickness for the south. She rushed to the dock with her luggage – but, being a Sunday, there were no ferries, nor any means of finding a boat in these Sabbath-observing parts of the Hebrides. Iona had been her fixation and obsession – she had by some accounts described succumbing to 'The Call of the Island'. But the island was, for her, a trap. She sat on the quays hoping in vain for a ship to materialize. It was perhaps her last chance to save herself. Eventually Netta returned to Traigh Mhor, locked herself in her room. The next morning her host opened the door of her room to find the two oil lamps still burning and her silver jewellery neatly arranged – but their owner was nowhere to be seen.

I passed by the dock on my way back from the bay and thought of the solitary figure of Netta Fornario sitting with all her luggage. For some people coming to Iona, no baggage was heavier than the weight of their own expectations. It was dark by the time I returned to the abbey. I was worn out from all the paddling. Before I went to my room, I took a detour into the graveyard, where my torch picked out a simple stone inscribed: M. E. F.

Upon it people had placed a small assortment of crystals, and also a small ankh – the Egyptian hieroglyph that is a symbol for life (perhaps a reference to the land of the deceased woman's birth). Newspapers reported that Netta's body had been found on Sithean Mòr the Tuesday after she went missing. She was naked but for a black cloak adorned with an occult symbol. She had used a ritual knife to carve a cross into the earth below her (interpreted as a way of opening a door, or making contact with the fairy realm). Her body was unmarked: scratches on her feet invited speculation she had been chased. There were rumours about a mysterious cloaked man who had been seen on Iona. Nothing more came of it.

READING AGAIN

After the evening services in the abbey I was a night owl: borrowing from the Community library, reading as much as I could about Iona in my room, fascinated by mysteries that overlapped and interweaved but rarely found resolution. It was only later after I re-read the same passages of some of the same books back on the mainland that my eyes sometimes turned to more factual aspects of Iona's history, which were unlike those that had first appealed to my imagination.

For instance: it is unlikely that there were anything like as many as 360 stone crosses on Iona, and it seems possible the number of kings buried there has also been exaggerated. The stories surrounding Columba were fantastic, to be sure, but they could also be placed in a specific historical context. Columba's hagiographers might have borrowed certain miracle stories from the gospels, and perhaps applied them to a more local figure (perhaps in a bid to convince potential Christian converts).

Celtic Christianity was a concept much discussed in Iona – often a byword for a more mystical, kinder and nature-focused faith. It is a term treated with suspicion by serious historians. The consensus now is that Columba and his followers were not a magical nature-worshipping offshoot of mainstream Christianity but a community that owed its origins to Rome. While solitude was undoubtedly part of the Celtic tradition, so too were rituals less likely to appeal to modern sensibilities, such as monks praying for hours on end until they shed tears of exhaustion. Then there was the matter of Columba's boat. The abbey housed a Welsh coracle, but a more convincing analogy seemed to be the currach – a similar but larger boat which evolved independently in Ireland, also made of cowhide but substantial enough to house a small crew and be fitted with sails. The seafaring capability of the currach had been proved in Tim Severin's 1978 book *The Brendan Voyage*, in which the author had hand-built a traditional currach 36 feet long and then sailed it from Kerry to Newfoundland in tribute to Columba's fellow saint Brendan the Navigator.

Fiona Macleod was a shy and elusive writer, never seen in literary circles. In reality, she did not exist. Fiona Macleod was the secret alter ego of William Sharp, a Scottish biographer and contemporary of Thomas Hardy and W. B. Yeats. Sharp may have based Macleod on a woman he had known and perhaps loved – the Celticist and translator of Breton folk tales Edith Wingate Rinder – and on his own repressed feminine self. Macleod's virtuoso prose was unlike the more measured tone of Sharp's own (far less successful) literary biographies.

Sharp managed to keep his double identity secret during his lifetime (getting his sister to write fake letters in her own distinct handwriting, posting them from random parts of the country). But the effort of this deception put a strain on his mental health. Sharp was part-Glaswegian and part-Swedish: he had not grown up on Iona, and nor did he have family on the island. He had only been there as another visitor, another pilgrim seduced by the mystical elements of Celtic Christianity. The folk stories of Iona he compiled under the name of Fiona Macleod are thus questionable in their fidelity to anything but his own inner visions. In other words, they may all have been made up. Sharp had suffered from poor health for much of his life, and died at the age of 50 in Sicily, where he is buried under an Iona cross made from Etna lava. He had met with the founders of Alpha et Omega the year after Netta Fornario was born.

Later accounts of Netta Fornario's demise offer counterclaims to the sensational newspaper reports offered at the time. The night she went missing it was cold: there was the risk of hypothermia. A physician ruled that she had died of heart failure. Through contemporary eyes, it seems probable that she was undergoing an acute mental illness that attached itself to a promise of destiny on Iona. Where the road ran out on her pilgrimage, it seems her mind turned in on itself. Other details of that Sunday in November were later refuted: it was not a ritual knife she held but an ordinary kitchen knife. And it was not on Sithean Mòr that her body was found but instead in a remote part of Iona's southern hills. The island, it seemed, could be a rumour mill and echo chamber. A confined space where devotion could turn to a dangerous delirium. In Netta's case, the ferry never brought her back to the real world.

Her pilgrimage to Iona had been inspired by the phantom figure of Fiona Macleod. Less than a century later, her own death – rather than being a cautionary tale – has unfortunately been a modern addition to the canon of Iona myths. It is often recounted on occult corners of the internet. Judging by the deposits on her grave, her story brings ever more misguided pilgrims on quests to Iona.

I had by then come to feel differently about Iona's myth-making microclimate, its self-renewing legends. I grew exhausted from the stories. Though one still struck a chord with me: the legend of Oran, who lent his name to the graveyard in which Netta Fornario was buried (along with all the Scottish, Irish and Norwegian kings). Oran was a companion of St Columba: his legend took different forms, but it began with Columba looking for a Christian to consecrate the ground beneath Iona's oldest surviving chapel – specifically by being buried alive. Oran volunteered for this (highly un-Christian) human sacrifice, and dutifully went forth into the underworld. Three days later – missing his old friend, nagged by remorse and wishing to see him one last time – Columba ordered the grave be opened up. At that point Oran appeared, opened his eyes and announced: 'There is no such great wonder in death, nor is Hell what it has been described.'

Columba cried out: 'Uir, ùir, air sùil Odhrain! mu'n labhair e tuille comhraidh,' meaning 'Earth! Earth! On Oran's eyes, lest he gossip any more.'

Oran was buried a second time, and told no more tales. It was probably for the best.

AT MARTYR'S BAY

I took a last paddle at Martyr's Bay, the beach where Vikings had landed in the ninth century and slain some 68 monks. It was beside the pier where the ferry now disgorged visitors from Mull and the mainland. In a few months as many as a thousand tourists a day would step ashore here (in preparation, I had spent the day pushing a Henry Hoover around corridors fuzzed with a winter's worth of dust). For the time being, though, a short period of peace endured.

The muddled weather of the previous days had resolved itself, so an even layer of cloud hung motionless in the upper reaches of the sky. A soft westerly nudged the packraft into the Sound, against which I pushed a gentle correcting paddle. First I set a course south, towards the white sand beach at Traigh Mhor, beyond which stood the cottage where Netta Fornario stayed. I continued a while under the cliffs leading towards Columba's Bay, then turned the boat back. When I landed, I saw Paul, the sculptor from the Netherlands, beachcombing on the shore. His hands were bloody. That day he had attempted to whittle an infinity symbol from a chunk of driftwood but accidentally cut himself. The wood was too soft.

It was at art school, he told me, that his life had changed. The small rituals of preparing materials for his work – paint, clay, wood – led him to consider the concepts of substance and spirit. He had been fascinated by transubstantiation, the idea that the bread and wine served in the Eucharist were the actual body and blood of Christ, and not just symbolic tokens. In the service that same morning someone had read the story from John in which Jesus heals a blind man by mixing spit with dirt; the thought of the dirt, the substance, had touched Paul. I deflated the packraft. We talked for a while on the beach. All kinds of motivation had brought people to Iona: impetuses of faith, dreams of isolation, the stories of Columba. But what was special for Paul was the substance of the island – its soil, its rock. That, it seemed, was enough for him.

Iona, it has often been claimed, is a place apart. In geological terms, this is certainly true. Looking at a map, I had supposed that Iona was a spare part of the Ross of Mull that the action of the waves had detached, and afterwards wandered off into the sea. In real life, however, you can see it is wholly distinct: while the cliffs on the Ross of Mull are a pink fleshy granite, Iona is mostly a darker Lewisian gneiss: a metamorphic rock that counts among the oldest in the world. This rock dominates the island's western coast in particular, and the mythical hills that flank the Bay at the Back of the Ocean. Its kinship is not with the volcanic hills of Mull over the Sound but with distant Lewis, Harris and the archipelagos over the northern horizon.

Lewisian gneiss withstood the forces unleashed by the Caledonian orogeny – the collision of continents that created the Scottish Highlands some 500 million years ago. Rather, Lewisian gneiss was first formed some 1,500 million years earlier in the Earth's crust, when intense heat and pressure turned igneous and sedimentary rocks into a coarse, banded stone. It was about half as old as the Earth itself. This story of Christianity's beginnings in Britain took place on the oldest rocks of these islands.

Paul said that being in the presence of Lewisian gneiss in particular shook his own inner foundations. The rock was a place where he could briefly forget the rest of the world and reconsider his existence in the context of deep time. He took long walks on Iona, sometimes by night. To the north you could sometimes see the green trails of the aurora. To the south were the spinning beams of two of Scotland's loneliest lighthouses, Dubh Artach and

Skerryvore, both perched on little rocks a dozen miles or so from the nearest inhabited island. They were monastic in their mission, starlike in their isolation. Paul said he had, during this time with the rock, started thinking about the Pleistocene – the period from 2.5 million years ago to 10,000 years ago – when humans were hunter–gatherers (when the Red Lady was stashed in a Welsh cliff). It was a fantasy that could be indulged on Iona's rugged west coast, where few people went.

'The majority of human existence was in the Pleistocene,' he said. 'It was the only time when humans were in balance with the natural world. When we stayed in one place it all went wrong: our diet went bad, we invented slavery. We lost our connection to nature. We are flesh and bone and temporary. Everything that stands still dies. What moves lives. Energy makes lives.'

Paul had read up on this. He was concerned that soon – through climate breakdown – we would be returning to an age that was a darker, more dangerous version of the Pleistocene: a future when humans would be uprooted from the homes of our habit, and we would be permanently on the move through the landscape.

It was getting late – we both had to get back to the abbey for dinner. As I steadied myself to stand up, the palm of my hand balanced on a well-rounded pebble. I later found out Fiona the Publisher was a fan of her namesake Fiona Macleod: it didn't matter if these things were made up, she said. Folklore and spirituality were being reinvented all the time. People could create their own stories. She had used a Fiona Macleod blessing to close her husband's funeral.

The next morning I watched the island retreat from the deck of the ferry, and – against my better judgement – felt that rising infatuation with the island again. Over a week on Iona I had eaten, prayed and hoovered in the abbey, and had many meaningful conversations with Community members. I had walked every road on the island and many of its footpaths, all of which led – one way or another – to the sea. And though Paul had fixated on the rock, my own abiding memory of Iona was of the shifting sea. The grey sea slopping against the rusty ferry. The white sea that had nearly sunk my packraft. The sea which – if you turned to the first lines of Genesis in the abbey bibles – was supposedly created before land and sky, light and darkness. By design or not, the theme of the sea had featured in many of the abbey services, though no stories of Galilee seemed to me as profound as the vision of a coracle on the Atlantic, and within it the Irishman who was said by his biographer Adomnan to know 'secrets hidden since the world began'.

I disembarked at Fionnphort, where the bus driver was still standing on the pavement smoking cigarettes. It occurred to me that during my entire time on Iona – speaking to visitors and pilgrims – I had only spoken to one Hebridean. And he had said: 'Can I see your return ticket please?'

5

An Archipelago

A Pilgrimage for a Hermit

Archipelago – the shore of St Herbert's

ST HERBERT'S ISLAND

Columba's followers and contemporaries cast off for other islands along the Scottish coast.

In the far north, St Ronan rode on the back of a great sea creature to the island of North Rona, where he lived with his sister on a tiny crumb of land 39 nautical miles from Cape Wrath. North Rona was inhabited until the seventeenth century, when a population of black rats (perhaps from a shipwreck) raided the islanders' food stocks. The 30 or so inhabitants perished, probably starving to death in isolation. The rats starved soon after. No one lives there today.

In the far south, Columba's confessor, St Molaise, lived as a hermit on Holy Isle, a steeply sided island off the eastern shore of Arran. In the early 1990s the island was the property of a devout Catholic named Kay Morris: in a dream, the Virgin Mary instructed her to sell Holy Isle so it might become a place for peace and meditation. She offered it to a community of Tibetan Buddhists for £750,000. They came back with a counter-offer of £350,000, and have been resident there ever since. There are stupas by the jetty, and prayer flags that whip about in the gales. The Buddhist community run retreats doing yoga, t'ai chi, meditation and mindfulness. Participants start their days with porridge. Here a tradition continues.

In the east, Inchcolm is known as the 'Iona of the East' – possibly founded by monks from Iona. Shaped somewhat like a fish hook, it lies in the Firth of Forth and is visible from Arthur's Seat. Like its western counterpart, it has a ruined abbey and was a place for noble burials. Like North Rona long ago, it is now home to a rare colony of black rats.

Of course, the most famous of Iona's island children lies over the border in England. Four decades after Columba's death, Aidan travelled from Iona to the tidal isle of Lindisfarne, where he founded his monastery. The night Aidan died in 651, Cuthbert – then a young shepherd in the Borders – had a vision of the saint being carried to heaven by a host of angels. Cuthbert succeeded him as bishop of Lindisfarne – and he, of course, was another island addict.

In this way, an archipelago of holy islands encircled Great Britain – the tradition extending to the Welsh islands of Bardsey, Caldey, Ramsey and others. I imagined these islands as being like a network of satellites – relaying signals along the seaboard, collectively beaming the word into the dark mainland. Among them, one English island stood out as an anomaly.

An hour's drive from Gretna Green and the border is the Lake District town of Keswick: a tourist hub set on the northern shore of Derwent Water. From the town's pebbly beach you might let your eye glide past the flotilla of pleasure cruisers onto the faraway leagues of the lake, which are graced with a little archipelago. Hogging the foreground is Derwent Island, home to an Italianate mansion owned by the National Trust. Peeking just behind it is the smallest member of the archipelago: the wooded Rampsholme Island. Take a brief potter around the bay and you can soon make out Lord's Island – where the earls of Derwentwater lived in the Middle Ages until their mansion fell to bits. This is *Swallows and Amazons* country. Bus tours clog the country roads of the Lake District and Duke of Edinburgh award groups crowd the fells, but even in the age of overtourism the uninhabited islands of Derwent Water still retain the feel of *terra incognita* – an ocean and continents rendered in miniature, beckoning explorers.

It was a warm evening in spring when I set out to reach St Herbert's Island, the largest island in Derwent Water. By seven o'clock the last of the pleasure boats had been fastened to the jetties and an audience was ambling along the lakeside to a performance at the Theatre by the Lake. A few men slung their blazers over their shoulders and paused to admire the sunset – a panorama of islands and mountains – perhaps knowing this view would be diminished by the interval and lost entirely by curtain call.

I inflated my packraft, stuffed a rucksack full of supplies inside. Soon the little boat was carving out a wide V in the water. For all its promise of solitude, Iona had been a place of endless conversations. Lindisfarne was, of course, overrun with crowds. Visiting the monastic communities of Holy Isle or Caldey would mean explaining myself, and even trips to remote Atlantic islands like North Rona would necessitate negotiations with sea captains. St Herbert's Island offered something else: a chance to sail to a holy island under my own steam and spend the night encased in its solitude. It would cost nothing. I would speak to no one. Perhaps this was part of the appeal for Herbert too.

Fairly little is known of St Herbert, other than that, according to Bede's *Ecclesiastical History of the English People*, he was a close friend of Cuthbert who lived on an island in Derwent Water. Every year Herbert crossed the Pennines so he might learn something from his friend on Lindisfarne (later they met up in Carlisle). In this way, St Herbert's Island might be seen as an island offspring of Lindisfarne – and a third-generation descendant of Iona. Where other holy islands stood in tempestuous seas, St Herbert's home was in a still lake, enshrined by freshwater fed from the fells.

Midway I stilled the paddle and looked up to the cauldron of mountains: the mass of Blencathra behind me, the last beams of sunlight clinging to Glaramara beyond the bow. Out to the west, a low sun almost met its reflection in the water – two suns blazing brightly together in union, dying almost as one as final rays folded over Catbells. It took about half an hour to paddle to St Herbert's Island. Apart from a long spit of pebbles at the northern end, its five acres were thickly, entirely wooded. I made a circumnavigation: the long arms of oaks reached out over the water, and beneath them submerged jetties slunk out from the shore. A pied wagtail followed behind me. There were no signs of human life.

Satisfied no one was going to stop me, I beached the boat and set up camp under a yew tree. St Herbert's Island was a magical place. The woods swam in aqueous light, the scent of wild garlic rich in the air. Ramsons shone like stars amid thickets of holly. There were no structures on the island: only the remains of St Herbert's hermitage – little more than a pile of rubble at the island's north end, knotted with ivy and clenched by roots. Not much had changed since Wordsworth came here and described it as a 'shapeless heap of stones':

This island, guarded from profane approach
By mountains high and waters widely spread,
Is that recess to which St Herbert came
In life's decline; a self-secluded Man,
After long exercise in social cares
And offices humane, intent to adore

The Deity, with undistracted mind,
And meditate on everlasting things.
William Wordsworth, 'Inscription: For the Spot Where the
Hermitage Stood on St Herbert's Island'

Almost a century later, the island had been the inspiration for
another writer. Beatrix Potter cast it as 'Owl Island' in *The Tale of
Squirrel Nutkin*. In the story, a tribe of squirrels paddle out to the
island in tiny rafts to make offerings to the owl named Old Brown.
I wondered if there was a hint of a Celtic monk in Old Brown, the
curmudgeonly loner, weary of visitors turning up in boats.

These days visitors come sometimes in kayaks and canoes –
empty beer bottles and bits of bog roll attesting to secret parties
on summer nights. There was talk of church groups making an
occasional pilgrimage. At the island's southern end was an oak onto
whose bark some people had carved their names – 'Jack 1971',
'CJM 1985'. With the passage of the years the letters had warped
some so that they resembled hieroglyphs or Cyrillic characters.
Some inscriptions were being carried upwards with the slow growth
of the tree, inching up from shoulder height towards the canopy
and the light.

I lay on the spit at dusk. Mountain ridges and hill farms lay
close by, their second selves reflected in the water. Later the lake
mirrored the turn of the constellations. Wild geese followed their
migratory flight path over Derwent Water – on Iona the birds were
said to represent the Holy Spirit, also reflecting the roving habits of
the Celtic saints. Iona and Lindisfarne were both sea islands: their
restless waters connected them to all the oceans of the world. But
around St Herbert's Island the waters were at peace: there was a
sense of a journey's end here. There were many kinds of pilgrimage.
An outward pilgrimage by boat to the island. An inward pilgrimage
of a soul in its solitude. But more than anything else, the story of St
Herbert suggested this as a place for upward pilgrimage: an island
as a launch pad to heaven.

According to Bede, it was at their meeting in Carlisle that
Cuthbert confided in Herbert that the two would not see each

other again. Breaking down in tears at this news, Herbert prayed that he might at least make his journey to God the same moment as his best friend. After a long illness, St Herbert died on his island on 20 March 687 – the exact same hour that Cuthbert passed away on Inner Farne. From two islands on opposite shores of northern England, Bede describes two friends carried aloft by angels (just like the vision of Aidan granted to Cuthbert in his youth). Perhaps, in this enclosure of water, the obvious way out was always up.

I would like to write that I fell into a deep sleep at my camp on St Herbert's Island. That I rose refreshed to a rosy dawn. That I carried some wisdom with me back to the mainland. But when I returned to my tent that night, the onslaught started. Mice – unaccustomed to or else undaunted by human company – flung themselves at the fly-sheet. I did my best to shoo them off, and in a moment of desperation ate all my food so there was nothing to tempt them. It didn't work. I woke at 3 a.m. to a chorus of squeaks and a pair of tiny yellow teeth nibbling at the canvas. Columba and Cuthbert had famously been friends to animals, so Herbert probably was too.

Grumpily, I flung my belongings back in the packraft. I paddled back through the grey light to Keswick, where the mountains slept under a quilt of morning mist. I shoved everything in the boot of my car and drove off. I dozed off in the car park of the Aldi at Penrith. Perhaps there was a sacred solitude to be found on St Herbert's Island. But it was not intended for me.

6

A Road

A Medieval Pilgrimage

The Regulars | The Churches | The River | The Old Road

A sign near Wrotham, Kent

THE REGULARS

Nobody was in the mood for a conversation – still less for telling a story.

I exited the tube into the scrum of lunch-hour London Bridge. Two security guards were arguing outside a corner shop. A cyclist thrust a middle finger at a cab driver who had cut him up. I entered Southwark Cathedral, where a small audience had gathered to hear the organist. As the last notes trailed off, they sat listening with continuing reverence to sounds outside: the wind hustling along the Thames, the trains screeching into London Bridge. They avoided eye contact with each other as they stood to leave. I went to buy a pilgrim's passport from the cathedral gift shop – a little booklet I could get stamped at stops along the Pilgrims' Way. The customer behind me in the queue huffed impatiently as I paused to stuff it into my rucksack. A little later I felt suspicious eyes on me as I stood outside an orthodontist in Talbot Yard. A blue plaque on the exterior wall read:

THE TABARD INN

Site from which Chaucer's pilgrims set off in April 1386

The Tabard Inn had been a real pub: it had existed in the Middle Ages and burned down not long after the Great Fire. A replacement of the same name clung on until railway travel called time for many of Southwark's coaching inns. This alleyway was one of the most famous locations in all English literature. Now it was a place of loading bays, fire escapes and extractor fans. People came here to have their teeth straightened. The Shard loomed above it. You needed a reason to be here, and I had one: it was a starting point for the Pilgrims' Way.

The Pilgrims' Way, as described in my Cicerone guidebook, was a two-pronged pilgrimage. The main highway travels east–west between Canterbury and Winchester: two ancient cities and Iron Age capitals at opposite ends of the North Downs. A second branch (also called the Becket Way) leads south-east from London, joining the main thoroughfare to Canterbury at Otford in Kent. It was about 90 miles from London to Canterbury: a Javelin train from St Pancras could chew through it in 50 minutes, a walker in seven to ten days.

Like the Ridgeway, this was another long-distance footpath into the past – though not to some numinous point in prehistory.

Rather, it was a way associated with the Middle Ages and Merry England – with chivalry and castles, bold knights and dishonest knaves, minstrels and mead. More than anywhere else in this book, it stood for the heyday of pilgrimage in England: a time when the land stirred with processions of travellers bound for an ecosystem of shrines. And none (for a while) rivalled the one in Canterbury. Chaucer chose this journey as his literary frame – the characters assembling at the Tabard Inn in Southwark, whiling away miles on horseback by telling stories. The carnival of human life trotted past. The road could be a leveller in a feudal society. The road coaxed out stories. At the time Chaucer was composing his masterpiece, the roads to Canterbury had already thronged with pilgrims for two centuries. People from afar came to the shrine of St Thomas Becket – the archbishop martyred by forces loyal to King Henry II – who had the power to work miracles in his death.

Then, as now, the road to Canterbury was part of a route from the capital to the continent: the London–Dover axis was one along which armies marched, merchants travelled, royals (English and others) processed on state visits from both east and west. St Thomas Becket's shrine was helpfully positioned along the way. More recently this has been the route for people heading off for booze cruises, for the Eurostar and HS1. It is a densely settled commuter corridor of dormitory villages and seasonal rail passes, known to anyone who has driven to a holiday in France.

In the midst of it was the Pilgrims' Way – a sociable path (without the aloofness of the Ridgeway) stopping at villages, pausing for a half in a country pub, briefly besieging the battlements of medieval castles before shuffling off on its merry meanders. And yet, as I was soon to see, the path never got too busy. I could track other Canterbury-bound pilgrims ahead of me by reading the names in one or two church visitors' books: there were a smattering of Germans, a trickle of Americans, a few Brits. A number of street signs bore the name Pilgrims' Way or variations on that theme. But oddly there were few signposts. Some locals did not know it was there at all. This was especially true in London, where long-distance walkers dissolved into crowds.

The blogs I had read mostly suggested a path leading through the leafy tracts of the Garden of England – they offered scant acknowledgement of the long march along the pavements of the Old Kent Road. My walking boots clopped on the tarmac as I set off from Southwark. Aromas of jerk and jollof mingled in the afternoon air. I passed a Cypriot social club, a white-collar boxing club, travel agents selling packages for Hajj and Umrah. There were the tourists at Southwark, art students at New Cross, bankers in Blackheath. Chaucer had revealed the spectrum of medieval society through his characters: to walk the path today was also to walk a cross-section of London and England too.

For centuries, the A2 had been a highway of inns – places for travellers to rest on their comings and goings in the capital (convenient when the Thames crossings closed for the night). The Tabard was long gone, but I soon saw that others – the inheritors of its tradition – had also fallen. The Bricklayers Arms lent its name to a roundabout, but the pub itself was nowhere to be seen. The Dun Cow had for two decades now been the Dun Cow Surgery. The Black Horse on nearby Great Dover Street became a private home in 2019. The Thomas a Becket was a palatial pub: it had an upstairs gym where the boxer Henry Cooper had trained. A pub sign still showed the saint in a green robe, though the building itself now housed a restaurant. Especially sad were the faded ceramic tiles outside The Kentish Drovers and Halfway House, depicting pastoral scenes of windmills and ruddy peasants with baskets full of apples. It was meant as an Arcadian vision of what was to come down the road in Kent, but the pub itself was no more. Recently, Covid and the cost-of-living crisis had hit pubs hard. It was tougher than ever to find one like the Tabard, in which you might meet characters and hear stories.

The only pub I could find on the Old Kent Road was the Lord Nelson: an old-school boozer where a fruit machine flashed beneath ornate Victorian mirrors. It did free sausages on St George's Day, and apparently the regulars cheered the Brexit referendum result. It stood close to St Thomas-a-Watering, the stream where

Chaucer's pilgrims stopped to draw straws and decide on the order of the storytellers (it was now a Tesco). I sat at the bar and chatted with regulars. Maureen was from Kells in Ireland, a town where monks from Iona had founded an abbey. She used Columba's Gaelic name, Columcille. John was half-Irish: he had moved to the Old Kent Road about 20 years ago. He said he knew his mum shouldn't have sold the old house in Notting Hill – today it would be worth a fortune.

I asked them to tell me a story – and after a thoughtful pause, they talked at length about the other lost pubs along the Old Kent Road: among them the Duke of Kent, where Maureen had once worked, and The World Turned Upside Down, which had been demolished. Something had died with those pubs, it seemed. When people did the Monopoly pub crawl of London (on which the Old Kent Road was the first stop) they had little choice but to start at the Lord Nelson. It was about the last pub standing.

'There's nothing on the Old Kent Road any more apart from pizza places,' said Maureen, wagging a finger. 'You have to get a bus or a taxi and go to Bromley.'

'I don't understand it,' said John. 'Surely all the tourists want to visit a pub?'

There were other problems on the Old Kent Road these days, they said. Everything had got worse after they stopped locking the park gates at night. As I left, they were talking about what they would do if they won the lottery: John said he would buy a house somewhere hot, and a pad in Notting Hill too.

I walked more miles along the A2. I walked past New Cross Gate and Deptford Bridge stations. I passed the White Hart, the White Swan – both barricaded and bolted, lost in the grim, publess days of 2020. Beyond the stubbly grasses of Blackheath lay the Sun in the Sands: an inn of eighteenth-century origins, so-called after the dust kicked up by Kentish drovers, caught by the setting sun. It was permanently shut and was down to become flats. Its shell stood where the route began its climb up Shooter's Hill, a thickly wooded rise once notorious for its highwaymen. This was the last place eastbound travellers could glance back over their shoulder to see the London skyline and catch their first sight of the promised land of Kent, over which the afternoon shadows advanced. The rays caught the plate glass of Canary Wharf. The arch of Wembley Stadium almost framed the setting sun.

I ended my first day's walk with a pint at The Bull: a pub still in business, set near the highest point of Shooter's Hill. It was busy. I asked the barmaid if they did stamps for pilgrims' passports.

'You definitely *can* get a pilgrim stamp here,' said a small man in the corner. 'It'll say Reebok, or Nike, and it'll be on your face.'

He laughed, said he was joking and then leaned in to shake my hand.

THE CHURCHES

Not only were so many pubs gone, but many churches along the Pilgrims' Way were locked.

The doors did not move an inch at St George the Martyr: a proud edifice of Portland stone in Borough. A little silver padlock was secured to the gates of Christ Church – a little Victorian structure on Shooter's Hill. I became hopeful walking the long avenue of horse chestnuts to St Margaret of Antioch, in Darenth – one of the oldest churches in Britain. The metal mechanism played a little in the door, and the timber began to yield promisingly in the frame, but it too turned out to be immovable. I approached these churches so often in hope – lifting the latches with the same anticipation as lifting the lid of a piano. But mostly I was disappointed, hearing the hollow clank of a latch echoing around the empty, sealed nave, like a single footfall. Canterbury-bound pilgrims of old would have paused and prayed at some of these churches. Today churchwardens played it safe by keeping them bolted. In the doors of a few churches were old sleeping bags, rugs and sandwich wrappers.

There were cobwebs on the door under the bell tower of St John the Baptist in Erith: about 15 miles on from Southwark. Instead

I found my way round to the main door, which was wide open. David, the churchwarden, was sitting inside quietly. I wondered if he was praying – but no, he had come to test out the Fire Escape signs in the church, to make sure the lights stayed illuminated for three hours non-stop. I was lucky my visit coincided with the annual test, otherwise St John's would also have been shut. David said they had experienced attempted break-ins in the past: you couldn't be too careful.

The church, despite some parts of it dating to the twelfth century, mostly looked after itself, he said. There was a bit of bother with pigeons. David told me a tale of a pair of green parakeets that had recently got inside. No one could get them out: they had squawked and flapped through a Sunday service – one nearly destroyed a piece of stained glass depicting the Lamb of God – but the congregation sang through the din. Later, one bird got stuck in one of the organ pipes, and the vicar had to fish out its corpse.

St John the Baptist was a beautiful church – part-swathed in ivy, with a pointy tower like a witch's hat. Yews shaded the listing headstones in the churchyard. Before the Thames changed course, the church had stood on the banks of the river. Pilgrims from Essex had landed on ferries here and disembarked to join the crowds heading to Canterbury. St John's could have been a church in any English village. Only, when you stepped beyond the lychgate, you saw this was an island of tranquillity in one of London's logistics hubs.

Next door were distribution hubs for Ocado, Tesco and Amazon – Scania lorries boomed along the dual carriageway just behind the graves. On the opposite bank of the Thames was the Rainham landfill site, where bulldozers shunted a small mountain range of rubbish, ostensibly fed by a fleet of rusty barges. A few miles along the path you passed depots, scrapyards, shipping containers stacked into little citadels. Seeing the limbering cranes and spinning turbines was like peering into the mechanisms of a clock. This was where the real business of the capital was done.

I followed the Pilgrims' Way along the edge of the saltmarsh to the headland at Crayford Ness. Escaped ribbons of paper from recycling centres were airborne in the breeze. Buddleias nodded over fly-tipped mattresses, which were themselves fraying into white wisps. It was late summer: the verges were all heavy with unpicked blackberries and busy with bindweed. The city shaded into countryside. The official boundary between London and Kent was the Darent, a muddy river that joined the Thames under a flood barrier. About 22 miles on from Southwark the river brought me to the Church of the Holy Trinity in Dartford – an eleventh-century church that had once contained a chapel dedicated to St Thomas Becket: it too would have been familiar to Chaucer's pilgrims, who probably would have spent their first night outside London in the town.

I went to try its glass doors, but in my heart of hearts I already knew it was locked.

THE RIVER

I had not intended to walk to Canterbury. This road was different from the places I had been before. Paviland Cave, the Ridgeway and Iona all were fogged in mystery: they left open questions, to which pilgrims brought their answers. It was these interactions between the ancient and the modern that fascinated me, these conversations across time on which I loved to eavesdrop. The road to Canterbury, by contrast, seemed neither ancient nor modern but something in the middle: a road ballasted with medieval history. So much about it could be said with scholarly certainty, I wondered what else I might learn from walking it.

The Darent had initially seemed like a grim tributary of the Thames: a river of capsized shopping trolleys and Dickensian mud. But soon it changed character. On the far side of a brick tunnel in Dartford it began to metamorphose into a chalk stream, willow-fringed and wild. Rope swings dangled from oak branches. Rainbow trout flitted under rickety bridges. The river babbled behind fishing lakes where fishermen hunched by green tents: it ran by a model aircraft club, where tiny Spitfires and Red Arrows barrel-rolled against a bright sun. It flowed too

under the great concrete bridges that carried the M25 and M20
– subterranean spaces that seemed cathedral-like in their echoes,
onto whose ceilings the river cast up its kaleidoscopic reflections.
Later the smell of lavender drifted in from the fields. Here the
path felt distant from the industrial estates downstream. I was
walking upstream, but I was also caught in an opposing current:
carried through a corridor of greenery, borne towards the source.
Pilgrimages often went in tandem with rivers. To make such an
upstream journey was in a way to travel back in time: to follow
the water to its origins, and rewind back to a place of genesis
and birth.

Along the Darent Valley, more churches seemed to be open.
At Shoreham a row of Irish yews brought me to the porch of
St Peter and Paul, in which there stood a blackboard that said,
'WELCOME, THE CHURCH IS OPEN.' Inside, columns of
sunshine – tinted and warped by stained glass – spilled across the
floor, reminding me of the liquid light of the river outside. The
doors at St Bartholomew's in Otford were automatic, springing
open with your mere presence.

Chaucer's pilgrims were prominent on the London stretch of
my walk: they featured in a window at Southwark Cathedral. They
had been depicted in a large mural by Adam Kossowski showing
the history of the Old Kent Road on the façade of the old North
Peckham Civic Centre. From Dartford, Chaucer's company
would have carried on east on Watling Street to Canterbury. The
Pilgrims' Way, by contrast, veered south, tracking the Darent on a
different, dog-leg route to Canterbury. Here you heard less about
the *Canterbury Tales*. Instead six men cast longer shadows: a king,
an archbishop, four knights.

Close to St Bartholomew's in Otford was the single remaining
tower of the Archbishop's Palace, a sometime residence of Becket,
who had probably travelled this route along the Darent Valley in
the weeks before his murder in 1170. Becket had initially served as
chancellor for Henry II, and in 1162 the king appointed his ally to
the vacant position of archbishop of Canterbury, possibly hoping
to ease tensions between crown and church. The appointment had

the opposite effect: Becket went native, pledged his allegiance to the Church, supposedly wore a hair shirt. He turned from ally to adversary.

The next church along the Pilgrims' Way was St Mary's Kemsing – also unlocked, its wooden door pock-marked with indentations supposedly carved by Canterbury-bound pilgrims. This little church was said to be haunted by a knight – possibly one of four who had overheard Henry utter the words 'Will no one rid me of this turbulent priest?' (or something like it) and made their way to Kent. The four knights interpreted the king's complaint as an order to kill, and upon arrival in Canterbury chased the archbishop into the cathedral.

Here they drew their swords, sliced off the crown of his head and splattered his blood and brains across the stone floor. The body lay there for some time. Pious folk began to gather his blood from the crime scene. Gervase of Canterbury noted that miracles took place first at Becket's tomb, 'then through the whole of the crypt, then the whole cathedral, then all of Canterbury, then England, then France, Normandy, Germany, [and the] whole world'.

Becket's cult spread fast: just two years after his death he was canonized. Less than four years after his death Henry II made a penitential pilgrimage to Canterbury, humbly removing his shoes for the last stretch (his tender royal feet bleeding) and praying through the night at his tomb (forgoing even trips to the loo). Fifty years after his death, Becket's remains were moved into a shrine.

Pilgrimages had certainly taken place in England before 1170, but St Thomas Becket's martyrdom was the herald for a new golden age of religious travel. His name resonated across Europe: chapels were dedicated to him in Salamanca and Toledo in Spain, Catania in Sicily and Esztergom in Hungary. He endures as the most famous of English saints, whose shrines brought a heavenly overlay to the earthly topography of the land. St Edmund brought people to Bury St Edmunds, St Alban brought them to St Albans and St Cuthbert brought them to his resting place in Durham. Monks squabbled for ownership of saints: old ones were dusted off from the annals of history. Christians prayed to saints as intercessors to God, their relics becoming objects of veneration: bridges between the material and divine. In Becket's case, it was often his blood that had the power to effect miracles – diluted and distributed far and wide, curing leprosy and blindness – the very blood that had been spilled on the cathedral floor.

Canterbury had been a centre of Christianity since St Augustine landed in Kent to convert the English in the sixth century AD – now it exerted a renewed, long-range pull. It was also the circumstances of Becket's martyrdom that meant the story travelled widely. He was an archbishop murdered in his own cathedral. As the knights pursued him, the monks of Canterbury made to bolt the cathedral doors, but Becket forbade them. He insisted the House of God should be locked to no man.

THE OLD ROAD

The doors did not shift at St George's in Wrotham, so I pressed on to where the Pilgrims' Way tracked the edge of a chalk escarpment. It granted occasional views out to the Medway, but in large part the path wound through woodlands, its passage cloistered by bushes and roofed by broadleaf. That tunnel seemed to narrow as the miles went on: at one point a badger bolted into view and then bundled off to a vanishing point. Drizzle descended on the Kentish fields beyond – dewing trellises strung with hops – but it could not penetrate the interior world of the woods where the path stayed dry.

In *The Old Road*, published in 1904, Hilaire Belloc recounted his travels tracing the Pilgrims' Way from Winchester to Canterbury. He acknowledged the pilgrims who had processed between the shrine of St Swithun's in Winchester and Kent's holy city. But his gaze, it seemed, was directed less at history than at cartography, noting that for much of the way between the two cities 'Nature herself laid down the platform of a perfectly defined ridge, from which a man going west could hardly deviate, even if there were no path to guide him.'[1]

As well as the ridge, Belloc also believed that Canterbury and Winchester were predestined to be important (even sacred) places by virtue of their geography. Both lay near seaports that gave access to the continent. Both were a day's march inland, with surrounding farmland to supply them and landward escape routes from invaders. *The Old Road* detailed a prehistoric road to Canterbury that had been plotted not by pilgrims but by the expediency of the terrain, deepened by so many coalescing journeys like a line thickened by many brushstrokes. Implicit in it too was Belloc's near-mystical belief in the old road itself: a thoroughfare with a sanctity surpassing the destinations to which it led. For him the road was:

> the greatest and the most original of the spells which we inherit from the earliest pioneers of our race. It was the most imperative and the first of our necessities. It is older than buildings and than wells; before we were quite men we knew it, for the animals still have it to-day.[2]

Belloc wrote of an instinctive need to tread in the footsteps of ancestors. He wanted to wheeze up the same hills as they had, to cross the same rivers – to find ancestral wisdom in the same accumulation of experience and feel their inherited blood quickening in his veins. Here again was the promise of the Ridgeway: stepping backwards in time by walking forwards, awakening something beneath with your footfalls – taking a homeward road to a nobler, uncorrupted time. But there was a difference: on the Berkshire and Wiltshire track you were mostly distant from everything, in the company of your imagination and the winds. In this part of Kent at least, you were continually thrust back to the twenty-first century.

At Birling Hill the path left the woodlands and picked its way among pylons, chalk quarries and a railway line. The rain grew heavier as I approached the village of Halling. Beyond it the Medway made a series of horseshoe turns, meandering amid a new housing development and a solar farm. It was walking here that I began to feel a sharp note of pain in my foot – a distant alarm that grew a little louder with every mile. I loosened my shoelaces, tried my best to ignore it. My bed for the night was only a few miles away.

The path eventually led past a sewage works to a cluster of wisteria-strewn medieval courtyards by the riverbank. It was late: there was no one to greet me at the Friars. I collected my key from a safe, located a heavy wooden door on which was inscribed 'St John of the Cross'. It creaked open to a little room whose low ceiling was supported by black and ancient-looking beams. There was a lamp, a Bible and a bed. Rain gurgled noisily in the gutters outside.

The Friars (otherwise known as Aylesford Priory) was founded in 1242 by members of the Carmelite Order arriving from the Holy Land. In the Middle Ages it was a place where Canterbury-bound pilgrims rested – and also a major place of pilgrimage in its own right. It turned into a stately home in the aftermath of the Reformation and burned down in the 1930s: only when the property was put up for sale in 1949 did the Carmelite Order purchase it back, picking up where they had left off in 1538. Today pilgrims to Canterbury stop here as their predecessors did. The medieval stones of the old priory merge with modern structures designed by Adrian Gilbert Scott.

By morning my foot had worsened: my right sock was streaked with blood. I hobbled over the courtyard to Pilgrims' Hall for breakfast, where just two other pilgrims whispered in conversation. I limped a little further on to explore the Friars' many chapels, one of which contained the relics of St Simon Stock, a thirteenth-century saint, who may have been from Aylesford, to whom the Virgin is said to have once appeared. I sat on the wooden benches in the courtyard to inspect my foot. I realized I could go no further.

I had imagined the Pilgrims' Way as a definitive path to Canterbury – in fact, it was one of many ways to get to the city. Chaucer's route probably went along Watling Street through Rochester. A continental route came from Dover. There was also the Augustine Camino, which connected Canterbury to Ramsgate and the shrine of St Augustine. In truth, medieval pilgrims did not create new routes: they followed existing ones. Perhaps there was nothing inherently special about this route from London – a motley mix of paths, riverbanks, tracks and hard shoulders – a path that only became coherent by my walking it. We each made our own road, and mine had been a mostly unhappy one. The churches that served the Pilgrims' Way were so often locked, the pubs by the wayside so often gone. I thought at that moment of the Leather Bottle in Belvedere, south-east London, which had been entirely destroyed, apart from a window on which there still hung a single curtain. Such places were there to service travellers on the road – without them some of the life of the Pilgrims' Way seemed to me to have ebbed away.

On my way back to the room I ran into a bald man who looked to be in his sixties wearing a utility vest and well-worn sandals: he asked me if I was the Tesco delivery man. It turned out he was one of the friars. He asked me not to write down his name. Things were not easy at the priory, he said: the place cost over £3,000 a day to run, which was why they hosted conferences, put on Shakespeare plays, offered rooms for AA meetings and suchlike. There had been 18 friars when he joined as a novice: now there were just five, he said. The friar was hopeful the place would never be sold, though I sensed this was his fear.

I explained that I had walked 50 miles from London, and my feet were in pain. He said he had been on a pilgrimage once – walking from London to Canterbury in the 1980s at a time when he had a full head of hair, then continuing on to the shrine of Medjugorje in what was then Yugoslavia over 77 days. He and a friend had slept rough along the way, taking just two days to cross Austria. I asked him how he felt in his heart at the end of a thousand miles of walking. He said, 'It was OK.' They didn't make a song and dance about it. He prescribed me surgical spirits to toughen my feet and, for wisdom on footcare, the Alan Sillitoe book *The Loneliness of the Long-Distance Runner.*

7

A Mountain

A Secret Pilgrimage

A Picture on the Pub Sign | A Picture at Our Lady and
St Michael | A Picture at Llanvihangel Court | A Promise

Mountain – Skirrid from a distance
(Photo by: © David Cheshire/Loop Images/
Universal Images Group via Getty Images)

A PICTURE ON THE PUB SIGN

It was dark, but you could still make out the crude picture on the pub sign.

It showed a mountain rising over the village – a crisp, pyramidal peak, almost like a stratovolcano in its shape. Above its summit, a bolt of lightning forked down from heaven – its spark illuminating the night-time clouds, which had been painted the rosy pink of a Baroque sky. This spear of lightning then shattered the mountain in two – splitting its rock, shaking the woodlands on the lower slopes, casting its sinister afterglow on the rooftops and spires of the ancient parish of Llanvihangel Crucorney (the sign seemed, rather oddly, to depict the village as it is today). Though they were not shown, implicit in this vision were the residents of the Welsh village woken from their slumber – rubbing their eyes, parting curtains to see the terrible destruction wrought on this part of Monmouthshire, where the Almighty had carved their local mountain in two. Below the picture was a short text for the attention of thirsty passers-by:

Wales' Oldest Inn
THE SKIRRID

Inside, the Skirrid Inn indeed felt ancient. A fire glowed in a sooty hearth, over which hung a single golden plate. A few midweek regulars muttered at the bar, but all made their apologies by nine – by which time the only sound was the crackle of the fire, whose shadows played weakly at my feet. On the coarse stone walls were signs erected for the benefit of tourists, detailing the many ghosts who were said to haunt this seventeenth-century coaching inn. One story went that the inn was once a courthouse, where some were hung on the spot (some returned in ghostly form, to make their innocence known). A replica noose was hung over the oak staircase to reinforce the point. The Skirrid Inn had become a place of pilgrimage for ghost hunters. Paranormal investigators came to place infrared cameras, to record creaking furniture, to hold séances with the dead. Online forums were preoccupied, among other things, with a vague, ghostly face that sometimes appeared at an upstairs window.

No one, by contrast, seemed very interested in the sacred mountain that rose just over a mile to the south – the mountain depicted on the pub sign – and which had indeed given the pub its name. I had arrived in Monmouthshire too late in the day to make a pilgrimage up Skirrid. But it was out there somewhere in the cold and the wet of the New Year night, keeping company with the passing clouds.

'What do you want me to say about the mountain?' asked John Smith, who was working behind the bar. 'The mountain is just a mountain. It's not had an impact on me. I climbed it once when I was 57, and I won't climb up it again – because nothing is going to change up there, is it?'

John said he was 67: he remembered people used to go up there carrying crosses when he was a boy, but they didn't do that so much any more. It was the 11th day of Christmas, but the decorations had already been taken down in the pub.

The Skirrid is a 486m-high mountain that is the easternmost peak of the Brecon Beacons. This particular part of the range, the Black Mountains, is defined by gently contoured hills which merge into each other – a place of heathery plateaux and curving ridges. The Skirrid is the exception, set apart from the rest of the hills. It is a singular spur of Old Red Sandstone – steep on its eastern, western and northern flanks, closer to sheer in places. Its geography means there is only one obvious approach for the walker to make – climbing the southern slope, following the backbone of the rock to where the north face falls away into thin air. From certain angles, Skirrid has the appearance of a pulpit, or a ramp leading to the sky.

Skirrid's Welsh name is Ysgyryd Fawr – taking its name from the Welsh word for 'shattered'. Folklore has it that the mountain was split in two at the precise moment of Christ's Crucifixion. As the Son of God bled on the cross at Calvary, God himself briefly directed his attention some 3,800 miles away to another mountain in south Wales – to split its rock with a fork of lightning. Or, according to another version, the destruction arose from a showdown between the devil and the archangel Michael. In a few accounts a seismic tremor shook the mountain at the time of the Crucifixion, as per Matthew 27.51: 'the earth did quake, and the rocks rent.' Some form of celestial commotion had gone on here. It depended who you believed.

But people *did* believe. Skirrid was known as the Holy Mountain, a place of pilgrimage for people in the Welsh Marches. Pious crowds would make processions to a little chapel on the summit. Some came here to pray that God would spare their homeland from Saxon invasion. The very soil of Skirrid was considered to be sacred too: stories tell of farmers who would scatter it on their land in the hope of rich harvests. There were rumours of coffins being sprinkled with Skirrid's earth, and (just out of living memory) of sick animals being led up here by farmers in the hope that they might be healed. The physical evidence of the lightning strike was a landslip that can still be seen on the western slope – some jagged rocks, and a section ruptured from the main peak. Geologists believe the landslip occurred aeons ago, when the ice sheets retreated and the weaker underlay of mudstones collapsed under the weight of the more substantial sandstone. To others, this was the debris of divine power. As Dr Hannah Cowell Roberts of Swansea University wrote in 2014: 'the local population [attributed] such formations to the interference in the physical world of the two most powerful beings they could imagine, God and Satan.'[1]

Skirrid is not the highest peak in the Black Mountains – but it has a property that snags the eye, and that directs your gaze upward. It is a central focus for the surrounding villages and fields. It edges above telephone lines, laundry lines and garden fences. In an age before drones, satellites or planes, the sense of 360 degree elevation a climber possessed there would have been rare. In the 1950s the south Wales historian and folklorist Fred Hando stood on top of Skirrid and wrote:

> Our holy mountain, the Skirrid, is guarded by a ring of five ancient churches ... Seen from the summit, they appear as outposts to a citadel; one could imagine the five patron saints

– Michael, Cadoc, James, David and Teilio, erecting a ring of prayer around their central shrine.[2]

Today the old summit chapel is a ruin. But of those five ancient churches below, three are now in the care of Reverend Julian Gray, a vicar in the Anglican Church in Wales. He explained that the boundary of the three parishes used to converge right on the summit of Skirrid, but as we spoke, they were being integrated into one single super-parish. A reorganization was taking place. The mountain was wholly in Reverend Julian Gray's domain. It remained important to him.

'Skirrid is separate from the other hills around it,' he told me. 'It's on its own. It's a bit like Ayers Rock – or Uluru as it's known now – in that it emerges out of nowhere.

'There's an idea of climbing mountains, reaching up to God and being closer to him. The Abrahamic faiths have thought of God being *up there,* and heaven being *up there.*'

Mountains can be a bridge to the heavens. And mountains can also be symbols of the everlasting. They can represent the world in microcosm – a vertical tapestry of ecosystems, from forests and meadows rising to bare rock and pure white snow. About their upper reaches blow weather systems – wind and rain – whose ferocity can suggest a divine power. Clouds are birthed from their peaks, and avalanches tumble from their slopes. For mortals, mountains can inspire yearning and awe at their base, vertigo and light-headedness on their high points – all sensations with an accompanying current of euphoria. Climbing them necessitates effort and devotion. And so mountains tower high in religion.

There is the mountain of cedars through which the hero passes in the epic of Gilgamesh. There are the mountains of the Hebrew Bible: Mount Ararat (5,137 metres), in what is now Turkey, where the Ark landed as the Flood abated; Mount Moriah (location unknown) where Abraham was commanded to sacrifice Isaac; Mount Sinai (2,285 metres,) probably in Egypt, under which Moses received the Commandments – all places of covenants and promises: deals done with the Almighty. There is the mountain

cave outside Mecca where Mohammed heard the word of God, and
Mount Meru – the centre of Hindu and Buddhist universes.

I have climbed sheer cliffs to the rock-hewn churches of Ethiopia
– some of the oldest churches in Africa – which are hidden in the
crags so worshippers could escape persecution. One winter I stayed
in the Hospice St Bernard – the pilgrims' shelter 2,469 metres
up in the Swiss Alps, where the dead were walled up in a little
mortuary, preserved by the same cold that took their lives. I stood
under the sacred cone of Mount Fuji the week a man accidentally
fell from the 3,776-metre summit and live-streamed his own death.
But of all the holy mountains I have seen, the one that appeared
the holiest to me was Machapuchare – the peak outside Pokhara in
Nepal, said to be a dwelling place of Shiva. It is a snow-encrusted
blade of rock vectoring up into the sky. No one has ever officially
received a permit to reach its 6,993-metre summit, meaning no
one has disturbed whatever resides among its ice.

By contrast, thousands of people walk up the piddly stump of
Skirrid – at 486 metres, the perfect height for a stroll after a Sunday
lunch. But in the topography of Great Britain it is regarded as a
mountain, and an unusual one too. Across the European mainland,
high places are adorned with crosses, chapels or statues of the
Virgin – one of the greatest sites of pilgrimage in Ireland is the
764-metre peak of Croagh Patrick, where St Patrick dispersed
demons by striking a bell. Great Britain has few holy mountains to
speak of (though Schiehallion in the central Highlands and Cader
Idris in Eryri/Snowdonia have vague mystical associations). But
Skirrid is exceptional: amid the low-lying farmland of the Welsh
Marches it is a shape distinct from the jumble of hills, a clean form
visible from the tower of Hereford Cathedral and the plains along
the Severn. It may be small, but it soars higher in the imagination.
Some neo-pagans believe the cult of St Michael was superimposed
on high places that were revered before Christianity took root. It is
impossible to prove. But it seemed to me Skirrid might always have
been a place set apart.

I wanted to know whether the mountain had any meaning for
locals today. Reverend Julian Gray told me he himself was not sure

that the lightning strike had happened. Perhaps it didn't matter, he said – perhaps it was enough that climbing Skirrid turned the walker's thoughts to the Crucifixion.

He gave me the telephone number of the vicar in the neighbouring parish of Llantilio Crossenny: the Reverend Heidi Prince. She was a keen hillwalker. Since her arrival in the late 1990s, she had presided over the revival of a Good Friday pilgrimage to the summit of Skirrid, leading parishioners to the top to say prayers. She found it attracted people who didn't normally go to church (she just didn't always like it when they chatted on the way up). I wondered if the ascent of Skirrid brought her closer to heaven.

'Looking down on things gives you a different perspective,' she told me. 'You see how small we are, in a way. But then I wouldn't say that heaven was up there. It's within you as well, isn't it?'

By chance, one of Heidi's parishioners owned a farm on the lower slopes of the mountain. Did anyone still collect the soil there: were the old legends of fertile fields true? She called up the farmers, and then called me back, sounding bemused.

'They had never heard of people taking sacred soil. In fact, this year the crops on the Skirrid all failed. I think because of the heatwave last summer.'

A PICTURE AT OUR LADY AND ST MICHAEL

By Twelfth Night a forest of discarded Christmas trees lined the pavements of Abergavenny. A few strands of tinsel clung to curtain rails, and a neon Rudolph remained affixed to a wet slate roof. But in its last moments the whole festive season suddenly seemed tawdry and forlorn, and decorations were anxiously being shoved into bin bags with a hungover remorse. An exception was the Roman Catholic church of Our Lady and St Michael, where a nativity scene still stood, assembled with some care in the nave. For the Feast of the Epiphany, little statues of wise men had gathered around the manger, flanked by two wonky Christmas trees.

I stood in the church for some time, listening to the shuffling footfalls of people arriving for a service, and the stifled coughs of

worshipers suffering winter colds. My eyes wandered from the
Virgin to a vision of the saint who had given this church the other
half of its name. In a gilt-framed painting from 1801, the archangel
Michael was depicted winged and wielding a spear, poised to sink
it into a devil he had trapped under his right sandal. The setting
for the battle was a range of dusky mountains. The hill over his left
shoulder suggested the triangular form of Skirrid, which was about
three miles away from the church. After a while, a man emerged
from a door nearby.

 'You're here to see the papal decree, aren't you? Come with me.'

Father Matthew Carney was thin and softly spoken, with a faint
Lancashire accent. He explained that he was a monk in Hereford:
he crossed the border to take services here and had the manner of
a man who did not have much time to chat. He led me through a
series of anterooms. Latticed windows looked out to a drizzly day
outside. A box of Liquorice Allsorts was set on a polished table.
We eventually arrived in a large chamber, where Father Matthew
pointed to a document framed on the wall. It was in Latin, with the
title: CLEMENS PPX. Below was a translation:

Pope Clement X grants a Plenary Indulgence to those who
devoutly visit the Chapel of St Michael on the Skirrid Fawr
on September 29th – Michaelmas Day. Anyone making this
Pilgrimage and wishing to gain the Indulgence is required, first,
to go to Confession and Holy Communion; then, on the Holy
Mountain itself, to pray 'for peace among Christian Princes, for
the rooting out of heresies and for the exaltation for the Holy
Mother Church'.

Given at St Mary Major's, Rome, 'under the
Seal of the Fisherman' on the 20th July, 1676,
and valid for seven years

Four centuries ago, in a basilica not far from the Colosseum, an elderly
pope affirmed the sanctity of Skirrid. Two days later he dropped dead
from gout. This plenary indulgence meant that anyone who climbed

the mountain would suffer no more temporal punishment for their sins. There would be mercy for those who made an ascent: at the summit, they could begin their lives anew. It was not clear what happened seven years after the policy expired, or indeed whether – in the eyes of the modern Roman Catholic Church – Skirrid was still a mountain on which miracles could take place.

'We don't really talk about indulgences as much now as a church,' said Father Matthew. 'And most people locally don't know about the mountain – with the majority of Catholics not coming to church any more.'

He sighed heavily.

'That is the way of it.'

There was, of course, the other reason the story of Skirrid had been forgotten. The sixteenth-century English Reformation saw Christian pilgrimage effectively become outlawed in England and Wales. It was a two-pronged assault: the theological underpinnings of pilgrimage were attacked, and the very idea of sacred journeys was dismissed as superstition. At the same time, the monasteries to which pilgrims journeyed were also destroyed – along with the shrines of saints like Thomas Becket. The mountain began to lose its divine aura to many who lived in its shadow. Many, but by no means all. A monastery could be demolished, but a mountain could not be.

At the back of the church, Father Matthew directed me to a banner showing St David Lewis – a man with a pointed nose, a scholarly squint and stringy, silver hair. Lewis was a son of the Skirrid. He was born in Abergavenny in 1616 to a Protestant father and a Roman Catholic mother, and attended the Royal Grammar School, whose successor lies further along the same road as the church of Our Lady and St Michael. Monmouthshire at that time was an area where Catholicism had to some extent survived the aftermath of the Reformation – with some people worshipping in a language the authorities could not understand.

Lewis travelled as a young man: first to Paris, where he affirmed his mother's Catholic faith, then to the English College in Rome, where he adopted the name of Charles Baker and became a Jesuit priest. The Welshman would have walked the banks of the Tiber near the college, surely moved by the splendour of the Eternal City, convinced by the righteous cause of Rome.

In his mid-thirties, David Lewis returned to his native Monmouthshire to serve a population suffering the effects of the English Civil War. Lewis persisted with his ministry as Catholics were persecuted. Preaching in both Welsh and English, Lewis earned the name Tad y Tlodion – 'the father of the poor'. He travelled by foot, visited houses by night (and suffered toothache for much of his life). He was officially denounced but unofficially loved by both Catholics and Protestants in the borderlands.

'We keep alive the memory of St David Lewis, our local martyr,' said Father Matthew. 'He is still a figure here. He probably said Mass up on the Skirrid. He's a link to the holy mountain. It keeps him alive, in my mind.'

Father Matthew pointed me to vestments hanging nearby: items that would already have been old by the time St David Lewis became the last Welsh martyr. One robe showed winged angels flanking the central figure of Christ on the cross.

'Maybe David Lewis wore these on the mountain – who knows?'

It was beneath this mountain that the saint spent some of his last hours.

A PICTURE AT LLANVIHANGEL COURT

I left Abergavenny on a Skirrid pilgrimage of my own devising – short enough to be done in a winter afternoon, arduous enough to be worthy of the mountain.

I parked up in the Morrisons car park, trampled through suburban housing estates and was soon striding through the oak and beech forests of Sugar Loaf, the starfish-shaped hill that is Skirrid's eastern neighbour. Rusty Land Rovers puttered through farmland. A kestrel turned through cobweb-thin mists. On the summit of Sugar Loaf my walking stick snapped in two. I sat on the trig point and tried my best to fix it but gave up, and spent some time looking over the landscape instead. To the west, rain clouds were thickening about the highest peaks of the Brecon Beacons. To the east, the sun was still shining on England: on the cider orchards and the hedgerow-hemmed fields of Herefordshire.

Almost directly on the boundary of the two countries was Skirrid. It was, in diverse ways, a place on a threshold. Sometimes my route dived into copses or burrowed through valleys. Once it passed through a ravine where I hopped across stepping stones. But most of the time Skirrid remained wholly in view – it was a point by which to navigate, like the magnetic north of a compass. As I drew closer to it, the daylight began to dwindle. By teatime, the mountain had flattened to a still silhouette impressed on hastening clouds. It would be pitch black by the time I reached the top. There was one last place I had to visit before I made my ascent.

A country lane branched off the A465 in Llanvihangel Crucorney, proceeding down a long avenue of trees. At the end it took a right angle at a formidable and ancient-looking wall, which enclosed the grounds of Llanvihangel Court. I walked along the tarmac. The tree cover overhead cancelled the last residual light of that January day. It did not seem like the right hour for a stranger to be knocking on the door of such a grand house, still less to be making inquiries about a painting. But it was worth a shot.

I had tried to get in touch with the owners of Llanvihangel Court, but the website was down. No one was answering my emails, and the phone number went to voicemail. From online searches I could tell that the stately home – in summer, at least – was used as a wedding venue. Pictures showed brides wielding bouquets and toddlers wearing tiny waistcoats. Now the house had a different atmosphere. Unlit windows mirrored the winter sky. I was not sure if I could see a faint pillar of smoke rising from a chimney.

Llanvihangel Court is a largely Tudor building flanked by rolling lawns on one side and a lily pond on the other. The timber columns of the stables were supposedly from the wreck of an Armada galleon, and erected by Spanish prisoners. Charles I had stayed here in the last years before his execution, in a bed emblazoned with the phrase 'remember thy origin' in Welsh.

This historic home had known many residents, but the most notorious was John Arnold, a seventeenth-century Whig MP who devoted much of his life's effort to suppressing Catholicism in Wales. He was a man with an instinct for violence, who savoured the assault and murder of Catholics. He once lightly slit his own throat as part of a plan to pretend an Irish Catholic had attacked him. Whether it was the cause of his ire or perhaps by coincidence, one of the great centres of Catholic pilgrimage lay right outside Llanvihangel Court. Skirrid rose barely a mile away: the alignment of its ridge seemed to point almost directly to his home. The façade of Llanvihangel Court, however, seemed to be oriented to the north: as if it had its back to the mountain.

Through years of persecution, Skirrid was believed to be a sanctuary for Catholics, who were said to secretly rally at the summit. I imagined John Arnold in the upper rooms of the house on a night like this, watching a firefly trail of torches leading to the summit, incensed at the papist gatherings happening right in his constituency, upon this heathen hill. In a report for the House of Commons on the activities of Roman Catholics in Monmouthshire and Herefordshire, Arnold affirmed:

> He hath seen a hundred papists meet on the top of an high Hill, called St Michaels Mount [Skirrid], where is frequent meetings eight or ten times in the year, as he is informed, Mass is said, and sometimes Sermons are preached there.[3]

Arnold's testimony was given in April 1678, on the eve of the Popish Plot – a conspiracy alleging that Jesuits were engaged in plans to kill Charles II. The plot was a fabrication, but it aroused a tidal wave of anti-Catholic sentiment, a hysteria that in turn precipitated trials and arbitrary executions.

Later that same year, David Lewis was to say morning Mass in the Monmouthshire village of Llantarnam when his whereabouts was betrayed by a couple, offered £200 as a reward by John Arnold. Lewis was found guilty of high treason and sentenced to death. He was taken at ten o'clock on a moonlit night to Llanvihangel

Court, whose upper rooms were to be his prison. Here John Arnold taunted his prisoner with a doll in the shape of the pope. It was noted that Lewis had formerly considered Arnold a friend.

Soon the little lane led into a courtyard. The windows on this side of the house faced towards Skirrid. I wondered if the condemned David Lewis might have stood somewhere on those upper floors, gazing up at the giant citadel-like mass of Skirrid – a rock whose holiness had been affirmed by a pope around two years before – and if his thoughts turned to the long-ago moment when the ground shook.

There was another reason I was here. A blog I had read said that Llanvihangel Court contained a painting of Skirrid that dated to the time of the Arnold family. I wanted to see it: I imagined some kindly figure welcoming me from the cold, guiding me around the building, telling me tales of Arnold, Lewis and the mountain that divided the two men.

Instead I found a tradesman chucking things into the back of a pickup truck. He explained he did odd jobs around the house. It was an unusual place, he said – facing north and surrounded by trees, which meant it was often dark. Who should I speak to about the painting? He pointed to a cottage on the edge of the courtyard.

I knocked on the door. A middle-aged man answered, looking impatient and flustered. Yes, there was a painting. No, the hall wasn't open so I couldn't see it now – and no, it wasn't possible to see the painting from the outside of the building either. He advised me to check the website for opening times. Or write him an email and he could send me a photograph of the painting. I understood from his manner that he wouldn't reply to me. And so I trudged back down the country lane, and onwards to the foot of Skirrid.

Eventually the Llanvihangel Court website did come back online. It advertised itself both as a wedding venue and as a film set. There was a history section – though it contained no mention of David Lewis, or of his execution and disembowelment under the auspices of John Arnold (which was delayed, because they struggled to find a willing executioner). Nor did the website note David Lewis's later canonization by the Roman Catholic Church in 1970.

Instead there was a promotional video showing Llanvihangel Court on a summer's day, with Skirrid looking green and glorious in the background.

A PROMISE

It began to rain: beginning as a gentle patter on my anorak, soon crescendoing to the thwack of droplets against Gore-Tex. Raindrops glimmered in the beam of my head torch. I walked with a penitent hunch, to keep the rain out of my eyes, to keep my eyes and my light on the path underfoot.

Skirrid today belongs to the National Trust. In recent decades the lower slopes have been planted with hazel, alder, ash and birch. This wood hissed with the pelt of raindrop on leaf as I passed through: it gurgled with sudden streams that spilled over the path. Once, a moth passed through the beam of my torch and then fluttered to somewhere unseen into the grim dank of the wood. I pressed on, to where the path climbed above the treeline, to where Skirrid shrugged off the woodlands of the lower slopes and exposed its spine of bare rock.

Skirrid had a strange spell, but it was also a melancholy mountain. No locals I spoke to over those January days seemed to know much about its story. It was known as a place for endurance challenges and charity fun runs. Most associated it only with the ghosts and Sunday roasts at the Skirrid Inn. Others seemed more interested in talking about the higher peaks of Wales, such as Snowdon, revered in its own way because its summit ecology had been altered by the volume of human ashes scattered there. Centuries after the Reformation, Skirrid's story still felt like one of dispossession. It stood for a wider landscape losing its enchantment.

Out in the open, sheets of rain whipped about the mountain. Low clouds wreathed the path ahead. Sometimes those clouds withdrew a little or the fibres of their mists thinned, and a window opened to the world below – a view of passing traffic on the A465 or the streetlights of Llanvihangel Crucorney. But no sooner had it opened than that window shut again, and I was alone again on the hill, the weather dancing wildly. Skirrid was the final hurdle for weather systems moving westwards from the Brecon Beacons. Sometimes, the rain seemed to defy gravity, hurtling upwards and arching over its ridgeline. Catholic pilgrims would have soldiered through such a scene, their eyes fixed on the summit: the place where they would be closest to the root of God's lightning, and within his earshot to make their promises.

My journey ended at the summit trig point, adorned by the signature oak leaf of the National Trust. So slight were the ruins of St Michael's Chapel on the summit that I stepped over them without realizing they were there. The chapel was first recorded in the sixteenth century, and may have been older – in any case, politics and weather had reduced it to a bump in the earth. I pulled my hood tightly around my face so it formed a muzzle. I hunched behind the trig – in the lee of the wind – waiting for the worst of the weather to pass. I wiped the rain from my watch. Nine p.m.

Then out of the darkness came a light. It appeared as if as a mirage or even a miracle – the beam moving along the ridgeline – becoming brighter, jolting about, belying the gait of the person who carried it. A fellow human had bothered to climb Skirrid, Ysgyryd Fawr, on such a grim January night! As they came closer, I imagined that they were bringing me some news: doing something momentous to mark the New Year.

Eventually a man stepped into the glow of my torch. His knees were mud-splattered, his face was obscured by an anorak, his words were inaudible in the roar of the wind. I could only catch snippets of what he was saying – grasped garbled syllables, as the wind carried his words off the mountain. Then there was a lull.

'I'm in training,' he said. 'Promised myself I'm going to do the Everest Base Camp trek later this year!'

8

A Well

A Pilgrimage and a Quest

The Crescent | The Water Temple | From the Tor |
At Bride's Well | Black Sheep | Dr Goodchild |
At the Chalice Well | On the Way Home

Well – Tudor Pole's marker stone at Bride's Well

THE CRESCENT

It was perhaps the most beautiful street in the city.

Royal Lancaster Crescent sat on the edge of a hill overlooking Bristol, its town houses orientated to the vista, like seats in a theatre. This street is supposedly the longest crescent in Europe, but its curvature is a gentle one – not a horseshoe, like the Royal Crescent in nearby Bath, but showing more of a shallow inclination, akin to a satellite dish, its radius suggesting a central focus somewhere in the thin air over the Avon.

Construction of the crescent began in 1791, a time when Bristol ships were carrying their cruel cargo of African slaves and American tobacco and merchants sought grand residences in this affluent hilltop suburb of Clifton. Soon after Royal Lancaster Crescent was completed in 1820, slavery was abolished: the Georgian sash windows looked out to the Victorian chimneys of a new age. At some point Royal Lancaster Crescent suffered a small stumble from grace, and its houses were cannibalized into constituent flats. And yet in the twenty-first century some of its grandeur seemed to have been renewed. (Zoopla said one property here fetched over £2.5 million.) And in those intervening years nothing had obstructed that original far-reaching view – so residents still enjoyed the Georgian architect's gift of a vista: down to the grid of streets, and to the comings and goings along the river. They could watch over the world of industry below, in which they had possibly earned the means to live on this hill.

It was spring when I walked through the streets of Clifton. Students were back from Easter holidays, and dandelions were sprouting among cigarette butts on the pavement. The neighbourhood was noisy with the sound of drills and hammers – the symphony of home improvements. A thin dust from building works hung in the air like pollen – the particulates suffusing that morning with a hazed light. Wrought-iron fences cast their spearing shadows on the tarmac. I felt queasy and apprehensive about what I was going to do.

Royal Lancaster Crescent was not hard to find – it lay just off a busy shopping street, past the Clifton Medi Spa and Defy Time cosmetic clinic. I followed a raised promenade above the street level, along the top of garages and basement flats. A few other people were out on their morning rounds: joggers, delivery workers, parents pushing prams. Out to the south was the thrum of Bristol: Spike Island, Ashton Gate stadium. The smell of freshly brewed cafetières and the chatter of Radio 4 wafted out from the first-floor flats. The impression was of ease of living: high ceilings, William Morris wallpaper, iMacs with dancing screensavers.

People seemed proud to live at Royal Lancaster Crescent. Plaques on the crescent commemorated former residents – an East India Company officer, the wife of Napoleon III (who once attended a boarding school here). The residents' committee notice board offered guidance for film crews wishing to use their street as a location for period dramas. Nothing acknowledged the brief, bizarre moment one century ago when 25 Royal Lancaster Crescent was a place of pilgrimage for people from as far away as the Middle East. I was doubtful whether any residents now knew that number 25 was said to house a magical object out of which sprang angels and celestial doves, whose arrival had been supposedly foretold by a bright star over the crescent: indeed, an object whose legitimacy had been affirmed by senior figures in the Church of England. This crescent was built at a time when human bodies were treated as capital. A century later it was home to an object supposedly connected to the destiny of all human souls.

And – another century on from that – there was me: trying to get inside the property to find out more. Number 25 looked no different from any other house in the crescent: partitioned into six flats, a bay tree placed by the front door. An empty box for a Dualit toaster had been propped on a downstairs windowsill.

I pressed the top buzzer. No answer. The next one down. No answer. The next one down. The static erupted into a breathless voice, which – when I explained what I was doing – suggested I speak to flat number seven, because number seven had been here the longest. Soon, an elderly, well-spoken voice piped out of the box.

'I'm sorry, but I'm very busy, and now is not a good time to talk. The newer residents don't know much – and I only know what I've only picked up over the years, and that the man, Mr Tudor Pole, yes, he thought he had a piece of the True Cross. Oh no, you're right, quite right of course, it was the Holy Grail, yes the Holy Grail. It was all to do with Glastonbury, and that sort of thing. I'm sorry but this really isn't a good day, but I'd be happy to ...'

I would have to try another time. I stepped back and looked up at the building. The upper windows reflected rectangles of blue sky. The confetti of cherry blossoms drifted over the crescent gardens. The builders at number 19 were having a fag break. The story of 25 Royal Lancaster Crescent was strange and little-known. And yet it was a modern retelling of an older, far more familiar tale – a legend about a quest, and an English holy land.

Partly out of curiosity, I took a walk to the Clifton Suspension Bridge, five-minutes from the crescent. The bridge had first opened in 1864 and was famously based on a design by Isambard Kingdom Brunel. Less famously, it was also the site of the world's first bungee jump. The pioneering feat was undertaken by two members of the Oxford University Dangerous Sports Club – David Kirke and Simon Keeling – on 1 April 1979. One of them glugged champagne and sported a morning suit for the occasion. Unlike subsequent bungee jumpers who generally linger theatrically on the brink, the footage of that April day shows no hesitation from the participants: both make a sudden leap of faith over the parapet, showing no fear as they hurtle towards the water.

THE WATER TEMPLE

Later that same day, I was naked in the upper pool of the water temple.

It had rained for some weeks previously, and so the water was in full voice: the current thundered through a spout, slopping in a little delta onto the bowed floors. The liquid echoes deepened under the brick arches, mingling with other noises from worshippers assembled inside. The ringing of a Tibetan prayer bowl. The plainsong-like cadences of female voices. And – obscured amid the booms of falling water – a low bass chant of *Om Mani Padme Hum*. This temple was dark, lit only by a few candles, and so it took attention to match these sounds to their originators. The chant was from a bald man bowing in honour of Gwyn ap Nudd, king of the fairies, the singing from a trio of middle-aged women spinning dervish-like on the rim of the lower pool. All were naked. Anyone entering this space might imagine they had time-travelled to a distant epoch – perhaps a mystery cult in the twilight days of the Roman Empire. In twenty-first-century England, however, everyone knew there was only one Somerset town where such a place could exist.

The White Spring, as the temple was officially known, was actually a fairly recent addition to the town of Glastonbury. The structure had been built over a natural spring in 1872, to serve as a reservoir for a town then suffering from outbreaks of cholera. Its initial career was short-lived: the water was too calciferous and kept blocking up the local plumbing. The subterranean cistern lay abandoned for almost a century until, around the 1980s, a local councillor bought it for £1. Its contents were drained, and doorways were installed: it became a little café. In 2005 a new owner turned it into a sacred space centred on the healing properties of water. The paint was stripped from the walls and pools were added. It was open daily (except Mondays). A steady stream of pilgrims of all kinds came to bathe here, each worshipping in their own way.

Among them was the White Spring's current custodian, Sol. He first entered the waters on his birthday a decade ago – an experience he described as being 'like a baptism in the waters of Babylon'. I had met him in the little garden outside the White Spring earlier that afternoon: he had a long grey ponytail and wore a T-shirt with a cartoon octopus on it.

His original pilgrimage to Glastonbury had been an accidental one. He was originally from Sussex, and worked as a bit part actor (or 'glorified extra', as he put it), playing a crime scene investigator on *The Bill* and a prison officer in *Bad Girls*. The journeys back and forth to London studios took a toll on him, and in 2005 he booked himself onto a meditation retreat in rural Herefordshire. At 8 p.m. on the orientation day a bell rang. There was to be no speaking, no books, no phones for nine days – you were to be alone with your thoughts. He shared a room with someone who snored like a freight train. Sol left on the second day of the retreat.

On the way back to Sussex he thought he might as well do some sightseeing and took a detour to Glastonbury on a sunny day in July. Something stirred in him. A few years later his landlord gave him notice: a voice in his head suggested he start anew in a Somerset town. Glastonbury, Sol said, was often considered the heart chakra of Planet Earth. Before he lived here, Sol had become jaded by failed relationships, had been at a point in life when he felt he had missed his chance to find love. Now he was happily married and, in his role as custodian of the White Spring, was helping heal the hearts of others.

'Some people who come to the White Spring cry. Some people light candles. You see people going through a process. We're creating a place of many paths. The spring can bring up things inside you. It can help you let go of them too.'

The White Spring was in one sense new, and in another very old. Holy wells were certainly among the earliest places of pilgrimage in Britain. They were generally assumed to be pre-Christian places of worship but, with moving water rather than datable matter being the object of veneration, their history was often hard to ascertain. They were themselves part of a broader flow of water through religion, a basin that encompassed the Ganges and the Jordan. With the dawn of Christianity, wells were linked to early saints: a spring had sprung up where the first Christian martyr in Britain, St Alban, had his head chopped off by a Roman soldier. Columba, Cuthbert and Aidan all had their wells. They were places of purification and miracle cures.

It was often observed that there was 'something in the water' in Glastonbury: it was a town of fewer than 8,000 people and over 70 different faiths, and thus many cross-currents of faith mingled at the White Spring. Catholic pilgrims wandered in sometimes and got frightened when they saw the altar to the horned figure of Gwyn (worrying that it was the devil). To calm them down, Sol directed them instead to a shrine of Brigid of Kildare, the Irish saint whose statue was placed in an alcove under an arch of twigs. It didn't matter that in Glastonbury 'Bridey' was often considered a goddess in her own right.

The White Spring was a modern invention, but the rituals it invited were ancient ones. They seemed to me twofold: first, a need to make an offering to the water – as instinctive as throwing a lucky coin into a well. And second, a sense that there was something else lurking in that water, something that might only be discovered if you stepped into the murk. One ritual seemed to serve the other. To deposit and to discover.

I spent a while sitting in the pools – watching the shadows play on the bare stone walls. Curious tourists peeked through the doorway, their eyes widening on account of the darkness (or maybe because of all the naked flesh inside). Meanwhile the water had been on its own journey – beginning as raindrops on meadow grass, percolating through soil and strata, chuntering through this cistern and then gurgling under manholes, flowing towards the town centre. All the pilgrims, by contrast, flowed uphill.

FROM THE TOR

Outside the White Spring a busy footpath led through gaps in the hedgerows and beds of nettles to Glastonbury Tor: the 158-metre hill whose slopes had granted its waters. Like Skirrid, this hill was associated with the archangel Michael. Like Skirrid, it was in the care of the National Trust. Unlike Skirrid, a sizeable chunk of church survived on the summit of Glastonbury Tor – a medieval tower, which seemed an upward embellishment of the steep slopes on which it stood. The Tor was one of the most famous sights in England, and a symbol or cipher for Celtic-ness. To some, the Tor was the holiest of holies: a bridge between upper, lower and middle worlds. The Tor was also the old logo for Clarks shoes – the nation's most sensible footwear brand. The April wind dried my hair as I climbed to the top, where a man in a suit of armour was holding his sword aloft.

'I bet you're wondering why I'm dressed as a knight!' he said to one passer-by.

But this was Glastonbury, so no one was wondering. Everyone was looking at the view, which eclipsed the panorama from Royal Lancaster Crescent in its loveliness. Out to the western horizon lay a smudge of the south Wales coast. To the north, in sharper focus, Wells Cathedral and the entrance to Cheddar Gorge. All around, the plains of the Somerset Levels lay patterned by field boundaries and cloud shadows. The intake of air and space on the Tor could be dizzying. In the late 1920s the artist Katharine Maltwood professed the existence of a 'Temple of the Stars' – an ancient set of zodiac signs imprinted on the landscape below the Tor, a star map extending halfway to Yeovil and Bridgewater. The Somerset zodiac theory fell somewhat flat when someone pointed out that it incorporated relatively recent drainage ditches, and that the eye of Capricorn was a haystack. But people on this hill saw what they wanted to see. In the words of Glastonbury historian Geoffrey Ashe, on the steep rise of the Tor, the mind 'interprets the landscape into something truly alien to common experience. The irrational scene loosens the grip of the Ordinary and gives scope to the Fantastic. Just by a matter of an inch, it jars open the magic casements.'[1]

I had my own theory on Glastonbury's geography. The first-time visitor might start to consider the town a series of circles – a kind of mandala – that could be traced from the Tor. At the centre of everything was the ruined abbey: discernible from the lower slopes as a pocket of greenery, with Gothic arches rising over lawns. This was where the story began. An abbey had been in existence here since the seventh century AD. By the Middle Ages, a legend spread that Christianity had been brought to Glastonbury in the first century AD by Joseph of Arimathea, the merchant who carried the body of Christ from the cross to the cave at Golgotha. As the apostles spread the news across the Mediterranean, Joseph made his way to Britain, carrying two vials of the saviour's blood. Borne by a miraculous wind, his boat rounded the cape of Cornwall in a single night. Joseph landed in south Wales, got booted out and was later granted sanctuary on the Tor by a merciful Celtic king. Here he lived out his years as a hermit, beside a sacred spring which healed the sick.

Thereafter this narrative was elaborated by multiple sources. The snowball effect never stopped. All legends were mutable, but this one was a Creative Commons. In one version Joseph of Arimathea carries the Holy Grail, the cup passed around by Christ at the Last Supper (it was concealed in the Somerset landscape, or perhaps handed to a secret fraternity for safekeeping). In another, Joseph found himself as a chaperone of Christ in his wilderness years, bringing the teenage son of God to Somerset, to walk the land of cloudy apple cider before his calling: William Blake wrote a poem about that version. To complicate things, the twelfth century saw the monks of Glastonbury Abbey announce the discovery of King Arthur's tomb – Arthurian romances and the quest for the Holy Grail merged and intermingled with the legends of Jesus and Joseph of Arimathea. Nothing much could be proved, though respectable historians had done much to divine droplets of truth in the whirlpool of Glastonbury legend. More level-headed (or cynical) voices suggested the stories were marketing material for an abbey that had burned down in the twelfth century, and which needed to attract pilgrims to fund rebuilding efforts.

In the sixteenth century the tidal wave of the Reformation lapped at the foot of the Tor, but Glastonbury had long been one of England's great centres of medieval pilgrimage and the elderly abbot, Richard Whiting, held out until his was the last monastery standing in Somerset. Whiting was dragged by horse to the top of the Tor to be hanged, drawn and quartered. The abbey was destroyed, but the old stories, invented or not, could not be.

Beyond the stout abbey walls lay a second concentric circle of Glastonbury: the town centre. Today – probably more than at any time since before the English Reformation – it existed to service the needs of pilgrims. There were shops selling healing crystals (many were offering 50 per cent off Madagascan stones) and figurines of Ganesh, Buddha and Odin sitting beside their price tags. There were New Age art works – landscapes where the sky was the purple of a Cadbury's Dairy Milk wrapper, and where goddesses rode white horses among rainbows. There were esoteric bookshops for a pilgrim's education: books about Nazi plans to colonize space and volumes on the Tantric nature of Jesus Christ. What Christ would make of this was unclear – though you could always ask him yourself: a man calling himself Jesus the Christ, the Buddha Maitreya, had an office on the High Street, halfway between the Boots and the Co-op. Online reports suggested he was originally known as Ron and came from California: his website had a link where you could help him rent an RV until 2033. Clouds of incense huffed out from every other door.

This incarnation of Glastonbury had its genesis in the years leading up to the inaugural Glastonbury Festival in 1970. The festival was (and still is) held at Pilton, seven miles away from Glastonbury town, though in its aftermath crowds of hippies gravitated towards the Tor (they preferred to be called 'freaks'). The freaks on the so-called 'scene' were largely male, well educated, took LSD and sincerely considered themselves pilgrims, confident that Jesus Christ would be making his return here in Glastonbury. What began as a trickle of summertime incomers had entered the bloodstream of the town 50 years later. Local people cited various watersheds for the conversion of Glastonbury from ordinary market town to fully fledged New Age capital. It happened when the old Woolworths was turned into an organic food shop. Or when the alternative shops crossed the Rubicon of a certain zebra crossing on the High Street. Or perhaps the defining moment was when the pubs took down the last signs saying 'No Hippies'.

A century ago the local industry in Glastonbury was the manufacture of boots and shoes. Now its commerce was souls rather than soles. There were healers of all kinds, and – just like the characters in Chaucer's Prologue – pilgrims of many priorities: red-faced revellers in the pubs, busloads of idle browsers from Bristol, superstitious teenage girls stocking up on crystals just as medieval pilgrims had craved relics. In the mix were a few robed individuals deeply immersed in the meaning of their own personal quests, many content to make themselves a spectacle for everyone else.

Glastonbury had been called an 'English Jerusalem'. But there was a key difference. In Jerusalem followers of the three main Abrahamic faiths clashed, and even Christian denominations squabbled for stewardship of the Church of the Holy Sepulchre. But in Glastonbury a coven of witches could join a shaman making his salutations to the sun. A man in a Runic hoodie and army trousers could meditate within the feminine sanctuary of the Goddess Temple. Christianity was in the mix too. You could follow any path in Glastonbury – one person's revelations only served to sustain and affirm the validity of everyone else's. There seemed to be a few basic guidelines: a belief in a past golden age, a confidence in an imminent new dawn for humankind – and a certainty that a certain Somerset postcode had something to do with it all. Oddly, no one seemed to be spreading the word and sending missionaries to Taunton or Shepton Mallet.

I much preferred the neighbourhoods beyond the high street – what might be considered the third circle of the Glastonbury mandala. Walking these streets, I felt real affection for the town. Here were suburban homes much like any in England: interwar estates, Fiestas and Focuses in the driveway and slides and swings in the garden. Only when you looked a little more closely did you see concessions to other realms: small signs that these residents too were searchers, or else people on a long-term pilgrimage. A dreamcatcher in an upstairs window. A Buddha keeping company with the garden gnomes among the lavender. It was in this third domestic circle that I lodged during my time in Glastonbury, in the Healing Waters Sanctuary (also much like any other suburban B & B, apart from the Buddha mural by the entrance and the intermittent 'self-actualization retreats' on offer).

There was just one other guest. Sonja was an RE teacher turned New Age priestess from Nuremberg, Germany. Kind eyes peered from under sandy hair. I met her the afternoon after I climbed the Tor: we sat in the communal kitchen and chatted over a pot of herbal tea. She said she had felt an inner calling to come to Glastonbury, to bathe in the waters of the White Spring under the altar of what she called the 'Hirschgott' (the deer god, or Gwyn). In Germany there were springs dedicated to the Virgin, of course, but nothing like the White Spring; indeed she had been nowhere in Europe like Glastonbury. Other pilgrims said the bombardment of cosmic energy in Glastonbury could get too much and they could only handle the town in small doses – but Sonja slept more deeply here than anywhere, feeling the motherly embrace of the ley line flowing under her bed.

She said it was the aim of her pilgrimage to foster a network of pan-European energy lines – through her travel she would soon be binding Glastonbury's energy to Chartres in France, and thence threading it homeward to Nuremberg. Later, we discussed the problems of Brexit in the communal kitchen, as she cooked courgette and onions on the hob.

AT BRIDE'S WELL

There was also a fourth circle to Glastonbury: a belt of retail estates on the western edge of town, with an Aldi, a B&Q, various garages and a sewage works edging the farmer's fields beyond. Early that evening I left the guesthouse, under cirrus clouds streaked the technicolour hues of a tie-dye T-shirt, and trod the long hump of Wearyall Hill on my way north. The late light flared in the dykes of the Somerset Levels. The sunset staged its last redoubt on the tip of the Tor. Up close it can be easy to be cynical about Glastonbury. But even from a short distance, its geography works its spell: the steep contours of the Tor coaxing an upward inflection of thought, just as the view from its summit seemed to open up the minds of some.

The Tor was said by some to have another, ancient name, 'Ynys Witrin' – meaning the 'Island of Glass'. There was a certain truth to it: the knuckle of the Tor once overlooked a waterworld whose flood had, in the greater measure of time, abated only seconds ago. The monks of Glastonbury Abbey helped drain much of the Somerset Levels, creating farmland from what had been a basin of reeds, rivers and wetlands. The area around Glastonbury was for millennia what Geoffrey Ashe called a 'British Venice'. Some of the oldest pathways in Britain had been found a few miles away – raised walkways over wetlands dating back six thousand years. It has been speculated that they were corridors to islands that might have stood for otherworlds. Or, who knows, perhaps the locals just wanted to keep their feet dry back then. Ashe postulated that, before the coming of Christianity, Glastonbury Tor itself represented an 'Island of the Dead' – that the water around it served as a barrier to keep the spirits in. Even now, Glastonbury Tor could revert to being an almost-island. The Bristol Channel flood of 1607 (the one that could have stolen the skull of the Red Lady) saw saltwater touch the Tor. Every winter or thereabouts the River Brue drowned a few fields around town. If you stood in the right spot, squinted and blocked out the telephone poles, you were granted a vision from a time before Christian legends orbited the Tor.

Beyond the Glastonbury ring road – past the Brewer's Fayre and a Premier Inn – a pathway led over a five-bar gate, through a young orchard and beside the sluggish current of the River Brue, speckled with lilies. Eventually it reached Bride's Mound: little more than a shallow undulation in an overgrown field, and a place associated with Bridey, or St Bridget. There was little to see. Bride's Mound was off the tourist circuit, though this hillock was also once one of Glastonbury's islands, a place where medieval pilgrims were thought to have arrived and rested before making the final journey to the abbey. Close to the mound was a marker, not unlike a gravestone. I read the inscription: 'This stone marks the traditional spot of St Bride's Well.' The stone had been commissioned by a man named Wellesley Tudor Pole. It was his story that had drawn me to the town.

Major Wellesley Tudor Pole was born in 1884 into a wealthy family of Bristol grain merchants. Photographs show a young man with dark eyes – almost handsome but for his receding hairline. It was said that, as a boy, Wellesley could see the 'colours of prayers' drifting up from the mouths of the congregation at church. He was something of a misfit – bullied at boarding school. By the age of 18 he experienced a calling, a dream that he had been a monk at Glastonbury – a town which he had never been before in his young life, despite its being little over 20 miles from Bristol. The first journeys he made to the town were a homecoming. Soon he received a psychic intimation – a message that there was a sacred object awaiting discovery in Glastonbury, and that it might reveal itself only to three maidens. Those three maidens, it then became increasingly clear, were to be his sister Kitty and her friends the sisters Janet and Christine Allen. The trio joined him on his many Glastonbury pilgrimages. Four Edwardian figures took picnics on Wearyall Hill. Kitty played her violin on the Tor.

'Almost from the first day that I was there on pilgrimage,' Wellesley wrote in 1907, 'I have felt convinced that a great find was about to take place and I have dedicated myself to the search for the "Holy Graal".'[2]

Had he been writing this in 2023, it would be at this point that eyes might glaze over, and the story of his grail quest would be lost in the noise of contemporary Glastonbury prophecy. Admittedly, in the words of one biographer, Gerry Fenge, we must still consider the possibility that Tudor Pole 'might, to put it bluntly, be a nutter'.[3] And yet the young man's quest began some 60 years before the freak generation arrived; nor did Tudor Pole fit the mould of a charlatan. Later in life he went on to be a skilled businessman and a respected army major who had the ear of General Allenby and Winston Churchill. He was lauded for his bravery in the First World War – shot by an Ottoman sniper hidden in a fig tree near Jerusalem. Respectable people remarked on his psychic ability to foretell deaths and to witness real-time troop movements on the Western Front, thousands of miles away. His was a life of visions – though he kept this interior world separate from his role as a dedicated and practical family man. His story is brilliantly told in Patrick Benham's 1993 book *The Avalonians*. What Tudor Pole discovered in Glastonbury in his youth was to influence the course of his life, but it seemingly made him little monetary gain, nor did he cultivate anything like a personality cult. His story, when I read about it, seemed both rapturous and ridiculous, hysterical but touching. It seemed to contain some of the essence of Glastonbury. His was the individual quest, blazing the trail for all Glastonbury seekers today.

In the autumn of 1906 Wellesley Tudor Pole was in a meeting at the family business when he experienced a sudden vision on an adjacent wall: a thorn tree, under which lay an object bathed in brilliant white light. The location he recognized as Bride's Well – he dispatched his team of 'maidens' to search the water (it later transpired it was less of a well, more of a sluice to drain the field). Pulling up their stockings and wading into the three feet of mud, the Allen sisters found something material.

Wellesley's prophecy seemed to have come true. Eventually a real, physical blue bowl was brought back to the Tudor Pole house in Clifton, Bristol, and housed in a specially prepared chapel on the upper floors of 25 Royal Lancaster Crescent. White curtains were suspended from the walls of the Clifton Oratory, and the bowl was laid in a casket on an altar. With the three women as its guardians, the object was treated almost as a human presence, according to Patrick Benham – the herald of a new, feminine kind of Christianity.

Pilgrims came to see it. Communion wine was poured from the cup. Miracle cures supposedly took place, and some professed to seeing lotus flowers and winged angels emerge from the vessel. Experts could offer no definitive verdict on the origin for the object – though it was accepted among attendees of the Oratory that this was the cup that had been with Jesus, and that had maybe caught his blood. Its discovery had something to do with the end times, and also with a new dawn. To hurry along the new age, the group contacted the archdeacon of Westminster and chaplain to the Speaker of the House of Commons, Basil Wilberforce (grandson of the abolitionist William Wilberforce, who had done much to end the Bristol slave trade). Tudor Pole took the cup to London, where Wilberforce affirmed its biblical origins, and was convinced it was the grail. He showed it to another visiting friend, Samuel Clemens, better known by his pen name, Mark Twain.

'I am glad I have lived to see that half-hour – that astonishing half-hour,' recounted the typically sceptical American.

> In its way it stands alone in my life's experience. In the belief of two persons present this was the very vessel was brought by night and secretly delivered to Nicodemus, nearly nineteen centuries ago, after the Creator of the Universe had delivered up his life on the cross for the redemption of the human race … and here it was at last, dug up by a grain broker at no cost of blood or travel.[4]

Wilberforce arranged for the blue bowl to be unveiled to an audience of dignitaries – including the American ambassador, the duke of Newcastle and staff from the British Museum. The *Daily Express* ran the headline 'Mystery of a Relic; Finder Believes it to be the Holy Grail'. One would expect the journalists to have scoffed at Tudor Pole, but the report was part-curious and part-credulous. The discovery had taken place in the aftermath of the Victorian crisis of faith, a time when English spirituality had been shaken from its dogmatic boundaries following the revelations of Darwin, and perhaps needed a new vessel in which to settle.

'Twenty years ago [Tudor Pole] would have been merely laughed out,' went the *Daily Express* editorial.

> Today, eminent men, among them divines and scientists, solemnly meet to discuss his story and to endeavour to discover what the vessel may be. It is good for the world to have really learned that 'there are more things in heaven and earth than dreamt of in our philosophy'.[5]

Perhaps the most significant person that Wilberforce introduced to Tudor Pole was 'Abdu'l-Bahá, the eldest son of the Persian prophet Baha'u'llah, with whom the Baha'i faith originated in 1863. Baha'i, which today claims up to 8 million followers worldwide, is a religion of consolidation: teaching the validity of all faiths, and emphasizing the unity of all peoples. It claims to be the fastest-growing of world religions. Like Tudor Pole, 'Abdu'l-Bahá was a man professing the dawning of a new age, and so the cup was of interest to him. From his base in Haifa, 'Abdu'l-Bahá made two pilgrimages to the Clifton Oratory, visiting in 1911 and again in 1913. A surviving photo shows the sexagenarian prophet, robed and white-bearded, sitting among his fez-capped followers outside the porch of 25 Royal Lancaster Crescent. A small rug seems to be placed at his feet. By his side stands Tudor Pole.

In the end, I never gained access to 25 Royal Lancaster Crescent. It was only some time later that I came to discover that the National Spiritual Assembly of the Baha'is of the United Kingdom had purchased one of the flats in the building just over a decade ago, with, I was later told, a view to restoring it as it existed during 'Abdu'l-Bahá's visit (it would probably entail guesswork – no plans or photos of the interior of the Oratory survived). I emailed them to asked if I could go inside, but they declined. Renovations were ongoing. They had recently put in a planning application to reinstate an original doorway. As a consolation, the Baha'i secretary, Patrick O'Mara, provided an extract from a letter written by Wellesley Tudor Pole:

> In 1911 in my Clifton home A.B. held the Cup in his hands for a very long time, saying nothing. Then he blessed it reverently and gave it back to me.

BLACK SHEEP

The last trails of twilight were beginning to leave the fields around Bride's Mound. I made my way back to my room at the Healing Waters Sanctuary. Few visitors I spoke to in Glastonbury had heard the story of the blue bowl: fewer knew it in detail, or of its connections with Mark Twain and 'Abdu'l-Bahá. More recently, Bride's Mound had entered local consciousness for other reasons: a travelling community had made their home in the orchards south of the hillock, arriving at a time when Prime Minister Boris Johnson was talking about 'flattening the curve' and everyone's attention was on Covid transmissions. Some said Bride's Mound was a sacred place for the travelling community. Others told me it just happened to be where there was room going.

In 2021 caravans were evicted from the Mound, but a huddle of vehicles lingered on in a field beyond Tudor Pole's well marker three years later. At the centre of them was a leather sofa and novelty bin shaped like a frog, of the sort seen in pub gardens. The caravans and campervans of New Age travellers were a regular sight in Glastonbury: vehicles with a hint of establishment to their names – 'Clubman' and 'Senator' – offset by the colourful murals on the side. Sometimes chimneys had been bored through the ceilings. They were – I was told by the group Friends of Bride's Mound – a fluid community, about which it was difficult and dangerous to generalize. The word 'fluid' seemed apt: fleets of caravans flowed down certain country lanes, forked off in little tributaries. Here and there business owners had placed rocky boulders on private roads, junctions and car parks – an effort to dam their flow. The caravans seemed to slip through.

A Conservative councillor on the Mendip District Council had accused travellers of shoplifting, and had advocated an order to evict them from certain sites. Travellers' supporters described this order as a form of fascism. Glastonbury was a popular place, so rents were high: some had nowhere to be but the road. It seemed to me they might be the inheritors of a tradition that stretched beyond the freaks of the 1960s, to those first pilgrims who had crossed the Levels.

The darkness thickened over the Somerset farmland. I left the field, opened the five-bar gate and passed a caravan parked under an oak tree. Clegg and Sheba were chatting in the shadows inside, drinking cans of Guinness. Clegg spoke in a broad Bradford accent. It was his caravan, and inside it he had installed a stove from a canal boat. Sheba lived in a shipping container around the corner. We talked about the story of the blue bowl. Sheba wondered if the Holy Grail was a thing, a place or even a state of mind. Then things went quiet.

'Everyone who comes to Glastonbury is a black sheep,' said Sheba.

'I'm not a black sheep,' said Clegg. 'I'm an alpaca!'

He laughed for some time at this joke. Then things went quiet again. There was truth to what Sheba had said. Seven years before Tudor Pole and his maidens, another black sheep had walked into this very same Somerset field: the figure of Dr John Goodchild. He was a key to understanding much of the mystery behind the cup.

DR GOODCHILD

One autumn day in 1897 Dr John Arthur Goodchild checked into his hotel room at the Hotel St Petersbourg, Paris – a well-to-do establishment still in business today, not far from the Palais Garnier. The doctor was in middle age and of a literary mind, soon to publish a book entitled *The Light of the West*, a search for the mystical in early Christianity. He was en route from London to his winter work as a doctor in Bordighera, an Italian Riviera town near the French border. In summer he mostly lodged with his father in Hampstead, north London, to whom he entrusted his belongings, such as a blue glass bowl he had purchased from a tailor's shop in Bordighera 12 years previously.

Suddenly Dr Goodchild reported experiencing paralysis and heard a disembodied voice in his hotel room. It informed him that the Bordighera Cup was the one carried by Jesus, and that it would shape the course of the century to come. Furthermore, upon the death of his father Goodchild was to place the cup at Bride's Mound in Glastonbury, where it would be retrieved by a maiden. Then Goodchild would receive a sign. The voice fell silent: a rosy light lingered in the Parisian hotel room. Weeks later, Goodchild senior passed away. Months later, Goodchild junior penitently brought the bowl to Glastonbury and placed it in the sluice in Bride's Mound. For some years from 1899 he made annual pilgrimages to that lonely field on the edge of Glastonbury, awaiting further instructions from a voice which never came. He worried that the farmer had drained the sluice, and the cup was gone.

The elderly doctor remained silent in the first days after Tudor Pole and his entourage made their discovery. But soon after, he confessed the cup's origins to Kitty Tudor Pole and, feeling joy at seeing his prophecy come true, made his own pilgrimages to the Oratory. He died in 1914, having seen the cup he had purchased at Bordighera reach the right hands.

There were many ways to read the revelations about the bowl's origins. It seemed to me a tragicomic accident, a story of two men who had cast themselves as characters in their own celestial dramas and of two grail quests colliding headlong in that Somerset field (propelled, in part, by the old Glastonbury legends). Another way to interpret it was as a hoax: the two men moved in the same circles and colluded over a period of time to create a headline-grabbing story, centred on a dubious antique. But it was a third interpretation that prevailed among many at the time: that Goodchild's visions vindicated those of Tudor Pole, and that the two were both small players in the greater destiny of a cup – an older man ordained to leave it there, the young heir appointed to collect it. Both understood the importance of 'maidens' and of femininity. Both were drawn to a body of water in an obscure part of an obscure field. Both may have been guided by the same unseen force on their pilgrimages.

These were the things I mulled over as I returned to the guesthouse in the gloom. The events were a little too recent to be a myth, too long ago to be scrutinized too closely. The precise location of the well was unknown – the River Brue had been re-routed, and the old sluice was gone. The whole matter would perhaps be too obscure to merit further inquiry – were it not for the fact that the blue bowl remained a presence in Glastonbury and that Tudor Pole's pilgrimage remains important to a few, even today.

AT THE CHALICE WELL

I slept fitfully that night, waking early the next morning. From my room at the guesthouse I could sit up in bed and watch the dawn on the Tor: the sunshine catching the tip of the tower, sweeping down the slopes, flooding the Somerset Levels in one radiant instant. After eating a bowl of organic cereal I was walking back into Glastonbury town centre. I had one last appointment.

Paul Fletcher spoke in soft south Yorkshire vowels and had long white hair that cascaded onto a blue Mountain Warehouse jacket. He looked to me like the fashion designer Paul Smith (though perhaps it was just because his name was Paul). He was one of the originals: he had been at the first Glastonbury Festival in 1970, and drove there in a 1945 Bentley – it was a great gathering of the tribes, he said, a great beginning but also an ending, for the festival did not resume in earnest for almost a decade afterwards. By that time Paul's attention had wandered to the town that lay miles beyond Michael Eavis's fields. He climbed the Tor. He heard the story of the bowl. In his own words, reading Wellesley Tudor Pole's writing 'lit him up'.

After living on Anglesey, Paul and his wife moved to Glastonbury two decades ago – it would be in this place they decided they would live out the last stage of their life. They had a son in London: a geneticist whom Paul described as living in a godless universe (though he said their different viewpoints always made for stimulating conversations). Paul, meanwhile, had devoted much of the effort of the past two decades to the mystical enterprise of the Chalice Well.

The Chalice Well was described on its website as 'a living sanctuary of healing, sanctity and peace'. It was, in essence, a garden snuggled in a valley under the Tor. The garden was enclosed by high stone walls that gave little indication of what lay within. Adult admission was £5. It was a major attraction: Prince Charles visited it in 1990. Signs asked everyone to switch phones to flight mode as they entered the space.

Paul had served as both Chalice Well chairman and as a trustee: he guided me through parts of the garden, which he described as being like rooms in a house. In one section, wide lawns were flanked by beds of sage, sorrel and soapwort. In another, the limbs of ancient yews lofted over a footpath edged by evening primrose. A great Turkey oak presided over the whole scene. And everywhere was the presence of water – pooling in the deep shadows of the Chalice Well itself, trickling out of a lion's head, careering through wandering channels. Little vials of Chalice Well water were also for sale in the gift shop by the exit.

The Chalice Well was the third and final holy well on my Glastonbury pilgrimage. It had been a water source for the medieval abbey and by the nineteenth century had become the site of a Roman Catholic missionary college. One dubious school of thought had it down as the place where Joseph of Arimathea hid the vials that caught Christ's blood; this, in fairness, had been said of many places in Glastonbury at some point or other, but the Chalice Well had undoubtedly been the town's saviour in the past. In the drought of the early 1920s the Chalice Well was the only water source in Glastonbury that never dried up. Now it was a place without any specific creed – simply a garden in which to contemplate, in the company of the currents.

'Research shows that water is a carrier of messages,' Paul explained to me as we peered into the well.

The water produced at the Chalice Well was distinctive: charged with iron oxide, which gave it a bitter, almost bloody taste and a reddish hue. Paul said no one was quite sure where it came from, but he thought it might be the hills of south Wales, and that it had flowed under the bed of the Bristol Channel. Water from the spring had been symbolically mixed with water from the Sea of Galilee, and tipped into the rivers around Chernobyl. Paul mentioned that his son didn't like the taste of the water here.

I loved the peace of the Chalice Well gardens. So much of Glastonbury was about extroverted spirituality – pulsing drums, trance states, nakedness – but noisy rituals were not allowed here. Paul explained volunteers had to devote time to untying votive ribbons from trees and digging up goblets and magic crystals deposited by misguided pilgrims on their many quests. Even local

Anglicans had suggested turning the Chalice Well into an English Lourdes – but Paul insisted that this garden was a place for individual meditation and not mass hysteria. Such was the intention of the man who had organized the purchase of the gardens and created the Chalice Well Trust in 1959: Major Wellesley Tudor Pole. He had seen a healing potential in the water, writing:

> When water wells up from hidden springs and sources and is brought intimately into contact with air, such water always possesses healing and vitalizing qualities which vary in strength, mainly according to the rhythm of the mineral substances through which the water has passed on its pilgrimage from darkness into the light of day.[6]

Eventually Paul took me to a bench on a meadow overlooking the gardens. It was another beautiful day. The Tor rose above us. There was the happy chatter of morning visitors below us, the notes of a rising wind and falling water. Until then our conversation had centred mostly on water. Now I tried to steer it tactfully to something else – an object that held liquid, an item that, I understood, was kept by the Trustees of the Chalice Well.

Paul shifted in his seat. He explained that when you become a trustee, there's a general policy that you don't talk about it. He asked me not to write about it too much either, because it entailed certain dangers. In 2015 the Nanteos Cup had been stolen, an item described as a 'Welsh Holy Grail', but thanks to an episode of *Crimewatch* it had eventually been returned. And yes, Paul said, it was still there.

The twentieth century saw Dr Goodchild's bowl ghost in and out of view. In those first years after its discovery the Bristol group took it to Iona to reawaken various holy sites. (Paul explained that, although they were both in the business of reawakening, Wellesley Tudor Pole and George MacLeod did not see eye to eye.) Eventually, press attention cooled, and Wilberforce went quiet. By 1913 the work of the Clifton Oratory seemed to have run its course. The Tudor Pole family had long been enthusiastic champions of the garden city movement: the cup went with Kitty Tudor Pole and her parents to a brand-new cottage on Meadow Road, Letchworth Garden City – it was entrusted to its female keeper as the war began and remained there on and off for decades thereafter. This, to me, seemed the most curious chapter of the whole story – an ordinary suburban home in Hertfordshire that quietly housed what was once sincerely believed to be the Holy Grail. I wondered if the neighbours knew.

Although he was often apart from it, the bowl remained in Tudor Pole's thoughts: he had perceived it as an instrument that might stop the bloodshed of the First World War. In the 1920s he also received psychic messages of a hidden chapel somewhere beneath the Topkapı Palace in Istanbul – a subterranean chamber whose contents would reveal the cup's meaning to the world. He caught the Orient Express to Istanbul but hit a dead end. He went into business selling, among other things, paper to Holland and suits to Hungary. After the Second World War he felt Glastonbury might have a role to play in saving humanity from a nuclear apocalypse. Tudor Pole passed away in 1968, considering the unrealized destiny of the cup to be his life's great failure. He died convinced it was the cup of Jesus Christ. Among his grandchildren was the musician and presenter of the 1990s game show *The Crystal Maze*, Ed Tudor Pole. I watched it as a kid. It was a programme about quests, of a kind.

'Wellesley Tudor Pole was in three minds when he died,' said Paul. 'Should [the cup] go to The Hague for European Peace? Should it go to China, because he believed China would be the dominant power of the twenty-first century? Or should it come to Glastonbury, because he had secured this site?'

At certain periods during its residence at the Chalice Well, the bowl seemed to be widely available. Someone who declined to be named said it was regularly used as an aide for meditation as recently as the early 2000s. Paul explained that since Covid the cup was stored somewhere, 'quietly being'. He worried we were at an especially 'hairy' period in human history. There was the spectre of fracking, and the dire state of British rivers. We talked too about the possibility of nuclear war – the same threat that had troubled Tudor Pole. On 23 April – St George's Day, which Paul noted as being the birthday of both Shakespeare and Wellesley Tudor Pole – a new government alarm would be trialled on our phones, what the papers were calling an 'Armageddon alert': a rehearsal for a possible end time.

I asked Paul if he thought the cup was authentic when he held it. He nodded.

'But I couldn't tell you what it is,' Paul said. 'Some people get knocked out and think it's a truly cosmic item, and other people go "What's all the fuss about?" It's very small. More of a dish than a cup.'

Paul had somewhere else to be. He said his goodbyes and asked me again not to write too much about the bowl – he didn't want to encourage grail questers. But I was already too far along the path by then, and so, Paul, I offer you my apology here. I sat for a while in that meadow, overlooking the gardens of the Chalice Well in the valley below. A red admiral danced through the morning air. There was the eternal music of running water.

The Chalice Well was different from the other pilgrimage places I had visited. Unlike a cave, a mountain or an island, the spring was a life force: it could be born in a deluge and die in a drought, it could be reborn, renew and relocate, usher up millennia-old waters from darkness and dormancy, and dredge other things into daylight. That alone was miraculous enough, but pilgrims here sought other properties in its flow. Everyone peered into the dark well in the hollow. Mostly they saw their own reflection.

Just over the garden wall was the White Spring, where I had bathed at the start of my pilgrimage. Nearby, a healer was explaining his own interpretation of these two opposite springs to a small audience of pilgrims. Apparently the white, calciferous energy of the White Spring represented the masculine, in balance with the red, blood-like feminine energy of the Chalice Well. The bowl also represented the divine feminine. Yet so many of the characters in its story seemed to be men. The healer asked if anyone had any questions, but nobody did.

ON THE WAY HOME

I took a short detour on the drive home.

The house was not hard to find: five minutes from the turn-off on the A1. It stood in an old neighbourhood that retained some of the early symmetry of the garden city – a neat arrangement of right angles, circles and ovals – laid out before a tangled profusion of streets muddied the original vision over subsequent decades. Not far away was the UK's first roundabout, out of which straight roads radiated to form a six-pointed star. Meadow Road itself consisted of a row of whitewashed houses built in 1909, each with subtle differences that would have been more pronounced, had they not been separated by the spacious lawns that were part of the city's character. Rose Cottage had a large bay window, looking at a row of pines. A single dormer gave the cottage a calculated touch of rusticity.

I knocked on the door. A tall, elderly man with kind eyes answered the door and, before I could finish explaining why I was here, welcomed me into his house. He took me past a flight of stairs where a stairlift had been installed, into a tidy living room. There was a painting of a snowy scene over the fireplace. A jigsaw of the Sydney Harbour Bridge was placed under the television. Patio doors looked out over a garden: a water feature had been placed in the foreground to draw the eye, the current babbling down an upright rock. Somewhere in the house, a clock chimed the hour. Glastonbury and Letchworth Garden City were in different universes. But this living room felt like the right place for this journey to end.

Peter was a retired management consultant; he explained that he and his wife, Jenny, had moved to Rose Cottage from Bristol in 2019. She suffered from multiple sclerosis and – with Bristol being a rather hilly city – they needed somewhere new to live. Jenny was originally from these parts and had family nearby: they were looking for somewhere clinical and modern. The visit to an estate agent led them astray.

'The moment we walked through the front door we knew we were going to buy it,' Peter told me. 'It felt like a special place. People said it was meant to be, but I don't believe in those things. I'm a bit of a cynic like that!'

After checking Jenny's wheelchair could move from room to room, they made the purchase. Jenny had passed away at Christmas, a couple of months before my visit. She had had a bad fall and two major operations. It seemed like the wrong time to be barging into Rose Cottage asking questions about the previous residents. But Peter said he was interested – he had time on his hands now to look into the history of the property. He knew about the Tudor Pole family. He didn't know that the blue bowl had been moved here from the Clifton Oratory – or that the 'holy grail' had been resident here in this ordinary suburban home, on and off, until it finally moved to the care of the Chalice Well Trust. He hadn't ever had any grail-hunters inquiring about it (though he did have a Jehovah's Witness knock the other week). Peter said he was only sorry he couldn't tell me more about the house's history when it carried its original name: Tudor Cottage.

I said goodbye. Feeling the need to move on, but struggling to find focus for my thoughts, I found myself driving aimlessly around Letchworth – along oak-shaded boulevards, lapping the roundabouts, doing three-point turns in cul-de-sacs. The garden city movement at its inception was a bold endeavour: a mission to balance industry and nature, to create healthy, tree-lined cityscapes for healthy residents. It was a bold experiment in a future way of living, though, oddly, many of the houses of these streets looked to the past in their architecture. There were gabled roofs and mullioned windows. The rough render of the Arts and Crafts movement.

And it seemed the residents (or perhaps the developers) could not resist giving names to their properties that hinted at imagined histories – or entirely invented mythologies – before the city's real origins, which in reality lay no earlier than the very first years of the last century. One was called St Brighid's. Another was called Avalon.

9

A Railway

A Pilgrimage Revival

Miniature Railway | England's Nazareth |
At the Anglican Shrine | A Station of the Cross |
The Holy Mile

Railway – Walsingham Station, aka St Seraphim's Chapel

MINIATURE RAILWAY

The Wells and Walsingham Light Railway was (a sign by the platform announced) the 'world's smallest public railway'.

The gauge was 10¼ inches, meaning the two iron rails were set apart little more than the width of an outstretched hand. A tiny steam engine pulled carriages wide enough to accommodate a single adult bum. You had to put your knees in your mouth and physically make yourself smaller to get inside the carriages. Old men were playing conductors and engine drivers – in their way they had become smaller too, little boys again. This love of small trains seemed to be particularly an English affliction, but I could understand it. Something about miniaturizing things made them purer, more perfect, like a Fabergé egg.

Of course, the trains here weren't always this small. For a century from 1857 full-size standard-gauge services chuffed along this same track bed. Then Dr Beeching wielded an axe, and only in 1982 did enthusiasts take over a four-mile section of the old line, installing a miniature recreation of what had been there before. The first trains were pulled by a little home-made green engine with a red nameplate, emblazoned *PILGRIM*.

I boarded the train at Wells-next-the-Sea, and soon we were puttering through the Norfolk landscape, the engine casting up its blossom of steam, the cuttings speckled with red campion and forget-me-nots. We crested an old embankment over golden rapeseed fields, passed under bridges from the old Victorian line, fitting the tiny train like a comically oversized pullover. Here and there were tiny stations where no one disembarked: little Adlestrops lost amid the weeds. The engine tooted grandly, announcing its intersection with lanes that no cars ever seemed to cross. It moved slowly enough for a little boy on board to pick fistfuls of grass from the lineside.

Midway through the journey I leaned into the next carriage to speak to Nigel Lavender, the train guard. He had started on the railway in February (he also worked part-time as an archery instructor). It was a fun job, he said. Most passengers on the Wells and Walsingham Light Railway were on a day out, followed by an ice cream and sandcastles on the beach. But for a tiny minority this journey was a sacred one: in its own small way, the miniature train continued a tradition of railway pilgrimages to Walsingham that had begun a century ago. I asked Nigel what he thought about Walsingham. He paused.

'A lot of passengers don't really know what Walsingham entails,' he shouted over the clatter of the rails. 'It is a bit of a ... niche interest.'

Eventually the train screeched to a standstill at Walsingham or – to give it its correct name – the village of Little Walsingham (population 800), where most passengers remained on board to make the return journey to Wells. Only a handful disembarked the miniature railway here. Had any of them been first-time visitors, they might have initially supposed this was an ordinary Norfolk village like any other. It had pretty flint houses with lace curtains, housing estates with wheelie bins out for collection. Rural buses ran intermittently past the primary school (rated 'Good' by Ofsted). For motorists, Walsingham is announced most noticeably by signs advertising the farm shop (which sells excellent pastries and sausage rolls). Walsingham made the news in 2023 after a 13-year-old boy was arrested for setting fire to the village hall.

'It's not something you'd imagine could happen,' one shocked villager told the *Eastern Daily Press*.

On the contrary, I could imagine few scandals more typical of rural England than the village hall getting torched by a bored teenager. It was much harder to imagine that it was in Walsingham – with its war memorial, its wisteria-strung cottages, its pub, which CAMRA praised for its 'proper pies' – that the Virgin Mary appeared in 1061 to bring a message to England. A ten-minute walk from the miniature railway station a sign noted the place the Virgin had marked as sacred, set on a green lawn near a little river. No one was paying it much attention the day I visited. After all, it was the weekend of the coronation: there was a duck race going on nearby, and it cost £1 to enter.

ENGLAND'S NAZARETH

In the story of Walsingham two chapters loomed largest – a first in the heyday of medieval pilgrimage, and a second that coincided with the heyday of the railway.

In the last days of Anglo-Saxon England, Walsingham was home to a noblewoman named Richeldis de Faverches. In 1061 she is said to have been visited by the Virgin Mary, who led her in spirit to Nazareth, showing her the house where the angel Gabriel had brought the news that she was to bear a son. The Virgin instructed Richeldis to build a replica of that holy house in Walsingham. Richeldis did as she was told, and soon a monastery grew around it. As the Crusades went on, it was sometimes impossible to make a journey from England to the Holy Land. Pilgrims flocked instead to the village known as 'England's Nazareth'.

Walsingham's rise to fame took place at a time when a network of pilgrimage routes criss-crossed England, from visits to local shrines (analogous to a commute) to long-distance thoroughfares to see famous saints' relics in mighty cathedrals. Routes converged and interlinked – wells and lesser abbeys became stopping points for pilgrims connecting onward to major hubs. Walsingham emerged as one of the greatest terminuses of Christian pilgrimage – ranking alongside Rome, Santiago and Jerusalem, rivalling Canterbury. Around its holy house grew a grid of streets, busy with wayfarers, the pious, the sick, the destitute (and probably conmen too). For three centuries from the reign of Henry III almost every English king and queen made a pilgrimage to Walsingham, travelling across East Anglian fields in their royal trains. It was the duty of every Englishman to visit once in his life, and the Milky Way was even known as the 'Walsingham Way', for its stellar path supposedly pointed across the night sky to the Norfolk shrine. Walsingham was a place at the centre of things – until it welcomed its last royal pilgrim, the 18-year-old Henry VIII, in 1510.

Three decades later Walsingham had embarked on a new journey into relative obscurity – the holy house wrecked, its buildings suffering the same fate as those at Glastonbury and elsewhere. Today a single swooping arch remains as a vestige of a thirteenth-century priory. Bluebells crowd around its base, and medieval staircases drop off into thin air. It is a reminder of the years after the Reformation, when this little village settled back into its slumber in the Norfolk farmland.

Later, it was awoken by the toot of a steam train. The Wells and Fakenham Railway had its genesis at the time of the 'railway mania', when competing companies scrambled to lay iron rails across the landscape. Walsingham station opened in 1857: passing trains carried shellfish from the North Sea and milk from local farms. Walsingham itself exported snowdrops in season, and cabbages and sprouts to Covent Garden. This was a very rural branch line, so cows sometimes wandered into the path of oncoming trains. When fog blew in from the North Sea, signalling was done by firing pistols. One evening in May 1879 a train from Norwich overran the platform and crashed into the station at Wells-next-the-Sea, killing a man who happened to be in the station toilets at the time. Otherwise the railway brought only good news. *The Official Illustrated Guide to the Great Eastern Railway* of 1865 recommended passengers to stop in Walsingham to admire 'the noble and stupendous pile' of the old priory. Now the village was plugged into a new kind of network.

In 1921 villagers would have likely seen the Reverend Alfred Hope Patten alight onto the platform of Walsingham station. He was the new vicar, and he had never learned to drive a motor car, instead relying on the intermittent train services (he also liked to ride a ladies' bike). Hope Patten was a complex character: sometimes aloof, other times playful, with a fondness for parlour games and medieval history – but a sensitivity about his dyslexia. In that decade of upheavals and awakenings he came to a Norfolk parish with a mission in mind: to restore Walsingham as a place of pilgrimage. He started out using incense in the church, set up a brand-new image of the Virgin and ultimately built a twentieth-century holy house for her to inhabit. These unsanctioned antics drew the ire of the bishop of Norwich, who wrote stern letters instructing him to change course. But the maverick Hope Patten was onto something. People visited Walsingham again, and new pilgrim lodgings were built. Now the railway was the means of pilgrimage: special trains ran from London Liverpool Street and sometimes King's Cross. The platform at Walsingham station was lengthened to accommodate them.

In the first centuries after the Reformation the Church of England had taught pilgrimage as allegory: a personal, interior journey towards God. Hope Patten gave this journey a physical destination, a place that could be found in the timetables of the London and North Eastern Railway. England's Nazareth had been restored. In this way Walsingham stood at a curious junction of histories: a holy place which in one way pre-dated the Norman conquest but – in another – was about as old as transatlantic flights, the theory of relativity and the BBC.

AT THE ANGLICAN SHRINE

'Pilgrimage is about stepping out of your routine into another space,' said Father Kevin Smith. 'It gives you an opportunity to reflect and to get things back in order in life.'

Father Kevin was the priest administrator of the Anglican Shrine at Walsingham, and as such was Hope Patten's successor. I had met him a year before, working on a story for the *Financial Times* marking the centenary of the restoration. He had a bald head, a big grin and a firm handshake. He welcomed me into his quarters in the shrine complex, where we sat on comfy armchairs beside a stone fireplace and drank coffee. Nearby was a picture of Father Kevin meeting Pope Francis. A bottle of Jura single malt sat on a table in the corner. It was a beautiful day outside.

Father Kevin had grown up beneath the Howardian Hills of north Yorkshire. He had first come down to Walsingham at the age of about 14 for the National Pilgrimage – the biggest celebration of the year, when congregations from across the country came to see Hope Patten's modern image of Our Lady paraded through the streets. He remembers the crowds, the devotion and, most of all, the ornate Malta lanterns.

'I'd never seen anything like it before,' he remembered. 'I was absolutely hooked. Coming here was just a whole new world.'

I too was visiting Walsingham during peak pilgrimage season: the National Pilgrimage was a week away, and a steady stream of visitors would be making their way to the village over the summer (mostly in cars, though some on coaches organized by parishes). A focus of Anglican pilgrimage was the shrine church outside the window – a red brick structure dating to 1938, within which Hope Patten's Holy House was cocooned like a Russian doll. The little structure was about the size of a garage, its walls black after a century of burning candles and accompanying prayers. These days Anglican pilgrims often came to Walsingham on a weekend itinerary – staying in simple lodgings, sharing meals, attending Mass and perhaps performing the Stations of the Cross around the immaculately kept shrine gardens. Father Kevin said pilgrimage was about fellowship: there was humour, banter too. There was free time so some people might go to the pub or maybe ride the miniature railway.

'People leave in tears because they've been so moved by the experience,' he said. 'Some want to stay forever. But you have to go back – to bear witness to what you've learned here, and to what you've experienced.'

Some places of pilgrimage might be understood in the context of their extraordinary geography: Glastonbury has its Tor, Iona stands at the end of the earth. Other destinations like Canterbury, Durham and St Albans were important cities before (and after) they drew great numbers of Christian pilgrims. Walsingham is unique in Britain in being a tiny village shouldering the weight of its holy past. It is set in a shallow valley amid the airfields and arable farmland of north Norfolk (the homeland of Alan Partridge). There are no legends of King Arthur here: no Celtic mysteries to be decoded. I doubt anyone goes to Walsingham to feel energy currents or be a shaman. It was a place in some senses remarkable for its unremarkableness. But similarly, according to Father Kevin, Nazareth was also a workaday town: he had been there twice on pilgrimages himself. There, in the so-called Arab capital of Israel, an icon of Walsingham was given pride of place in the basilica.

The more time you spent in Walsingham, the more you saw it had another, more subtle quality of holiness – one that might be understood by daydreaming Anglophiles. It looked like the setting for Hovis adverts, Enid Blyton books, Miss Marple mysteries. Its music was the clink of china in a tearoom, the coo of a morning wood pigeon, the clunk of a croquet mallet and the whistle of a steam train on a bank holiday. Its sacraments were scones, Sunday roasts, cask ale. Its via dolorosas were country lanes, potholed and garlanded with cow parsley. It was famous for its Holy House. It also felt homely.

'Most of our pilgrims come from urban centres,' said Father Kevin. 'To come into this beautiful part of the world is a wonderful thing for people who don't have that space, that beauty to enjoy. It speaks clearly to people about the goodness of God, and the gift of life.'

Of course, as Nigel had told me on the miniature train, Walsingham was a bit of a niche interest. Low-church elements of the Church of England were still wary of its high-church, Anglo-Catholic, 'bells and smells' tendencies brought here by Hope Patten – what they saw as an infiltration by Rome. Militant Protestant groups (particularly from Northern Ireland) came to protest during the National Pilgrimage, holding aloft placards that read 'No Popery' and 'Thou shalt not make unto thee any graven image (Exodus 20.4–6)' and, best of all, the deranged 'BEHOLD THE WALTZING HAM SHOW WITH ITS WOBBLING HIGH DOLL. MIMIC PRAISE TO JESUS. SATAN'S FARCE.' Not long ago there used to be about 30 protesters who annually crossed the Irish Sea: there were moments when the Norfolk Constabulary had to separate them from the procession. At last count, Father Kevin said there were three or four troublemakers. He suspected their visits would eventually fizzle out. It would be a relief.

But there was also a bigger worry. When Father Kevin first visited as a boy, around ten thousand pilgrims came for the National Pilgrimage – today the numbers were down to about two thousand. Almost all the pilgrims I saw during my two visits were elderly. Covid-19 had dealt Walsingham a hammer blow – the buses that had brought pilgrims had dwindled in favour of cars (there was a lower risk of transmitting the virus in a car, but a smaller feeling of solidarity too). Since the pandemic, accommodation at the Anglican Shrine has been offered to tourists on Booking.com to help cover costs: 'wasn't told we had to be silent when we booked,' wrote one online reviewer (all the other customers were very happy).

Walsingham may indeed be a place of miracles – but was not immune from the ongoing decline in numbers happening across the Church of England. Even before the pandemic, church attendance nationwide had fallen by as much as a fifth in the decade to 2019. The 2021 census was a landmark, showing that for the first time less than half the population of England and Wales identified as Christian. It seemed that, in the long term, Walsingham's story risked being forgotten, as it had in the wake of the Reformation.

Across the road from the Anglican Shrine were the grounds where the medieval priory had stood. It being the weekend of the coronation, the £6 entry fee was waived – picnicking families had laid rugs and hampers on the grass beneath the surviving Gothic arch. Red, white and blue balloons were tied to a yew tree, and children cheered on the plastic ducks that bobbed along the River Stiffkey. Someone had printed out pictures of Charles and Camilla on respective sheets of A4 paper and stuck them in a window nearby. Hope Patten had been a little bit out in the positioning of his new holy house. Three years after Hope Patten's death (he collapsed during a service at the shrine in 1958), excavations unearthed Richeldis's original site about 80 metres away from the current shrine – now identified by a little sign propped on the lawn. I sat down by the sign, watching day trippers and pilgrims amble past. Few were distracted by this plot of Norfolk where the Saxon noblewoman had once built her holy house – to a patch of turf whose holiness, like Lourdes and Fatima, had supposedly been affirmed by the Mother of God.

Since its revival, Walsingham had never quite seen the millions of miracle-hungry pilgrims that flocked to Lourdes and Fatima. That could be explained by the legacy and hangover of the Reformation, by the turn and tangle of English history. But I wondered too if it was to do with an Anglo-Saxon temperament: a conservatism and coolness, a reluctance to see miracles in the countryside (especially in twentieth-century Norfolk). In any case, this was beside the point. In the twenty-first century Walsingham's story was no longer an Anglo-Saxon one.

A STATION OF THE CROSS

The last (full-size) train from Walsingham to Wells ran late in the evening of 5 October 1964, a year Britain lost more than a thousand miles of railway. It was a British Rail Eastern Region railcar, of the bone-shaking kind that worked rural lines, where it didn't matter so much if passengers grumbled.

A black-and-white photograph shows a few suited men on the platform, grimly observing that final departure. Goods trains rumbled on for a little while longer, but their day of reckoning came soon. Eventually the grass grew tall on the old track bed. The heavy wooden furniture in the station waiting room went unpolished. In later years the signal box was torn down, and a Wolseley was abandoned on the line – a sign, perhaps, that the era of the motor car had dawned.

Walsingham station suffered the fate of many others in the years after the Beeching axe until 1967, when some new tenants took out a lease from the local council. Soon passers-by noticed unusual embellishments to the old station: a little onion dome installed over the porch and, above it, a cross with the three horizontal crossbeams of the Russian Orthodox Church. Today the Wells and Walsingham Light Railway stops a three-minute walk short of the original Walsingham station, which is now the Orthodox pilgrim chapel of St Seraphim's. Nonetheless, all miniature railway passengers are welcome inside the old station. It is a curious building, set at a junction of Walsingham's railway and pilgrimage history.

'Most of the station is still here,' said Sylvia Batchelor. 'Creating the chapel means we've managed to keep the station too.'

Sylvia was the custodian of the chapel. She showed me around, speaking seriously and studiously about its past. The Orthodox Church had a tiny presence in Walsingham from the start of Hope Patten's revival, and that continued throughout the Second World War, when Eastern Europeans interned in nearby camps came to visit. Later, an Orthodox brotherhood came here with just £25 in the bank and set up a chapel in the only building they could afford to rent, which was the recently abandoned station.

It was at St Seraphim's that Sylvia was received into the Russian Orthodox faith in 1978. She had first encountered the Orthodox Church while a student in London, and something had resonated. There was the use of candles to remember the dead (Sylvia explained her mother died suddenly when she was young). She also felt drawn to the icons – the gilded paintings of saints with their beautiful, baleful eyes. Icons, Sylvia said, were known to speak to people. In the Orthodox world, icons could themselves be the focus of pilgrimages.

The chapel's previous occupants – Father David and Leon Liddament – had passed away in 1993 and 2010 respectively, but together they had made St Seraphim's a unique British hub for icon-painting. St Seraphim's is still the UK's only icon museum: depictions of saints are on display along the old platform. These art works were not worshipped as physical objects but rather served as portals, or 'a window or door between two distinct realities', as a sign explained. Inside the old station the two painters mixed powder pigments with egg yolk for their paint: applying it to gilded MDF and plywood. The method was an eastern one, but their subject matter was often the early saints of the British Isles. One icon showed about a hundred saints dotted about a stylized map of Great Britain – Aidan and Cuthbert stood on an oversized Lindisfarne, a smattering of saints perched along the Hebrides. St Columba sailed in his sensibly sized coracle, and Christ hovered somewhere above Cape Wrath. Sylvia said the early British saints were important to her.

'I'm hoping we can find our way back to our roots really,' she said, quietly.

The Orthodox Church in Walsingham broke with Moscow some years ago (it had become more of a branch of the Russian Foreign Office, according to the parish priest) and is now under the Ecumenical Patriarchate of Constantinople. Ukrainians, Romanians, Poles and Cypriots still come to Walsingham for services (along with a few former Anglicans who left the CoE disgruntled at the ordination of women). Sylvia showed me around the station grounds where railway workers once kept allotments: it is now a community garden, with a little hut used for gatherings and a resident goose called Wanda. We ended our tour in the chapel itself, where the Great Eastern Railway station fireplace was still intact. There was a residual smell of incense.

In this room – over the course of a century from 1857 – people had idled away their time in stillness and contemplation, sitting quietly on summer afternoons and snowy Christmases. Weeks passed, punctuated by services. A lifetime of arrivals and departures had been observed by the stewards of this building. Now it was an Orthodox chapel rather than an English country station, but I suspected some quality of its silence had endured. The iconostasis marked the symbolic dividing line between heaven and earth – 'earth' being the old waiting room, 'heaven' being the old ticket office where tickets for onward journeys were once granted. Curious pilgrims of all kinds visited here, Sylvia said, and she did not know what seeds had been sown in their minds when they left. In any case, they saw how Richeldis's vision had brought strands of Christianity from around the world to converge in this part of north Norfolk. She remembered one visitor in particular: a man who had worked at Liverpool Street station when pilgrim trains were running.

'He said that one whole train – all the carriages and the guards vans – was given over to the sick, and there were children in iron lungs. As a young man he asked to be taken off that route. He found it too much.'

Beyond the chapel's iconostasis was the sanctuary, most of which was out of view, though above it a patch of ceiling could be seen, painted dark blue to stand for the night sky. Sylvia said she planned to get someone in one day, to paint it with stars. At the time of writing, I learned she herself departed the world in September 2023.

THE HOLY MILE

A number of country lanes converged on Walsingham: hedgerow-flanked roads that muddled about the countryside, making sharp turns at farm walls, scaling small hills, making their accommodations to the modest demands of the East Anglian contours. Just outside the village were two fords where the tarmac slunk under the quacking ducks and tadpoles of the River Stiffkey, climbing out soggily the other side.

The Pilgrims' Way was different: it did not climb or descend; it begrudged only the most incremental curves. Instead, it was the other way around: the landscape seemed to accommodate the Pilgrims' Way – facilitating its passage through cuttings, buttressing its route with embankments, supporting its journey with iron bridges. You knew instinctively from its smooth, stately procession that this route, known by some as the 'Holy Mile', was no road, nor (as its thin strip of tarmac might suggest) had it even begun life as a footpath or cycle path. This had been a railway line.

The track bed of the Pilgrims' Way began at St Seraphim's – where the old Wells and Fakenham Railway had departed Walsingham station – and swept south to Fakenham. It passed the old goods shed (a sign warned you to keep out). It passed the site of the old sidings (now a car park, where bus drivers twiddle their thumbs waiting beside coach charters). Its onward route would be the natural continuation for the miniature train line from Wells, but those little rails were never extended south – perhaps because this part of the old line had been charged with a deeper meaning in the decades after the Beeching axe. Although pilgrims came to Walsingham in cars and buses, many left the village to ritually walk along the old railway line. In doing so, they briefly summoned both the ghostly masses who trod across England in the years before the Reformation and also the pilgrim trains of the twentieth century.

It was a bright afternoon as I walked the Pilgrims' Way south from St Seraphim's. Soon the village felt far away. A woodpecker rattled away in a nearby copse. Cows mooed over the walls of Abbey Farm, and from across the fields a gust of wind carried a single audible 'cuckoo'. This was one of many such abandoned railway lines that criss-crossed East Anglia: within a few decades there would be no one alive who remembered travelling it in a train. It had been a relatively modern artery in the body of Britain – circulating blood vessels of trade and travel – but in its way it felt as timeless as a Roman road. At its southern point, the Pilgrims' Way ended beside the Catholic national shrine and basilica of Our Lady of Walsingham, where the old railway disappeared into impenetrable thickets.

The Anglicans and the Orthodox Church had a presence in Walsingham, but the Roman Catholics (the first to revive Walsingham pilgrimages in 1897) were a mile away in the village of Houghton St Giles. Liverpool Street trains had halted here too – on some pilgrimages children dismounted onto stacked orange boxes. After Beeching an idea of sanctity had attached itself to the old, abandoned track bed, for it connected the modern Roman Catholic basilica to the medieval ruins of the priory. Catholic pilgrims walked it in procession carrying rosaries and crosses. Some walked their Holy Mile barefoot. A villager in Walsingham had told me about a recent encounter she had had.

'I see you are doing it the hard way!' a villager had cheerily observed. The barefooted pilgrim pointed to the sky. 'I'm doing it God's way.'

As I neared the end of my Holy Mile, I heard new sounds travelling along the line. The chime of bells: the beat of Indian drums. Soon the music of Sri Lanka and Tamil Nadu were breezing down cuttings dug by the navvies of the old Victorian railway. Closer still, smells of cardamom and tamarind wafted up the embankments. A chatter rose among the birdsong.

The weekend of the coronation also marked another festivity: the Tamil Pilgrimage. It was perhaps the biggest event of the pilgrimage year in Walsingham, when thousands of members of the Tamil community came, mostly from London and the Midlands, to Houghton St Giles. Several thousand were milling about the basilica, queueing to see the Catholic image of Our Lady. Parasols were held above her.

In 2023 the idea of 'pilgrimage' in England could summon up images of walkers with hazel staffs – revivalists striding through the landscapes in tribute to the wayfarers of old. But the Tamil Pilgrimage felt like a truer continuation of all those Walsingham pilgrimages that had gone before. Families in Sunday best – men in suit jackets and women in sarees – shuffled along the old track bed. A farmer's field was full of parked BMWs, Audis and people carriers. Bored teenagers (dragged along by their parents) loitered behind, or snuck off to test out the car sound systems (someone was playing 'Candy Shop' by 50 Cent). Curious Hindus apparently sometimes came along for the ride. Here there was family, fellowship – and picnics too. On the orders of his parents, a teenager from Harrow gave me a tupperware box full of chicken curry. A man from Jaffna handed me a slab of Sri Lankan butter cake.

Walsingham's Anglo-Saxon pilgrims may have been declining – but others had come in their place. In this village at the heart of UKIP-voting Norfolk, a great diversity of people gathered. Filipinos and Latin Americans arrived in buses at the Catholic shrine. Irish travellers drew up in their caravans. The railway was gone, but Walsingham was now plugged into another network – a galaxy of Marian shrines around the world.

Many at the Tamil pilgrimage would have also been at Velankanni, a little town in Tamil Nadu where the Virgin had also appeared. Among her miracles was the rescue of seventeenth-century Portuguese sailors caught in a monsoon surge. She had also appeared to a buttermilk seller who rested beneath a banyan tree. Set by the Bay of Bengal, the town was known as the Lourdes of the East: immense crowds gathered there.

Shajil Paul and Siji Lonappam had been among them: following in the footsteps of their parents and their grandparents in making pilgrimages to Velankanni. The couple were not from Tamil Nadu but from Kochi in Kerala, a 15-hour train ride away. During peak pilgrimage season Indian Railways organized special pilgrimage trains from Kerala (with festival fares). The pilgrims moved as one on board the broad-gauge train, eating, chatting, dozing to the lullaby of the rails – and then disembarking to form pedestrian trains: long lines snaking to the basilica. Shajil and Siji's pilgrimages ended abruptly in 2010, when they moved to Spalding, Lincolnshire. Here Shajil worked as an engineer for a company making small engines (including jet skis). Siji was a nurse in a rehab hospital.

At first they missed home, but family friends mentioned another place a little bit like Velankanni but quieter, about an hour and a half's drive across the fenlands. Ever since, they had come to this Norfolk village two or three times a year. I fell into conversation with them later that afternoon back in the gardens of the Anglican Shrine, where they were taking selfies with their two teenage sons. They had originally intended to go Mass at the Catholic shrine, but hadn't realized it was the day of the Tamil Pilgrimage. Wanting peace and quiet to reflect, they went to the Anglican site instead. There wasn't a big difference, they said: as children in Kerala they had mixed with their Muslim and Hindu neighbours, and everyone went to each other's festivals.

'Velankanni is very crowded,' said Shajil. 'It's more peaceful here. There you do not reach this same spiritual level.'

Siji explained that their Walsingham pilgrimages had aided them through their first decade in the UK. They had prayed to Our Lady that they might buy a house – those prayers were heard. They had prayed too that their young son might get into a Lincolnshire grammar school – he got one of the highest scores in the entire county.

'Possibly he would have passed it otherwise,' said Siji. 'But we need that support from God.'

Today they were praying for good GCSE results for their older son, writing intentions on a piece of paper that was carefully folded away. Just as previous generations had gone to Velankanni, so they hoped that this next generation of their family would pattern their lives with journeys to this Norfolk village where an Anglo-Saxon noblewoman had built her holy house long ago.

I had never been to Velankanni. And so – after I said goodbye to Shajil and Siji – I sat on a little bench in the Anglican Shrine gardens and googled it. The results showed Our Lady of Velankanni, clad in a golden sari. There was the basilica of Our Lady of Good Health – a whitewashed structure strung with neon lights. But what caught my eye was Velankanni station, adorned with Gothic arches and crowned by two blunt spires so that, to a first-time pilgrim, it might easily be mistaken for a church.

10

A Pub

A Secular Pilgrimage

The Walk to a Pub | A Continuing Path | Coming In from the Cold

Pub – The Old Forge

THE WALK TO A PUB

Seb was an outdoorsman from Victoria.

He had traversed the Du Cane range of Tasmania and climbed the snows of Kosciuszko in New South Wales. In his mid-twenties he moved to London for a job, and was given a desk on the other side of the water cooler to my own. On free weekends I showed him the British outdoors: Snowdonia, Scotland, the South Downs. In mid-Wales he insisted he had the bush skills to make a campfire anywhere in the world, and laboured in vain over a sorry heap of sodden logs. He liked the OS maps, the drystone walls. But what he liked most about our British walks were the pubs: those inns we descended on after a slog through the hills, with their roaring fires, Yorkshire puddings – and golden pints whose first sip felt like a consecration. The best pubs, said Seb, were the ancient, tumbledown ones that allowed dogs. There were pubs in Australia, but they weren't quite the same. Indeed, it was possible there was nothing quite like British pubs anywhere in the world. In these hostelries, the effort of the journey was redeemed.

After a few years in the UK, Seb decided he would head back down under to start a family. To mark his departure we went for one last walk in the hills – this time, to the pub to end all pubs. The Old Forge was, according to the *Guinness Book of Records*, the most remote pub in mainland Britain. It was a semi-mythical establishment, set on the Knoydart peninsula – a wild corner of the West Highlands sometimes known as 'The Rough Bounds' and more poetically as 'Britain's Last Wilderness'. Sharp mountains and deep-gouged glens severed Knoydart's road system from the rest of the entire British network. To the north of the peninsula was Loch Hourn (poetically translated as the loch of 'hell'), while to its south was Loch Nevis (the loch of 'heaven'). The country that lay between was a test for mortals. There were only two options to get to the pub: either catch a tiny boat from the port of Mallaig or else set out on a two- to three-day walk through the Highland wilderness.

To go hiking in the densely inhabited United Kingdom you generally had to contrive your route – to pick one thread from the dense web of footpaths, to decide on your own arbitrary starting point and finishing line. This for us often meant plodding a path to a pub which could otherwise be reached by car or rural bus in a fraction of the time. But the Old Forge was different. It stood in the village of Inverie, which was more or less where the land ran out. The path leading there from Glenfinnan was a path of necessity: the only means of access on terra firma. In setting out on the 27-mile hike to Knoydart (what the locals called 'The Walk In') you were suddenly committed to traversing rainy passes, fording ice-cold rivers, scrambling over rugged terrain. You were flung into an age before cars, buses, trains. Mobile phone reception too was elusive: there was no one to help you if you so much as sprained an ankle. The finishing line was the way out.

It was ostensibly a feat of endurance, but the path also had a lesson. Over a few days you banished yourself from society and lived off your own wit and supplies. Its empty tracts had some of the solitude that Aidan and Cuthbert might have sought. At the end you arrived in Inverie, a village whose beating heart was its pub. Here you returned from exile, came back into society and felt its warm embrace all the more keenly. You felt gratitude. Later I wrote an article about 'The Walk In' for *Outside* magazine, and the editor settled on a title: 'A Pilgrimage to the Pub at the End of the World'.

Seb and I set out for Inverie in February 2018, on the eve of the great snowstorm that became known as the Beast from the East. We caught the sleeper from Euston to Fort William, our ice axes clanking as the train rolled through the night. Disembarking, we set out under the Victorian arches of the Glenfinnan Viaduct, where the railway ended and the footpaths began. The viaduct was itself a place of pilgrimage: this was the bridge that carried the Hogwarts Express in the Harry Potter movies. Fans in Gryffindor scarves parked up for a selfie. The backdrop to all their pictures were the mountains of Lochaber – their slopes of heather and bracken rising to compacted neve. It was into this Narnia that we were headed.

We fixed crampons, tracked the great ridge from Sgùrr nan Coireachan to Sgùrr Thuilm, Arctic-like under its lingering crust of snow. There was a heaviness in the clouds that foretold the coming storm, but also a silence and stillness. To the east, Munros extended out to the Great Glen, white peaks becoming blue in the distance. To the west you could see Hebridean islands known to Columba. At the top, Seb Facetimed his family in Melbourne, told them he loved them. We pushed onwards to the pub.

To this day – when suffering from boredom or waiting in queues – I close my eyes and try to imagine myself pacing 'The Walk In' to Inverie in real time. Leaving Glenfinnan, I descend from the saddle of a pass into the pine forests of Glen Dessary, in whose glades there is the thud of deer hoof on pine needles and a sense you are being watched. I imagine a numbness around my ankles as I ford the frigid River Pean, the feeling returning as I later tread under Sgùrr na Cìche, a lone pyramidal peak that guards the entrance to the Rough Bounds. Sometimes I idle in the bothies – those simple shelters found across the Scottish Highlands, three of which line the route into Knoydart. Bothies are little huts that are free to use without heating, electricity or (often) a watertight roof and within which you can find candles, half-used gas canisters, a few bits of firewood and rodents. They are often old crofters' huts abandoned during the Highland Clearances – relics from a time before this part of Scotland was emptied of its people in enforced eighteenth-century evictions. They carry a taunting echo of the society from which hikers exit on 'The Walk In' – and into which they hope to return.

My favourite bothy of them all was Sourlies – a lonely hut on a seaweed-strewn sea loch where hikers rest the final night before reaching Inverie. There were seashells pressed into the walls. The only sound was my bubbling stove.

Over those days doing 'The Walk In' the pub loomed ever larger in my thoughts – the prospect of it became a balm against blisters, a spur through exhausted miles. For years too the fame of the Old Forge travelled across Scotland and the world – folk musicians often carried their instruments across the mountains. Upon arrival, bows were rosined and strings tuned: the music played until dawn. Patrons climbed on the tables to strip the willow. It seemed like the ultimate place to come in from the cold, an enclave of hospitality in inhospitable territory. Though we did not know it, by the time Seb and I set out on our own walk to the pub in the winter of 2018, the Old Forge was also on its own difficult path.

When we finally arrived that winter, the doors were locked shut. The lights were out. Having a can of Stella sitting on a bench was not the same. It seemed this pilgrimage had lost its shrine.

A CONTINUING PATH

The English Reformation was followed centuries later by revivals such as at Glastonbury and Walsingham. But in another sense, the pilgrimages never stopped being made.

Between the seventeenth century and the early nineteenth, some 48 spas were founded across the UK: like the holy wells that preceded them, they centred on the healing possibilities of water to restore body, mind and maybe soul. The towns that grew around them were centres of intrigue and entertainment to which people travelled from afar. Around the same time, affluent upper-class pilgrims set out on the 'Grand Tour' – a journey to Florence, Venice, Rome and other places undertaken for its edification and cultural enrichment. These journeys often centred on churches. They were also a rite of passage. By the time the Baptist missionary Thomas Cook was offering tours in the late Victorian era, such a trip, to Italy and beyond, was not only the preserve of the elite. An era of mass tourism dawned: the distinction between holidays and holy days blurred. Even now, it can be hard to disentangle spiritual travel from travel to raise the spirits.

Today, 'meaningful' journeys often imply the original act of walking. 'Pilgrimage' is a word sometimes used by those following the route of the Kinder Scout mass trespass of 1932, retracing the steps of the few hundred working-class Mancunians who defied landowners by striking out into the Dark Peak of Derbyshire. They tussled with gamekeepers, and six martyred themselves by getting arrested. Some were sent to prison. Their actions helped lead to the creation of the National Parks and enshrined a right to roam. The boom in long-distance paths ensued. Among the first was the Lyke Wake Walk: a 42-mile, 24-hour challenge hike across the most windswept parts of the North York Moors National Park. First conceived in 1955, it was not explicitly a pilgrimage route, yet it stirred associations with mortality, taking its name from coffin bearers who carried the dead over the moorlands. The Lyke Wake Club (who administered its records) had its own body of folklore dwelling on the afterlife, drawing on the prehistoric burial mounds that lined the route. Here was a modern path with meaning.

The Pennine Way became the first of Britain's official 'National Trails' in 1965. Such routes often overlapped with pre-existing pilgrimage routes – the North Downs Way is in large part concurrent with the Pilgrims' Way route between the cathedrals of Winchester and Canterbury, while the Ridgeway became its own National Trail in 1972. These are secular paths primarily for leisure, but the people that walk them have similarities with pilgrims from the Middle Ages. Notably there is a dress code – less often a cloak, a wide-brimmed hat and a hazel staff, more often a North Face jacket, a merino beanie and carbon fibre walking poles – all signals you are a wayfarer. Among long-distance walkers there is often a tendency to accrue, collect and 'tick off' routes as pilgrims did and still do – conquests made explicit by Facebook posts, Strava medals, made material by patches sewn onto bags. Even now, people invest meaning in walks, cycles and runs in the form of charity challenges: fundraising for organizations that might have helped friends or relatives in need. Such challenges are still undertaken 'in memory' of a loved one, much as pilgrims made journeys to pray for the departed. In all these ways, the symbology and language of traditional pilgrimage have percolated or found parallels in secular journeys of meaning.

For me, an idea of 'pilgrimage' affixed itself to that most remote Highland pub, which seemed to stand for the sacred institution of the 'pub' more generally. Treading those lonely glens en route to Inverie, I dreamed – as pilgrims did – of a paradise at the end of the road. That winter it was not to be.

COMING IN FROM THE COLD

Inverie is a huddle of whitewashed houses, poised between the stony shore of a sea loch and forests that cling to grey mountains. It has a population of about 100, a tea room, a primary school and a post office and shop. Here you technically stand on the mainland of Great Britain, and yet feel you might have been on another island in another time – you can roam for miles in most directions and see no one, and not often observe even the faintest imprint of modernity. Knoydart is a yearned-for wilderness, all the more rare and precious for being in one of the most densely populated countries on the continent.

Knoydart, like Iona many centuries before it, was another little Highland world whose geography allowed people to do things differently. A landmark community buyout in 1999 led to the creation of the Knoydart Foundation: 17,000 acres of the peninsula now counts as community-owned land. The foundation runs a hydroelectric scheme, operates a sustainable timber business and reinvests profits into housing and employment projects for locals. For many, Inverie is a model community – an experiment in green living, forged in a cold corner of the country. At its centre is its shrine: a simple whitewashed cottage with a slate sign that reads 'The Old Forge'.

The Old Forge evolved out of a social club in 1992: the original landlord, Ian Robertson, successfully marketed the pub to walkers while also ministering to locals in the quieter periods. In 2012 he sold it to J. P. Robinet – a tall, bearded Belgian who first came to Knoydart as a deer stalker. Robinet claimed he had previously been the manager of a five-star hotel in his home country at the age of 27: his CV lists positions at grand Arc Deco hotels and illustrious lodgings in the Swiss Alps. Upon taking control of the Old Forge, he pivoted its offering to fine dining. The food hitherto had been bad, he said. Soon something went awry.

Over the course of almost a decade, the Highland press charted a series of disputes between Robinet and the Knoydart community. It began with reports of locals being barred for muddy attire. It escalated into reports about a police raid on the Old Forge for unlicensed firearms and of an Old Forge employee taking Robinet to an employment tribunal. There were articles detailing unpaid utility bills. Robinet shut the Old Forge for the winter season – doors were locked over the short, dismal days when the pub was needed to raise spirits. This was why the lights were off when Seb and I arrived. It might have been an insult to locals – were it not for the fact that by then many had stopped coming. Robinet, for his part, insisted he had only barred a minority who exhibited 'bad behaviour'.

'It starts by acting with politeness,' he told me in a 2019 article for *Outside*. 'It starts with not burping; it starts with just using the toilet properly. It also starts with having a shower.'

Robinet attributed the animosity to the fact he was an outsider, that others were jealous of him. He had previously catered for Richard Branson and Björn Borg.

In any case, his opponents hit back by creating their own rival 'pub' in 2019. The Table was a rickety wooden structure somewhere between a bus stop and a garden shed – provocatively sited on a patch of grass outside The Old Forge. It was adorned by a disco ball and Scottish saltires, and had a pizza oven and giant Jenga. Robinet accused the patrons of The Table of being drug users and others of being unemployed and having 'Empty Life Syndrome'. But it was frequented through the winter months (and summer too): it had no licence, and indeed no doors, so you could walk in any time. I visited The Table, on a second Knoydart 'walk-in' during the autumn of 2019, researching an article for *Outside*. A chill wind was blowing in off the loch when I arrived soon after sundown: locals rubbed gloved hands together and puffed into their collars. Inside was some of that warmth and companionship I had craved in the Highland wilderness. The village shop was shut, but someone handed me a can of beer anyway. Music played on a bluetooth speaker; stories were shared. Weariness eased in my limbs. Conversation turned to the building on the other side of the road.

'To lose a pub is to tear out the heart of a community,' said one local, who declined to be named. 'If the pub was the beating heart of the community, this is the new left ventricle. That's all we've got, one chamber out of four. We're trying to fill the gap. It keeps us sane. We all work hard, we gather.'

At the core of the dispute around the Old Forge was the semi-sacred institution of the public house. A feature of pilgrimages, past and present, was the pub – which granted succour and sanctuary along the road. Walsingham had once had about 20 pubs – now there were just two, and senior clergy grumbled to me that they were not what they used to be. You could catch a faint echo of medieval Glastonbury in the abbey, but perhaps a louder one in the George and Pilgrims, a fifteenth-century inn over the road, built under the orders of the abbot. Unlike its neighbour, it had survived the Reformation intact: pints were still pulled here, shamans and druids milled about under its battlemented parapet. Alcohol was not allowed in Iona Abbey, though there was a Wednesday night trip to the Argyll Hotel. According to its local Rotary Club, St Albans still has the highest density of pubs anywhere in the UK – a hangover from the days when vast numbers of pilgrims flocked to the shrine of St Alban. The town is also the HQ of the Campaign for Real Ale (CAMRA). Across the country, congregations often adjourned from churches to pubs over the road. The numbers of churches and pubs in the UK were evenly matched (about 40,000 each), and both were in sad decline.

The mythology of the British pub began with the 'gentil hostelrye' in Southwark, where pilgrims gathered before heading to Canterbury. And, it seemed to me, there was another old story ghosting about Inverie that autumn I visited – of two people who had walked far on a lonely road, seeking a room at the inn. The Table may not have been a pub. The Old Forge may or may not have been a shrine. But hospitality was sacrosanct.

Shooting stars wisped over the patrons of The Table that night – there was also the green blur of the Northern Lights. The Table was essentially a few planks of wood, but it had some of the spirit of a pub: not a business, but rather something that had arisen of its own accord, to meet a need to gather. When babies were born on the 'mainland' and brought back to Knoydart, it was to the Old Forge that they were first carried. The story I wrote about the pub for *Outside* magazine travelled further than any I had written before. It was published in January 2020 – for some time after, no more 'Walk Ins' were undertaken.

It was during the course of the pandemic that I heard the news about the pub – that J. P. Robinet was putting it up for sale, and the Knoydart community were attempting to buy it and run it themselves. A third of local residents volunteered their time to help. There followed a period of fundraising through the lockdowns when all pubs were shut. With additional grants from the Scottish Land Fund and Community Ownership Fund, the pub was finally purchased by the community in March 2022.

That summer of 2022 people began once again to travel through the Rough Bounds for a pint: bands played, fiddles reeled once again. More visitors on social media started using the word 'pilgrimages' for their journey – and outdoor companies offered guided 'pilgrimages' to the pub. In 2023 the BBC ran a documentary about folk musicians travelling to the Old Forge – entitled 'A Pilgrimage for a Pint.'

I messaged my friend in Australia: we would try again one day. After a period of renovation the Old Forge would now be open through winter: best of all, there were plans to offer a free beer to everyone who walked in.

The beer in question would be supplied by the Knoydart Brewery – a small operation I had visited during my 2019 visit, set up a winding lane from the pier at Inverie. Its owners, Sam and Matt Humphrey, described the long-distance walkers who bought bottles from the door as finding their 'Holy Grail' here. It was the UK's most remote brewery and an unusual operation too: casks had to be sent on a boat across the five-mile sea crossing (which, Matt noted, gave the IPA a slightly different flavour).

Also unusual was the setting for the brewery. St Agatha's Chapel was a Roman Catholic Church – first dedicated in 1886. For years it had been a storeroom for the adjoining manse, but in more recent times the pews had been cleared: you could see fermentation tanks through the Gothic windows. There was a table adorned with bottle tops where the altar might have been. St Agatha's was deconsecrated in 1990 – two years before the Old Forge first opened as a pub.

11

A Stadium

A Football Pilgrimage

The Saturday Pilgrimage | Three Cathedrals |
You'll Never Walk Alone

The tower of Liverpool Cathedral

THE SATURDAY PILGRIMAGE

It is Bill Shankly, the greatest of all Liverpool FC managers, who is credited with speaking the immortal line: 'Some people believe football is a matter of life and death, I am very disappointed with that attitude. I can assure you it is much, much more important than that.'

It is ostensibly a joke. But academics – among them the sociologist Dr Anne Eyre – have devoted effort to analysing the parallels between football and organized religion. In a 1997 paper entitled 'Football and Religious Experience: Sociological Reflections' Dr Eyre noted that not only did some clubs grow out of parish and church teams, but that football in the late twentieth century (and now the twenty-first) performs some of the same roles as an organized faith: 'religion is part of the overall quest for meaning and transcendence in contemporary society. That quest takes many forms – some more traditional, others more secular.'

The more I read, the more plausible it seemed that football had some of the functions of a religion. Being a fan gives you a sense of shared identity, a membership expressed in colours and kits. There is the profusion of symbology (badges and banners) and holy relics (signed shirts and silverware). There are small superstitions too – the lucky socks that are never washed. The leaders of this Saturday congregation were the managers, who – like Shankly – sometimes became canonized in retirement or death. Players too had their power: Maradona had the 'Hand of God'. Robbie Fowler, among Liverpool fans, was nicknamed 'God'. There were the anthems – which, when sung in unison by thousands, brought about a tingling of the spine that edged towards transcendence. The word 'faith' seemed important – keeping an unconditional *faith* as your club's fortunes fluctuated, clinging to an (often misguided or irrational) belief they could be raised from the underworld of the lower leagues and ascend to glory. Around it too, Dr Eyre identified the idea of pilgrimage: of Saturday journeys made by generations of fans to home grounds. And also to rainy away days in February – the nil-nil draws that demanded even greater devotion.

There was the endless journey of the league – but pilgrimage was a better fit for the FA Cup, where fans spoke of being on 'the road to Wembley'. Its anthem was the hymn 'Abide with Me'. Here teams did not know which opponents they would face until the draw was made – giants or minnows, David or Goliath. But a long run in the cup would mean being tested in far corners of the country.

On 15 April 1989 Nottingham Forest fans travelled to Sheffield for the FA Cup semi-final. Those northbound on the

M1 would have passed the collieries – then in their last days – while fans going by train trundled under the crooked spire at Chesterfield. Supporters of the opposing team, Liverpool, had more choices – they could follow the M62 on a dog-leg route via Huddersfield (it was busy with traffic that day). Other options were the wriggly Pennine passes across the spine of Northern England, over the watersheds and the moors. Among them: the Woodhead Pass and its chain of reservoirs; the sharp bends of the Snake Pass under the bulk of Kinder Scout; or the Hope Valley, which led to the great gritstone edges, and the city of steel which lay just beyond. One special train left Liverpool for the occasional matchday station at Wadsley Bridge, over the road from Hillsborough Stadium.

Typically, one team would have continued their FA Cup journey that day, but instead a tragedy ensued. The aftermath of the Hillsborough disaster saw what became known as the 'Anfield Pilgrimage' – journeys of meaning, which continued through the spring days of 1989, and which, in a much wider sense, are ongoing today. Dr Eyre had written about this too.

When I called her up on Zoom, I understood that her interest was not purely academic. She was drinking from a Liverpool FC mug. She explained she had grown up in Barnet, north London, and had started out as a Chelsea fan, but switched to Leeds during the glory days of the 1970s, when Johnny Giles and Billy Bremner ran amok. When Liverpool beat Newcastle 3–0 in the 1974 FA Cup final she switched allegiance one final time. Her headteacher told her not to talk about football in her interview at Liverpool University, but she did, and won her place.

'From the minute I got there, I felt at home,' Dr Eyre told me. 'It's something that's relevant to pilgrimage. It's as if I'd been there before. I've never been able to bottom that out: I've thought about that deep mystical stuff. I haven't got a firm view about reincarnation.'

She completed her PhD in March 1989. A month later she was in Pen 3 in the West Stand of Hillsborough, with her then boyfriend. As things became more constrained, she prepared to 'ride it out'. She worried she was being too 'girly' and looked at the clock. People don't realize they're in a fatal crush while it's happening, she explained. She was saved by being pulled up to the stands above. The next day, Anne and her boyfriend stepped off the train back in Liverpool, and joined vast crowds thronging towards its Catholic cathedral. A nun had stitched together an LFC banner to be placed beside the altar.

'There was some real desperate need to get home: to be among your people,' she said. 'The symbol of the community was the Catholic cathedral. There was a loudness in the silence there. I can remember even now: people going up and putting scarves on the altar. It was inclusive, embracing, spontaneous. Over the next few days I felt absolutely held.'

THREE CATHEDRALS

Liverpool has a skyline like no other. Many industrial cities have hidden their churches: mills, chimneys and warehouses crowded out the medieval spires centuries ago. More recently, plate glass towers have come to define the silhouette of Manchester, Leeds, Birmingham and others. Liverpool is unusual in being both dominated and defined by its twin cathedrals – two structures set on a hilltop. Both are mighty, and both are modern.

In the first summer after the lockdowns I spent a week in Liverpool working on a story for *National Geographic Traveller* – staying in a B & B in a Georgian terrace. From my window I could see the hulking tower of Liverpool Cathedral, the Anglican place of worship. It is impossible to miss, being the biggest cathedral in Britain (and by some measures the eighth largest in the world). Its tower rises like an immense lighthouse over Mersey shipping. Inside, local sandstone gives the space an earthy feel. In the nave, you sense you might be standing in a canyon between two red cliffs. It was one of a few religious buildings I had been to – Hagia Sophia and Seville Cathedral were others – that seemed big enough to accommodate a concept of the almighty.

Liverpool Cathedral was designed by a Roman Catholic architect, Sir Giles Gilbert Scott, and finished in 1978. Around 700 metres away stands Liverpool Metropolitan Cathedral, the Roman Catholic church designed by Sir Frederick Gibberd (who also designed London Central Mosque), which was consecrated the decade before. Where Gilbert Scott's design was neo-Gothic, Gibberd's design seemed almost intergalactic – a cone rising to a space-age tower. Light filtered in through sapphire-hued stained glass that encircled the nave. When I stepped in one August afternoon, the blue light made me think of an aquarium. To others it looked more like a tent, and was nicknamed 'Paddy's Wigwam', on account of the Irish Catholics who made up much of the congregation.

The two stood at opposite ends of a thoroughfare named Hope Street, which seemed allegorical (but was actually just an accident, being named after the merchant William Hope). In another city – Belfast or Glasgow, perhaps – these neighbouring cathedrals might have seemed adversarial, but in Liverpool they were brotherly, thanks in large part to the Catholic Archbishop Derek Worlock and his Anglican counterpart, Bishop David Sheppard, who struck up a friendship from the 1970s into the 1990s. There was no competition or resentment when the population settled on Liverpool Metropolitan Cathedral as the first place to express its grief in the wake of Hillsborough. The Anglicans held another memorial service with the prime minister in attendance. Two bishops worked as one to minister to the bereaved.

There were other places of worship close to Hope Street. I spoke to the caretaker at the Princes Road Synagogue, a magnificent Moorish Revival structure consecrated in 1874. Across the road from it was the sadly dishevelled Welsh presbyterian church, and a few doors down the better kept Greek Orthodox church of St Nicholas – designed as a replica of the church–mosque of Vefa in Istanbul. The neighbourhood they stood in – Toxteth – was a home to the oldest black community in England, present here since the early eighteenth century. The German church nearby was locked, but I did manage to get inside the Nordic church down by the docks, next to the oldest Chinatown in Europe. Further away was a terrace that had housed the first recorded mosque in the UK.

Liverpool may be Britain's original multicultural city. In the early nineteenth century some 40 per cent of world trade passed through its docks: later the city was known as the 'New York of Europe' for its vigour and diversity. Much of its wealth in the eighteenth century came from slavery – a past confronted in the city's International Slavery Museum. Slave ships gave way to steamers in the mid-nineteenth century as Irish refugees landed, fleeing famine. Later Liverpool boomed as the second city of the empire: the foghorns of ocean liners also boomed along its streets. It was England's gateway to the world, but as more immigrants set foot on its quays, it became less like other English cities. Liverpool was both a rich mix of identities and something proud and distinct in its own right. It was almost a city–state – a European Singapore. For some, being 'Scouse' transcended boundaries of religion and nationality. I often saw graffiti with the old slogan 'Scouse not English'. According to a 2021 poll in the *Liverpool Echo*, some 53 per cent of respondents said they would not be supporting England in the final of the Euros.[1] They had other allegiances.

Towards the north of the docks were two major football stadiums: Goodison Park and Anfield (which, like the two cathedrals, were set roughly 700 metres apart). Anfield, in particular, is legendary – but it is also unusual. Old Trafford is surrounded by car parks, and the Etihad Stadium is the centrepiece of a vast sports complex. Emirates Stadium sits on a tarmac island ringed by railway lines, while Stamford Bridge is flanked by some of the most expensive property in the world. Like all of these places, Anfield is home to a footballing titan, but it conforms to the old archetype of an English ground, its stands rising over the terraced houses out of which fans would pour on a match day. It stood at the heart of a community.

After the war, the city beyond the stadium went into decline and by the 1980s had reached its lowest ebb. Containerization had decimated Liverpool's docks. Unemployment soared. A heroin epidemic took hold. Liverpool City Council was at war with the Thatcher government in London, furthering a rift. Amid the urban decay, Liverpool FC continued to soar under their manager, Kenny Dalglish, winning trophies and giving citizens something to be proud of – in this context, Hillsborough hit the city hard.

On Sunday, 16 April 1989, the club opened its doors at noon and became the focus of the 'Anfield Pilgrimages'. Over the week of mourning that followed, people from Liverpool and beyond flocked to Anfield – it, rather than the scene of the disaster, offered itself as a place of pilgrimage. The focus of their grief was the stand beloved of home supporters: the famous Spion Kop. According to the Catholic Pictorial:

> Liverpool became a Three Cathedral City on Hillsborough Sunday. In addition to the Metropolitan and the Anglican we added the Anfield Cathedral with its two acre liturgically green sanctuary and the Kop altar bedecked with countless flowers and festooned with red and blue stoles and albs [scarves and shirts] which had been sacrificed by the laity in memory of their dearly departed. The cloisters approaching the Anfield Cathedral were crowded all day Sunday, the only sound breaking the silence being the tread of the pilgrims' feet approaching the main door of the Cathedral, the Bill Shankly gates.[2]

Inside the stadium, rival Everton supporters had left scarves and shirts in solidarity. It was not unusual to see grown men crying. Religion and football blurred: players and coaching staff had the job of consoling people, serving almost as priests to mourners. It was a place where the goalposts had been changed – indeed, they had been covered in flowers. Anne Eyre made the pilgrimage to Anfield that week, and has written extensively about the events.

'That is what happens with collective trauma,' she told me. 'People go to where it feels right, and not even in a conscious way. It was instinctive: their home was the ground. Both the cathedral and the stadium were, in a sociological sense, sacred – spaces set apart for dignity and respect. They had unspoken rules. You knew they were sacred even if you weren't a Liverpool fan, or even if you weren't Christian.'

Over a week in 1989 a million pilgrims came to Anfield, catching trains and buses from near and far, walking the last leg among the terraced houses to the stadium in a sad echo of match days. The Anfield pilgrimages had a lasting effect on the club. Two flames were incorporated into the club's badge in the wake of the Hillsborough disaster, and a real eternal flame was placed at the permanent Hillsborough memorial to the 97 victims, under the Main Stand. Through years of grief and injustice it became a shrine.

Anne Eyre has since cultivated a field of expertise in trauma and disaster management. She now lives in Coventry and feels in exile from her spiritual home in Liverpool, but remains part of the Hillsborough Survivors Support Alliance (HSA). A year before she spoke to me, she had been on a charity walk around Liverpool organized by another survivor, Mike Wilson. It was partly to raise money for the HSA, but it also brought about a sense of togetherness. They had started at Anfield, worked their way around the city – passing Goodison Park, following the Mersey north, veering inland to Aintree racecourse, returning to their starting point 20 miles later. Pilgrimage was the right word to describe the walk.

'I've now realized, personally speaking, I'm never going to heal. But things like this can make a difference – and I can evidence-base it with trauma research. Things like making connections with people, the ability to ritualize and commemorate an event. To continue to make meaning. Pilgrimage is about making sense of something. But it is also about making meaning.'

YOU'LL NEVER WALK ALONE

Mike Wilson sent me a Microsoft Excel spreadsheet, detailing the 265-mile walk he was planning from Nottingham to Liverpool.

It was not an ordinary map: nor were there coordinates. Rather, it was a list of 41 sports clubs and the distances between them. Most were football clubs; a few were cricket clubs. There was a smattering of rugby union and rugby league. Collectively this archipelago of grounds formed an upside-down U shape – leading from the banks of the Trent at the City Ground (home of Nottingham Forest), reaching its northern extent around Elland Road (Leeds United) and Valley Parade (Bradford City), and then turning south-west across the Pennines to the Mersey. There were titans of world football en route, and there were also teams from the seventh rung of the pyramid, where the stands were just four rows deep. Listed on the spreadsheet they sounded almost like Saturday afternoon scores: 'Blackburn Rovers: 10.42 miles, Preston North End: 3.53 miles.'

Mike worked in IT for a bank – but much of his time was dedicated to organizing charity walks between sports clubs. He knew these grounds from previous events. There was Sheffield FC, the oldest football club in the world, who made coffee whenever the fundraisers walked through. Accrington Stanley, which gave them a ball and let them have a kickabout. Sheffield Wednesday were always helpful.

Mike had organized and undertaken three walks from Hillsborough to Anfield (2012, 2014 and 2019), but the 35th anniversary walk in 2024 would be different, with the teams made up of Hillsborough survivors. They would raise money for the HSA. Teams walked in a relay as a support minibus travelled alongside them, swapping participants in lay-bys, petrol stations, Costa Coffees. Mike knew survivors who would not want to go to stadium 8 of 41: who had never been back to Sheffield. According to the spreadsheet, they were due to arrive at Hillsborough at a 5.35 on a Thursday morning. The schedule allowed a ten-minute stop. They would arrive at Anfield at 2.45 the following Sunday afternoon: Mike said he often went quiet on the approach to the stadium. Even though it was a place some went week in week out, it came with a 'different feeling' when you walked from afar and stood by the flame.

'When you kind of do something like this it will feel like a pilgrimage,' said Mike. 'It's very much about solidarity. You've these people come from very different walks of life – dockers, tradesmen, teachers – and they understand what each other have been through. It will feel like we're bringing something home. What it is, I don't know.'

Many other Liverpool fans had made pilgrimages between Hillsborough and Anfield over the years. Some hikers had taken a direct route through the Dark Peak, passing under the summit of Mam Tor and the Great Ridge, ending at Anfield a symbolic 97 miles later. Cyclists too traversed the Pennine passes. I knew many of the routes they had taken. But I felt this was not my road to walk.

Mike crossed the Woodhead Pass with his dad and a friend on 15 April 1989, travelling from Manchester, where he had been working at the Co-op. His father, David, was a headmaster – Liverpool born and bred, having attended Dovedale Primary School and then teaching there in the years after John Lennon and George Harrison left.

Mike had a plan to get the best view at Hillsborough. There was a curved section of the ground which he describes as being 'like a Subbuteo stand', accessed via the Leppings Lane entrance. They got only as far as Pen 4, at which point 'you went where you went'. Mike was 24 then: he was agile, found a railing and ultimately helped others clamber over. He was separated from his dad: it was 50 minutes before they saw each other again. Later that day, they drove back over the Woodhead. In the village of Tintwistle, where the Pennine moors slope down to green farmland, Mike remembered old ladies placing telephones on occasional tables, with home-made signs inviting fans to call home. He remembered everything that day, though not quite as much as his father, who was 'meticulous' in his memory, down to the colour of the houses in Tintwistle. In old age, his dad remembered the small details of Hillsborough long after he had forgotten his granddaughter's boyfriend's name.

Mike said his closeness to his father was the reason he had escaped the worst of the trauma suffered by other Hillsborough survivors, a large number of whom had tragically taken their own lives. Father and son spoke to each other almost every year on 15 April. Mike knew it affected his father deeply, but he never saw him cry, and described him as his 'rock'. At the age of 83 David turned up unannounced on the final stage of the 25th anniversary walk from Hillsborough to Anfield.

'He could barely walk to the kitchen at home – but he insisted he was going to walk that half a mile from Everton to Liverpool. He couldn't walk again for about three weeks after that.'

David passed away in 2022 – part of the reason that Mike wanted to do a walk in 2024 was so that he could sponsor a stage of the walk in his memory. Although the end destination was Anfield, the grounds on the way also were important – something like Stations of the Cross, where you could feel solidarity from rival clubs, and compound the sense that you were not walking alone. It seemed important to get inside and get a photo by the pitch.

'When we're at a ground – doing a photo with a banner with the names of people who were at Hillsborough – it means something,' said Mike. 'It means that they're there: they're with you.'

12

The Stones

A Countercultural Pilgrimage

Golden Age | Dial House | Savernake Forest |
The Old Pilgrims | The Once and Future King |
The Shortest Night

Stones – Summer Solstice 23

GOLDEN AGE

It was late afternoon when I woke from my nap.

Opening my eyes, I saw figures falling from the clouds above me – becoming more distinct as they fell to the imminent earth, acquiring limbs, helmets and holding what looked like they might be little guns.

Parachutes sprung from their backs, and soon they scattered like pollen in the wind – swooping and helixing out of sight. There was a whine from the aircraft that dropped them: mingling with other sounds that drowsy, dead-still day on the Wiltshire downs. The buzz of fat bumblebees in the verges. The hush of the River Avon sweeping slow over the weir. The wingbeat of dragonflies that switched course about the millponds. And beneath it all – in a low, bass register – explosions on the plain. When you lay flat on the ground, you could feel the vibrations in your bones: a shuddering as if somewhere down in the Earth's crust some reckless act of destruction was being authored. In fact, it was the artillery again. The war was ongoing: the British Army was still training the Ukrainians on Salisbury Plain.

It had been too hot to walk earlier that afternoon. Instead I had lain in the shade of a hawthorn tree and made a pillow of my rucksack. By five o'clock the sun peeked under the branches and I was on my feet again, walking south as skylarks sang. This was the final part of my pilgrimage. It had been a circular one. Over a week I had made a convoluted loop around Wiltshire. Now I was following the Avon downstream from the Vale of Pewsey – passing gardens of honeysuckle and hyacinth, war memorials around which old military men tended to flower beds. Sometimes I stopped in thatched pubs. Once a column of armoured vehicles passed by, and a soldier saluted. One evening I swam in the inky waters of the river and thought I saw the technicoloured streak of a kingfisher light up the dusk. At night I made a secret camp in the woods, and I felt again faint tremors under the ground sheet, summoning me from sleep. Mostly they were irregular, but once or twice they had a rhythm – like a pulse in the soil. With each mile I felt I was drawing nearer to their seismic centre.

The next morning I passed the barracks at Larkhill and Bulford. For a week I had talked with people about the stones; for longer I had read about them. Some hours went by when I thought of little else. But still the sight of them caught me off guard. I lifted the latch of a five-bar gate, looked across a field and there they were: grey and bone-like, about a mile or so away. There were marquees pitched around them.

Thousands of pilgrims were heading to the circle that same summer evening – caught in their gravity. I expected a few – the older ones – would be turning their minds back to the much-repeated story. That long ago these stones were an expression of a nationhood: a temple for a new kind of society. That they were a place where people gathered to mark the turn of the year, and a time of solar ascendancy. Tribes from distant places and of diverse character had made pilgrimages to this temple on the plain and mingled peacefully: there was ritual feasting, music and song. It was a golden age. But later something changed. A new kind of people had come to displace the old ones, or else their priorities altered. In any case, the gatherings ended. Today the wreckage of the stones and their fallen altar were a reminder of a golden age that had been lost and which, in the minds of the committed, might one day be regained.

The narrative was all rather hazy – but that was the general gist of it. Some months previously I had met a man who had been there from the very beginning of the whole business. He was almost 80. And he lived in Essex.

DIAL HOUSE

There was a knot of interchanges where the M11 met the M25. At junction 7 I took the turn off – passing golf courses, and mock-Tudor mansions with AstroTurf lawns. A raggedy England flag was jammed in a bedroom window. In North Weald – between a tattoo studio and the Scruffy to Fluffy pet grooming parlour – the satnav pointed down a country lane that snuck off behind a village hall.

This lane was unlike any I had ever driven on the outskirts of London: narrow and potholed, with almost no junctions on its one-mile length. It felt oddly remote as it ran through Essex farmland, passing an abandoned wireless station where Morse code messages were once relayed to Paris. The lane stopped in a farmyard beside a single-track railway line. This railway had formerly been the outermost extent of the Central Line: grimy trains from the City and Stratford had travelled through fresh countryside air to the old terminus at Ongar. In 1994 the Central Line was shortened to end at Epping, and since then a heritage railway had taken over this bucolic section of track. On holiday weekends, when steam engines still chuffed past, anyone in the farmyard might imagine they had been transported to a long-ago summer in post-war Britain. The passage of the decades had done little to change a red-brick cottage on the edge of the farm.

This was Dial House. It had been described as a hippie commune, a centre for alternative thought or, according to Wikipedia, a 'self-sustaining anarcho-pacifist open house'. Stepping through the gate into the garden, it was also convoluted – a cluster of outbuildings and sheds gathered around a sixteenth-century cottage which had itself been embellished by Victorian architects and was partly obscured by foliage. The gardens too were intricate and immaculate – divided into meandering pathways and secret lawns. Tibetan prayer flags fluttered over a mural of a smiling sun, which watched over a vegetable patch. I wandered around for a while, and thought I heard the notes of a wind chime. Dial House was an unlikely oasis of beauty in those often drab fringes of the capital.

I caught a whiff of incense from one shed, and knocked on the door. The man who opened it had snowy hair that fell to his shoulders, and a face cragged with wrinkles – but there was a litheness and a quickness to him that it did not feel wrong to call youthful. Penny Rimbaud welcomed me into his writing hut, where cut-out paper fish hung from the ceiling and a stick of incense smouldered in a corner. I sat on a rocking chair on a kilim rug. Rimbaud spoke slowly, in a low, gravelly voice.

'Since the beginning in 1967 – when I first found this place – I just wanted to allow life to happen here. And I'd help "life" in whatever way I could. Like making a vegetable patch or pruning the trees. Doing whatever comes out. Poetry, painting, music.'

Jeremy John Ratter was born in outer London suburbia in 1943. As a toddler he hid from German bombs in his mother's arms under the kitchen table. His father returned from the war, and years later was disappointed when his grown-up son left art school without a degree. Jeremy, however, considered himself a philosopher and so changed his name (by deed poll) to Penny Rimbaud. He needed somewhere to live and one day wandered down a country lane to find a cottage being used as a den by local children. Its rooms were burned out and there were holes in the floor. In his early twenties he had found what he described as his Shangri-La.

The landlord let Rimbaud stay at Dial House rent free on the understanding he fixed it up: a job which he said was like painting the Forth Bridge, inasmuch as it could never be complete. The doors never fitted their frames. None of the windows was square. The floors were wonky too. No matter: Rimbaud worked at it, kept chickens, grew vegetables, made it a home. Initially the house was cluttered with Victoriana – particularly antique clocks which, Rimbaud told me, came with their accompanying cast of ghosts. Sick of the hauntings, he cleared out the clocks and kept nothing but a bedside table, a cooker and a book by one of the Greek Stoics. With ghosts banished, real people came to Dial House instead. Some of them had seen a funny-looking place from the window of a passing Central Line train and decided to join the commune.

'If you open the door, someone will walk through it,' Penny Rimbaud said. 'The original idea behind the house was to open lots of doors and see what happens. And that's still how I live. I don't plan anything. I learned that the key to an unlocked door is an unlocked heart.'

One May day, one particular individual walked through the doors of Dial House: a man Rimbaud recalls in his autobiography as a 'smiling, bronzed, hippy warrior [with] eyes the colour of the blue skies that he loved. His neatly cut hair was the gold of the sun that he worshipped.' It was a warm May day, and yet Penny Rimbaud remembers a freak snowfall in the wake of that smiling man – the flakes settling on the herbaceous borders of the garden. The man's name was Philip Russell. He was known to everyone as Wally Hope.

Hope was in his late twenties and had a troubled childhood: his father passed away when he was 12. He was raised by a guardian – a BBC newsreader – in Ongar but learned to eschew all authority from the start. By 1974 he was already a figure in the British counterculture scene, naming himself Wally after a dog that had gone missing at the final Isle of Wight Festival in 1970.

Wally Hope had identified Dial House as the launch pad for a great endeavour – the creation of a new, pioneering free festival. In the early 1970s the free festival movement was already in full swing – Glastonbury Festival had taken place, followed by the Windsor Free Festivals from 1972. They were organic gatherings of people, free in every sense of the word – costing nothing to enter, free from the intrusions of capitalism, free from the need to get landowners' permission or wear clothes or observe social norms. Free festivals lacked a central authority – the ethos was that you 'bring what you expect to find'. Hope's plan was for a free festival with a spiritual impetus – pilgrims would assemble at the great Neolithic temple on Salisbury Plain and, at the summer solstice, join him in worshipping the sun as it rose from the horizon. Rimbaud remembers Hope's words as he walked into Dial House that May day.

> 'I have a dream,' Phil continued, barely looking up from the intricate patterns of the oriental carpet, 'that one day the children of Albion will play again together in the shadows of the great stones.'[1]

Rimbaud thought it was a bloody stupid idea. He had himself been to the stones before: he thought it was just the place you stopped for a piss on the A303 on the way to your holiday in Cornwall. But he saw that Hope was serious about sun worship. And so, together with other commune members, the two started printing leaflets advertising the event, making posters adorned with pyramids and mysterious symbols. Rimbaud set about baking bread. Hope saw that dignitaries were welcomed on this revolutionary inaugural pilgrimage: letters of invitation were extended to the pope, the duke of Edinburgh, John Lennon and the Dalai Lama. The date was set in June. The address of the stones was provided as: 'alternative UN headquarters, care of God, Jesus, Gandhi and Buddha, Garden of Allah, Sacred Heart of England, Wiltshire'. Wally Hope also invited British Airways air hostesses (with whom, Penny Rimbaud said, he had an unhealthy infatuation). It would be a reawakening of the temple, and of the country in which it stood.

'Phil was a sun worshipper,' Rimbaud said, 'and not in the Costa del Sol sense – the sun was his energy, his centrepiece. He was aware instinctively, intuitively, of the meaning of that place.'

———

I gazed out of the window of Penny Rimbaud's hut, out on to grey Essex fields. His story was beguiling, but it is worth considering those preparations at Dial House in a broader context. Many of Penny Rimbaud's assertions about Wally Hope were outlandish: the strange weather that followed him around (in particular, the rainbows he could summon from nowhere). Wally Hope himself seemed something of a hippie caricature – he saw LSD as his sacrament, drove around in a vehicle he called the 'cosmic armoured car', dressed in the uniform of the Cypriot National Guard. He was a prankster and a dandy, though most thought him sincere in his devotion to the sun and his belief in the power of that temple on the plain. Others thought him vulnerable, with a fragile grip on reality. In truth, Hope belonged to a long dynasty of dreamers that had entered into the orbit of that monument.

The infatuation arguably started with the eighteenth-century antiquarian William Stukeley, a friend of Isaac Newton. He was the very first to understand that the stones were aligned to the summer solstice – and that on the morning of 21 June dawn rays followed a long avenue to enter into the horseshoe of monoliths. It was not the only ancient monument oriented to the sun -- though it was the most famous. Stukeley romantically associated the place with Druids, the priestly caste present in Britain at the time of the Roman invasion. He was, of course, a few thousand years off the monument's true Neolithic builders, but he was correct that it pre-dated recorded history and was a relic of an almost unfathomable past.

In any case, Stukeley's speculations became self-fulfilling. By the beginning of the twentieth century neo-Druids were gathering at the stones at the summer solstice, marking the passage of the year with their own re-imaginings of ancient rituals. They wore long robes and some wore fake beards: the competing orders squabbled for prominence. Ken Barlow from *Coronation Street* once joined them. However imprecisely and inauthentically, they aimed to rekindle a flame there: to put the temple to something like its original use. Summer solstices became shindigs: the sacred mixed with the profane, the cosmic with the comic. Between the wars there were jazz performances at the stones. By the 1950s someone had brought a dancing skeleton to entertain visitors. The pubs in nearby Amesbury did a roaring trade on midsummer's eve, and scuffles broke out with squaddies from the army bases. Some came to the stones for a spectacle, others for a party, a few for a fight. But among them there emerged pilgrims – people earnestly using the stones as an instrument to understand their home planet's place in the solar system, and in turn their own station in the universe. More than anything, the stones seemed to be about belonging. It did not matter who you were. The stones had no written creed: they asked nothing of you. For those who considered a building too small to contain God, they were open to the skies. This was a place people sought answers to the greatest questions – finding comfort in crowds, and clarity in the first rays of a solstice dawn. Unless it was cloudy and rainy. It often was.

It could never be known for sure, but it seemed possible that Wally Hope's free festival was the first time since the Late Neolithic period that vast crowds of seekers had congregated at that monument. He understood that something lay dormant in post-war Britain, and that he might stir it back to life. As Penny Rimbaud once wrote:

> Phil had travelled the world and had met fellow thinkers in every place that he'd stopped, but none the less, he always returned to England. Perhaps it was his love of the mythical past ... Perhaps he felt as I did, that real change could only be effected in the place that you most understood: home.[2]

It was a slow start. The 1974 festival saw about 500 hippies pitch up, with music from the synth band Zorch. Rimbaud went back to

Essex, but Wally Hope and a few disciples – the so-called Wallies – stuck around in a teepee encampment close to the stones, named Fort Wally. They were evicted by court order by August. Hope, spying an opportunity, addressed the press outside the court:

> 'We won, because we hold Stonehenge in our hearts. We are not squatters, we are men of God. We want to plant a Garden of Eden with apricots and cherries where there will be guitars instead of guns, and the sun will be our nuclear bomb.'[3]

Hope by now had the kindling for a much greater fire. By 1975, three thousand attendees came to the festival. In 1976 the press jittered about fifteen thousand people coming to Wiltshire (in reality, it was far fewer). But as the decade wore on, ever more buses, vans and motorbikes began to flow down the A303 with every summer solstice. Pilgrims were drawn by Hope's message of a temple built by the people for the people (and later stolen by the government). At night, when campfires twinkled along the plain, the festival had the aura of something from scripture, a caravan out in the wilderness of Salisbury Plain. Penny Rimbaud had written of the sounds of Indian flutes, the scent of wood smoke, the drifting kites, tethered horses and old men 'muttering prayers to their personal Gods'.

> Every night leaping flames illuminated a tireless storyteller whose vision of Eden cast splashes of iridescent light across the plain landscape of the plains. He told tales of how it was that of all the places on Earth, this fire had come to be lit in this place at this time.[4]

At its peak in 1984 the festival had become an ephemeral city of 30,000 residents (70,000 at solstice). It had its own systems of economics and trade, its own highways and byways, its own system of justice and enforcement too – drugs were widespread, but heroin dealers were not tolerated (at the entrance there was a burned-out vehicle with a cautionary sign that 'This was a smack dealer's car'). Police hovered around the fringes but reputedly rarely entered, recognizing the free festival was a de facto autonomous territory within the United Kingdom.

Some identified the Stonehenge Free Festival as a blueprint for a new society. To cross its threshold was to enjoy untold freedoms. Different tribes – hippies, students, bikers and later punks – mingled mostly peacefully through summer solstices, dancing, singing, taking drugs, disrobing and swimming in the nearby Avon. They listened to bands at the rickety stages (the rampaging guitars of space rock pioneers Hawkwind came to define the festival sound). Crowds looked with reverence to the Druids, now inaugurated as priests of this temporal metropolis on the plain, officiating over ceremonies at sunrise. Weddings took place. Children were named within the stones. The Neolithic monument was now a shrine around which pilgrims converged at a certain time of year, like another more famous one in a desert far away. There was no theological cohesion. That was the point of the free festival.

The ideas of the Stonehenge Free Festival threatened to break free from Salisbury Plain and escape into the rest of the world. By the 1980s the rise of the festival coincided with the growth of the New Age traveller movement – new nomads who, at a time of mass unemployment, eschewed a life of materialism in Thatcher's Britain for the liberty of open road. They moved in convoys between a calendar of summer free festivals – of which Stonehenge remained the primary and pre-eminent event. The writer and Earth mysteries advocate John Michell asserted the rediscovery of Stonehenge as a pilgrimage site 'fulfilled a human need which had been repressed by the Reformation'.[5] Newspapers scoffed at all the nonsense and nudity. When I told people I was writing about the Stonehenge Free Festivals as a pilgrimage, they sometimes laughed. It is clear to me that this was a new English pilgrimage in the mad, molten moment of its first creation.

Penny Rimbaud told me he was contacted by the IRA, the remnants of the Baader–Meinhof group and other underground organizations, all seeking an alliance with festival organizers. He declined the offers. In any case, as the years went on, the Stonehenge Free Festival was less of an event that could be organized, more an unstoppable force that moved under its own momentum. Its founder never lived to see his vision flower.

I spent an afternoon listening to Penny Rimbaud in his shed until the incense burned down to a nub and daylight began to wane outside. He had many memories of Wally Hope at Dial House: the time they sat communicating through the movement of embers in a fire; the time his friend went into a trance at the kitchen table. The saddest was when Wally arrived at the cottage for the last time in summer 1975, a shadow of his former self.

'He couldn't walk and could only vaguely talk. He was desperately disconnected.'

Hope had taken 36 hours to drive to Dial House from Wiltshire (he kept parking up in lay-bys because he was passing out). He was by then on a steep downward spiral: Hope had been caught by police in possession of LSD at a squat in Amesbury in May 1975, whereupon he had been sectioned and admitted to a psychiatric hospital in Salisbury. Here, Rimbaud claims, Hope was administered with a lethal cocktail of drugs that turned him into a 'zombie'. He was detained for the duration of the second free festival, released only when the last hippies drove home on the A303. Rimbaud said the authorities were frightened of what he had created, of what he might do next.

'Dr [David] Kelly was taken out because he knew too much,' Rimbaud said. 'Wally was taken out, because he felt too much.'

Others said Wally had long struggled with his mental health. Curiously, a slogan for the Stonehenge Free Festival was 'You're never too old for a happy childhood.' For a while Wally Hope sobbed in his bed at Dial House: Rimbaud wrote that his hands shook 'in the way that old men's did on a cold winter's day when the bus never came'. One day he tried to leave, but as he headed to the back door, that weather came again: a monsoon-like rain poured down, and Rimbaud remembered a bolt of lightning striking the vegetable patch. It was a sign that Hope did not heed.

Wally Hope died at his guardian's house in Ongar in September
1975: the coroner returned a verdict of suicide, which Rimbaud
disputes. Penny Rimbaud says that after losing his friend he lost the
last dregs of faith in the 'system'. Colour drained from his world,
and skylarks no longer sang. He later found fame as a member of
the anarcho-punk band Crass. In death, Hope became a martyr for
the Stonehenge Free Festival – his ashes paraded around the stones
in a little wooden box over subsequent solstices, in the manner
of a medieval saint's relics. Penny Rimbaud said he himself felt a
resonance in the stones – a silence and depth like an old oak tree
– but he became disillusioned by the worshippers that gathered
around the box, and their shouts of 'Wally Lives'. The free festival
blazed on for a full decade before it suffered its own painful death
at the so-called 'Battle of the Beanfield'. Fifty years later, Rimbaud
wondered if it had all been worth it.

'Wally would have cried his way to the grave if he had known
how it all ended. It wasn't what he wanted. If he had thought that
the Beanfield was going to be the end result, he would never have
done it. No question.'

I said goodbye, passed the vegetable patch where the lightning
bolt struck and followed that strange country lane from Rimbaud's
Shangri-La back to the tailbacks and tedium of outer London. But
Penny Rimbaud's words came to me again, months later, when I
found myself in a Wiltshire forest on the trail of the last pilgrims
of Stonehenge '85.

SAVERNAKE FOREST

It is easy to find the Savernake Forest on a satellite image of southern
England.

The New Forest is the muddy green of its heathlands. The Forest
of Dean is greyed by the settlements and roads in its midst. The
Savernake Forest, though small, seemed to me to be the darkest
hue of them all – a dense triangle of old-growth greenery, cornered
between two A-roads outside Marlborough. It has a concentration
of ancient trees almost unsurpassed in Britain. Thirty-two

specimens – the aristocrats of these woods – have been given names and identities.

The grandfather of them all is the bulbous Big Belly Oak – thought to be 1,100 years old, having perhaps taken root in the twilight years of the Saxon kings. Perhaps a shade younger is the millennia-old Cathedral Oak – with mighty, elephantine branches, it could have been a sapling when the Normans placed Savernake in the charge of a warden, one Richard Esturmy. His descendants – 31 generations later – still own the forest. It has not been sold in a thousand years. Somewhat sickly now is the Queen Oak – planted to commemorate the marriage of Henry VIII and Jane Seymour in 1536. Henry VIII came hunting in the forest: he may have met his third wife while staying with her father, the warden Sir John Seymour, at his nearby home at Wulfhall.

More junior are the avenues of beeches planted by Lancelot 'Capability' Brown in the eighteenth century. Brown was commissioned to carve sightlines from the mesh and tangle of woodlands – notably the Grand Avenue that extends for four miles from the ancestral pile of Tottenham House. Today long, straight roads continue to divide the forests into quadrants and right angles, slicing it like a piece of a cake. But branching away from those forester's tracks, into its thicketed recesses, Savernake can still feel unruly and wild. I was walking here a few days before the solstice. Outside the sun beat remorselessly on farmland, but the forest swam in coolness and quivering green light, like a shallow seabed. Stray beams of sunlight splintered through the ceiling of oak leaf, catching the gables of branches, lighting the path ahead.

A few days before, another pilgrim had passed through the Savernake Forest. Self-described 'tree pilgrim' Martin Hügi was en route from Land's End to John O'Groats: he devised a walking route whereby he would visit 2,700 ancient trees along the way (he also hoped to add unrecorded specimens to the Woodland Trust's Ancient Tree Inventory as he went). Martin was a qualified arborist: he told me his love of trees took root growing up on a country estate in Hertfordshire, where his mother was a nanny. Later, at university in Nottingham, he found a cedar of Lebanon on campus – it had a fork big enough to lie down on without fear of falling off. He read books there for hours at a time. For him, trees were sacred places.

'And I think that's not uncommon,' he told me. 'Humans have been treating trees as sacred places for millennia. Ancient trees really are like a fusion of the earth and of livingness.'

He had wandered off the beaten track in Savernake, and found new specimens to add to the register here too. Although he walked alone, Martin sometimes spoke to the trees. Sometimes, in the quietest places, he thought he heard a response.

'Whether it's a sentient tree talking back to me or it's just my psychology – I'm not sure. I'm a scientist and a chemist at heart. But I also have had deep spiritual experiences. I can flip-flop like that.'

As a pilgrim, he said the most important thing he had learned was to trust in the flow of the road ahead of him. It was a potholed road that led me a mile through thick summer woodland to Savernake Lodge – more remote still than the one that led to Dial House. Beds of nettles grew tall by the roadside. There was no one around: only an Asda delivery man who was looking lost in his van, jabbing at his phone. The track emerged into a clearing and made an abrupt right turn. The lodge had once been a stable: it had a grand clock tower (though the time was wrong). It was now the home of David Brudenell-Bruce, the earl of Cardigan and the current warden of the forest. A septuagenarian with thin lips and cool grey eyes, he said little as he opened the door, and showed me along a long corridor where oil paintings of aristocrats hung on the walls. We sat on opposite sofas in a large living room. A fire alarm was beeping in the background, wanting its batteries.

Brudenell-Bruce often seemed to be in the news. There were reports of legal cases centred on the sale of his family silver and stories related to Tottenham House – the stately home on the edge of the Savernake Forest in which his forebears had resided until 1940. Against the earl's wishes it had been sold to a hedge fund manager a decade ago. But I wasn't here to ask about that: I wanted to hear about the events in the forest in 1985.

'I haven't played this out in my head for a long time,' he said in a clipped Etonian voice, looking at the ceiling. 'You might think I am deliberately not giving you eye contact – which is rather unusual in conversation. It's only by looking at something else I can replay those pictures across the brain.'

On Friday, 31 May 1985, officers of the Wiltshire Constabulary contacted the earl of Cardigan, letting him know that a convoy of New Age travellers (by some accounts 140 vehicles strong) was squatting on his land. They knocked down a barrier to gain access to the forest. The earl paid them a visit: 'Sorry about the pole,' one of the travellers had said to him. The convoy was headed to Stonehenge. None of the travellers cared for the notices that had been distributed by the National Trust and English Heritage, or the adverts in *Time Out* announcing 'the free festival will not be allowed on the land at Stonehenge cared for by them this year or in future'. The reason given was damage to the ancient site. There was a truth to this, although some archaeologists said it paled in comparison to damage done by the MoD. In any case, the Wiltshire establishment had for years been wanting to end the carnival on the plain, which was expanding with every year and getting out of hand. In the eyes of the travellers, it was not in the power of English Heritage, the National Trust or anyone else to withhold access to the stones, which belonged only to the people.

'The two parties were absolutely on a collision course,' remembered Brudenell-Bruce. 'Something had to give.'

The following morning, curious to see what would happen next, Brudenell-Bruce and a friend got on their motorbikes and tracked the convoy south towards the A303. They wore motorcycle leathers and helmets so no one could identify them. The convoy kept stopping and starting: Brudenell-Bruce remembers a naked traveller getting out to stretch his legs in the village of Shipton Bellinger. The police remained insistent the convoy would not reach the stones, and close to the A303 had set up a roadblock – two cars parked in a chevron shape. The officer in charge that day was the deputy chief constable of Wiltshire, Lionel Grundy: he assembled an army of officers in riot gear, enforcing a high court injunction to stop the festival. A reckoning came.

Brudenell-Bruce saw a convoy truck ram the police barrier, then disappear off into a field of beans by the A303. Things escalated: Brudenell-Bruce says he saw police officers set upon the vehicles parked on the road, smashing the windscreens one by one. The first was a converted ambulance.

'Sitting in it was a blonde girl who might have been in her twenties. She was pulled out of the vehicle by her hair. Ambulances have a certain meaning to society: they're there to help the sick, injured and the dying. It was a really brutal, horrific sight that makes me feel yucky even now thinking about it.'

One by one, more vehicles drove into the field to escape the police. The ensuing events became the so-called 'Battle of the Beanfield' – what would turn out to be the biggest mass arrest of civilians in post-war Britain, with 537 people detained. After a long stand-off, the police, aided by circling helicopters, entered the field. The earl, still anonymous under his helmet, served as the foremost of the few witnesses that afternoon: he alleges that he saw one policeman hit a pregnant woman on the head, and officers smashing vehicle windscreens with stones gathered from the field. Ordinary British bobbies seemed to be losing all control. He alleges too that policemen concealed their collar numbers, setting on civilians in a manner he described as being more typical of North Korea or East Germany than Wiltshire on a Saturday afternoon. He recalls a woman with her child attempting to surrender.

'She put her hands under the baby and lifted it up like something out of the Old Testament. And she shouted to the police, "Look: I'm carrying a baby, for God's sake!" Someone had found a lump of something and flung it at this stationary vehicle where this woman was holding the baby. It exploded into 20,000 pieces of glass. Both mother and child were completely covered in broken glass.'

'Stunned, astonished and appalled are words that are far too weak,' he went on. 'Of course there was malice. I can never see a policeman in the same light ever again. I've never seen the world the same way ever again.'

Bloody images of the Beanfield circulated over the following days – travellers bruised, bandaged and stretchered off. In the aftermath, social services were on hand to take travellers' children into care, and dogs were destroyed. Immediately after the arrests, Brudenell-Bruce says he saw policemen with sledgehammers smashing up buses from the convoy, reducing dashboards to powder, destroying homes. The police sought the earl's permission to clear a few remaining New Age travellers still on his land: he withheld it, and was in turn derided by the press for being a figure of the establishment giving refuge to people they labelled 'Giro Gypsies' and 'Sponging Scum'. As the chairman of the Marlborough Conservatives, Brudenell-Bruce says he found himself in later years sitting on committees with a fellow Tory, Lionel Grundy. He says he could never bring himself to speak to the man. Despite widespread allegations of police brutality, no official inquiry has ever taken place. One policeman was convicted of actual bodily harm.

The Battle of the Beanfield took place in the midst of the upheavals of 1980s Britain – the miners' strike had only just ended, and the Battle of Orgreave had happened the year before. Mrs Thatcher said her government was 'only too delighted to do anything we can to make life difficult for such things as "hippy convoys"' – it seemed that the Battle of the Beanfield was part of an ideological crusade.[6] It marked a watershed for the New Age traveller movement, whose numbers declined in subsequent years. The free festival was now over: authority had reimposed itself on a tribe of nomads who, over a few heady summers, had escaped its grasp. The Beanfield was won by the forces of conformity. But the battle was also about the magnetism of that prehistoric monument on Salisbury Plain, a Neolithic temple to which pilgrims had, for ten years, brought their motley vehicles and motley interpretations. A sacred shrine rediscovered, now taken away. In the ITN footage of the Beanfield – amid the violence and commotion – a young male traveller can be heard shouting in the background, 'This is a religious war.'

The earl said goodbye as coolly as he had said hello. After leaving Savernake Lodge, it took the rest of the day for me to trace the route of the convoy south: out beyond the long rides and glades of the forest, beyond the solar farms with panels pointed reverently to the blazing June sun. I was gravitating ever closer to the expanse of the plain, whose guns that day were still. The Beanfield itself was a paddock by the A303, set between a cattery and a café called the Dinky Diner (which did bacon baps and paninis). After a long time scanning the verges, I eventually found a small green sign that had been installed a few weeks previously:

This marks the spot of the BATTLE OF THE BEANFIELD,
  June 1st 1985.
You can't kill the spirit.

THE OLD PILGRIMS

The narrow boat people said it was their favourite stretch of the canal.

For over 15 miles between the Bruce Tunnel and the town of Devizes there were no locks on the Kennet & Avon Canal. That meant there were no interruptions to its slow, stately procession through the Vale of Pewsey, so a captain might spend meditative hours sat at the tiller, letting their gaze skip among trailing willows or considering the green rise of Tan Hill above. The canal was busy with weekend boats the day I trod the towpath westward from Savernake, chugging motors scattering fish that shoaled in the shade under red-brick bridges. The canal wandered under the hooves of the Alton Barnes White Horse and – further west still – passed the All Cannings Long Barrow.

I stopped a few miles short at the Barge Inn, a pub close to the midway point of the canal. It had once served as a general supply base for boats carrying merchandise between London and Bristol. This midsummer it had again become a staging post, this time for pilgrims en route to the stones. A small crowd sat under parasols in the beer garden. The sound of dub and a waft of herbs came from a camping field beyond. That day, the Barge Inn was hosting the tenth anniversary celebration for the Stonehenge Festival

Campaign, the group that had placed that commemorative sign at the Beanfield a few weeks previously. There were, at a guess, about two hundred people there. It was not – as someone made very clear on Facebook – a 'festival', presumably in case the Council were paying attention. It was a gathering of people. These were the ones who kept the spirit alive.

The closest thing they had to a leader seemed to be Paul Sid Hope Hegarty – known as Sid. I met him under an awning attached to a Toyota Hilux, where we sat with his friends Lisa (also known as Lemon), Noggin and Russ (also known as Baz). Overhead flew the flag of the Free Festival Campaign. Next to us was a giant cut-out of a flying teapot. Sid was nearing 60, wore a black beanie hat and a Rasta wristband: his dreadlocks entangled with the beads strung around his neck. He was from the Brixton area, and he first heard about the free festival in a south London squat four decades ago. He and a friend first came to the stones for the winter solstice of 1985: they parked in Fargo Woods and partied through the night with hippies.

'Coming from London, I'd never been out of the city before,' Sid said. 'Stonehenge felt really remote. I felt I was in the middle of nowhere. It was a really spiritual experience. Since then I just couldn't stop coming back. I just wish I'd found out about it earlier.'

Sid's timing was bittersweet. In 1986 he returned to Stonehenge for the summer solstice: despite the events at the Beanfield the year before, some hoped against hope that the free festival would rise from the ashes. What they found instead was a so-called 'exclusion zone' – a four-mile perimeter enclosing English Heritage and National Trust land. There was now fencing, floodlights and police roadblocks: Stonehenge had become Checkpoint Charlie. Sid tried his best to rush to the stones and almost got arrested.

'Basically I came back to London on the National Express coach crying because this festival never materialized. So I went back to the rat race, back to the inner city, back to Babylon with all my dreams crushed. My world was fucked. It was then I started using hard drugs, smoking smack. I just want to give you an idea what this thing means to people. But the flame was always there.'

Sid found his salvation in a series of long-distance walks that came to be known as the 'Stonehenge Pilgrimages'. Through the years of the exclusion zone – through the late 1980s and into the 1990s – travellers and others embarked on summer solstice walks from cities such as Bristol, Southampton and London. In doing so they were campaigning for the revival of the festival – hoping to 'Avenge the Henge' – commemorating the victims of the Beanfield, expressing devotion to the stones. Sid said it took about two weeks and the pilgrimage route varied every year. So did the numbers: sometimes it was tens of walkers, sometimes hundreds.

Sid remembers starting out at the Battersea Park Peace Pagoda, camping the first night at Ham Common. The pilgrims then followed the Thames upstream to Runnymede, where they talked about Magna Carta. Sid said the group eventually left the river behind and pitched up among the Roman walls of Silchester. They carried tents and camping supplies, ate vegetarian food, grew wary of undercover police in their midst (they were easy to spot). Beyond Newbury, police helicopters buzzed overhead. One helicopter allegedly followed a pilgrim behind a hedge to watch him pee. The journeys ended on the cusp of the exclusion zone on the eve of the solstice. Sid and others peered through barriers, reflecting on a paradise lost.

Sid saw parallels between the 1980s and today: the Tory government, the energy crisis. These days the campaign for the free festival saw him petitioning English Heritage to offer a suitable site for a festival somewhere near the stones. But they didn't want to know – nor were other landowners willing to offer any land on which he might put a sound system and reignite Wally Hope's fire. This got him down.

'We're only small. We're not a huge number of people anyway. We're not doing anyone any harm. None of us are getting younger now, and a lot of people from the old days, they're not with us any more.'

The spirit was still alive, but it had changed. Some people I spoke to at the Barge Inn had been at the original festivals, camped amid technicoloured buses and tumbledown vans. By contrast, the caravans and camper vans in the campsite today were largely shiny white, suburban-looking – some were luxurious. His and hers folding chairs were set by stainless steel barbecues. Someone was singing the praises of his handheld coffee grinder.

The Hilux we were sitting beside belonged to Noggin – he joked he was Sid's chauffeur. He was roughly the same age: with sun-tanned skin and a tattoo of a moon and sun on his wrist. He had been at the free festivals from '82: tried mushrooms, felt the power of the stones, remembered a bloke dragging a tarpaulin behind his motorbike, charging 20p for a ride around a field. Noggin had been a festival devotee: in the years after the Beanfield he jumped the fence at Glastonbury, until the year that Robbie Williams headlined, and Noggin saw it had become like the Radio One roadshow and understood something had been lost. He said it was still a pilgrimage for him driving up to the Barge Inn from his home in Dorset, passing the landmarks from years gone by, but he said quietly he didn't think there could ever be another free festival. That was OK. Now he had a successful landscape gardening business. He owned a house and a boat.

'Now I can sleep in my own bed, have a bath and cook up something nice to eat. Maybe it's an age thing.'

Evening descended on the Vale of Pewsey. Bands played in the function room of the Barge Inn – strains of ska slipped out into the still Wiltshire night. Propped on top of a guitar amplifier was a little box that read: 'Wally Hope, Died 1975, A Victim of Ignorance'. Painted on a nearby wall was a mural of Stonehenge. Here, 18 miles away, some of the old crowd were back together again.

Among them was Russ, aka Baz. He was from the same part of Dorset as Noggin: he had a silver goatee and a lizard tattoo on his arm. He had worked in printing and in traffic management and had undertaken spiritual journeys in India. He spoke with great intensity, rarely blinking. His first Stonehenge was 1983, when his mate passed his driving test and drove everyone up to the plain. He stepped within the festival and was 'blown away'. In '85 he arrived in time to see police vans chasing people from the scene, but by then seeds had been sown. Stonehenge changed Russ: it showed him not to live in fear of authority, that he was free to make his own way.

'I was a very angry young lad,' he said. 'I was in borstals, detention centres. Stonehenge started me on the path that led me to where I am now. I own a house. Not a big house or anything. I've brought up two sons who've not had the problems that I had. And I'm happy.'

His boss didn't give him annual leave for the celebrations at the Barge Inn, so Russ took the drastic step of quitting his job to be among his friends. It didn't matter, he said – he could find another job. He'd had a breakdown a few years previously when his mum died, and he realized it was at gatherings like this that helped him recharge, regroup, before heading back into the real world.

'It's a tribe,' said Russ. 'It is our identity. Something we lack in English society. This is it. Stonehenge is our history, who we are. Most cultures cling on to that. The British government is stopping us from being ourselves.'

The free festivals ended for good after the bloodshed of 1985. But in truth the exclusion zone was also history. For two decades the stones had been open for a kind of celebration and worship at the summer solstice. This wasn't really discussed. Russ wasn't going. Nor was Noggin (he had to get back home because he was getting the builders in). Perhaps they did not want to disturb the ghosts of the past – or override memories of an enchanted youth. Noggin also said you had to pay £15 to English Heritage to park your car at summer solstice. Where was the freedom in that?

THE ONCE AND FUTURE KING

I found the deer about six o'clock. I was walking down a country lane by a housing estate not far from the stones, and there it was – a roe with its back legs flattened against the tarmac, looking up at me with pain and panic in its eyes. It was moving its neck in frantic clockwise circles, jabbing at thin air with its antlers, the movements slowing as the minutes went by and life emptied by degrees from its half-crushed body. The hit must have happened just a few minutes before. I thumbed at my phone and was put through to the Wiltshire Constabulary. The woman at the other end asked the location, my name and then detoured from the script.

'Oh my goodness, the poor little thing. I do hope it don't suffer.'

I waited with the deer for a few minutes, listening to the swish of a breeze in the cow parsley. I wonder now if I should have killed the deer out of mercy. Eventually blood ran into the whites of its eyes, and the neck stiffened then dropped. A police car was on the way – but I was gone before it arrived. On the eve of summer solstice, it seemed the force had capacity to deal with such an incident. That was because things were more peaceful at the stones these days.

Around the same time, fellow officers had been assigned to the Airman's Corner roundabout, watching a procession of brake lights inch their way through the dusk to the solstice car park. This was by now a tightly choreographed operation. In the weeks beforehand, lay-bys and roads around the stones had been blocked by traffic cones and concrete barriers: PCNs slapped on any offending cars, all traffic marshalled under austere, faintly insincere-looking signs that read 'WELCOME TO SOLSTICE'. Police vans were also parked where solstice attendees were having their bags frisked. Prohibited items included (but were not limited to): alcohol, camping equipment, Chinese lanterns, fireworks, barbecues, tea lights and sharp or pointy things that could conceivably be used as weapons.

An exception seemed to be made for Excalibur – a sword that belonged to Arthur Uther Pendragon. Arthur Uther Pendragon had been born Timothy John Rothwell in 1954: his sword had allegedly been a prop in the 1981 John Boorman film *Excalibur* before he spotted it in a shop window. Arthur was, of course, an enduring staple of British silly season news. He sincerely believed he was the reincarnation of the once and future king and dressed flamboyantly in flowing white robes that went with his flowing white beard. At other times he rode an equally flamboyant 1100cc Moto Guzzi California motorbike which he described as his 'iron steed'. He turned up at various protests and seemed willing to pose for a photograph. He was self-deprecating, but there was a seriousness about him too: he was the figure most associated with the campaign for solstice access in the wake of the Beanfield. Earlier that same evening, he had refused to pay English Heritage's £15 car parking charge – and so, on principle, caught the 333 bus from Salisbury to the stones. It was dark when I located him and his entourage, members of the 'Loyal Arthurian Warband', three or four blokes standing under their battle standard near the portaloos. They were looking for a bloke called Dave who had a van. Traffic delayed them: the warband had missed their chance to hold a sunset ritual in the circle.

'As with any pilgrimage, it's about getting there,' said Arthur. 'I had quite a journey here. I left Salisbury on the bus at half six, and got here at, what? Ten o'clock now! I can do it in 15 minutes on my motorbike! But that's all part of the quest.'

Arthur first came to the stones at the age of ten, en route to a family holiday at Butlin's Minehead: he doesn't remember the holiday, but he remembers the stones, which shaped the course of his life. Later he was discharged from the army after sustaining an injury jumping out of a plane in Hong Kong. He joined a biker gang and attended the final free festivals from 1983; in 1985 he was escorted out of Wiltshire carrying Hawkwind's equipment on his bike, unaware that violence was erupting at the Beanfield (otherwise he and his cavalry would have ridden to the rescue). It was during the wilderness years of the 1990s, in his guise as Arthur, that he became a thorn in the side of English Heritage – a group that he still calls 'English Heretics'. Through the 1990s he kept his vigil by the stones, braved chill winters, accepted takeaway cups of tea from tourists and slept under a tarpaulin in the woods. Over that decade he was often arrested trying to breach the exclusion zone, and in 1995 was successfully defended against charges of trespassory assembly by a young lawyer named Keir Starmer. In 1997 he chained the doors shut at English Heritage headquarters in London. In 1998 he went to the European Court of Human Rights, citing his right to freedom of thought, conscience and religion. Soon afterwards a separate legal ruling meant the decade and a half-long exclusion zone enforced by the Wiltshire Constabulary was effectively deemed illegal. Arthur was ready when the walls came crashing down.

In the first summer solstice of the new millennium, pilgrims came again to the stones: Arthur walked into the circle to applause, declaring, 'This is your henge. This is your temple. Do not let anyone tell you otherwise.' After what were (in all seriousness) called 'round table' discussions between Arthur, English Heritage and other parties, a kind of truce had been struck. It had endured over the decades. English Heritage's programme of 'Managed Open Access' saw the site open to the public at 7 p.m. on 20 June and shut 13 hours later. Solstices and equinoxes were a brief, blessed hiatus during which there was no admission fee: unlike ordinary visitors, pilgrims were free to walk among the stones and touch them. But Arthur still wasn't happy. In recent times he had campaigned for the reburial of human remains found at Stonehenge, and was now taking English Heritage to court over the £15 parking charge – which he said was a de facto case of 'pay to pray'. There was also the spectre of the Stonehenge Tunnel. He had devoted his years on earth to this great temple of time. I sensed he would continue until the final battle.

'Stonehenge is a great sundial,' he said. 'But it doesn't tell you the time of day, it tells you the time of year. People have been coming here on the longest, the shortest and the equal days for thousands of years. We're here in continuation of that. So by any token you like, this is a pilgrimage. This is as much a pilgrimage as any of your Christian pilgrimages or any of your visits to Lourdes. It's a gathering. Over a million people this weekend are going to be at the Hajj and they can accommodate it. So why can't they accommodate us here?'

I followed Arthur and his warband towards the stones. It was a warm night, giddy with anticipation. Over several hours, several thousand people ambled the mile from the car park to the circle. A drone buzzed overhead. TV cameras were there. This was emphatically not a festival, though there were some of its trappings: stewards in hi-vis jackets, vans selling oven-baked pizzas and cheese toasties, a stall flogging souvenirs. The souvenir stall, in particular, seemed to offend Arthur.

'I like free gatherings. I don't like commercial gatherings. They've got their tent here selling their stupid T-shirts aimed at Americans that say "Stonehenge Rocks!" on them. First time they put it in, they had to put a security guard around them because I said: "Guess what! I'm gonna be the one turning over your bloody trestle table. And that puts me in good company because a certain Christian done exactly the same with the money changers on the temple steps." You know what I mean?'

Arthur said he drew strength from the stones, just as they still drew strength from the people that gathered among them. Moreover he knew they had the power to change people. He had seen drunken louts climbing the monoliths – but over the course of solstices and equinoxes he had seen the same people return, becoming pilgrims who revered the stones, protected them and told off other people for climbing on them. I saw him on and off through the night. Sometimes he was performing rituals with Excalibur. One time he was having a selfie taken with Chinese tourists.

THE SHORTEST NIGHT

There were floodlights on the perimeter of the solstice site, yet their beams did not quite penetrate the stone circle.

Instead people brought their own lights to the stones: handheld iPhones and Androids cast an electric glow into the inner sanctum, illuminating figures who danced to the beat of seven African drums. The beat never stopped, though sometimes it surged, and in tandem the light intensified as new pilgrims were drawn by its ecstatic crescendo. There was whooping and chanting. Clouds exhaled by vapers sailed through the midnight air. Fairy Liquid bubbles drifted and popped against the highest trilithons. The closer you inched to the fallen altar stone the more you felt rather than heard the pulse of those seven drums – perceived the incendiary percussion in the pit of your stomach. It was loud – some could only take it for a short while before seeking respite beyond the enclosure of the circle, out in the cool vastness of that short night. Out there people sat on blankets, chatted, smoked. Shadowy figures pressed their foreheads against the outer stones in private prayer.

It was out there, in the small hours, that I fell into conversation with Rajkumar and Bishal. They were from Gurkha families, and this was their first summer solstice at the stones. Rajkumar was nearing 30 and had just married: he had first seen Stonehenge on a video at school in Nepal. For Bishal the connection seemed to go deeper. He was several years older and wore a black North Face jacket. A slow smile broadened with every word he spoke, so he beamed at the end of every sentence – before his face reset again. He was not wearing shoes.

'You have to walk barefoot here,' he told me, speaking quietly. 'So you get the energy from Mother Earth. You can't feel it – but you know, deep inside, it's doing something. It's just not going to happen straight away.'

Bishal said he was from a small mountain village that you could spot from planes descending into Kathmandu International. He had been born into a family where there wasn't enough money for shoes: as a kid he remembered villagers returning home from jobs in Hong Kong, showing off flashy gadgets. He vowed he would never be like them. In his teenage years he became a 'gangster', somehow fell off a bridge and broke his leg – it was a mad time of what he called 'young blood'. In 2008 he moved to Nuneaton with his family, and fell into an even worse crowd. He started using heroin – he remembered stealing from his mother. He remembered her tears. His older brother threatened to send him back to Nepal for rehab.

Instead he moved with his soldier brother to Tidworth, an army town on the eastern edge of Salisbury Plain. Here, far from the Midlands, even further from Kathmandu, something changed within him. Under the vast Wessex skies he searched for the strength to quit heroin and endured the pain of withdrawal, which he described as being like a 'rattling' sensation. That pain came even years later – there were times when he thought he could not take it any more. But then he made a pilgrimage across the Wiltshire fields, carrying with him a stick of incense. He sat down to meditate in sight of the stones.

'Stonehenge attracts you. When you first see it, it's all in your mind all the time. That's what happened to me. I used to come here all the time. I brought seeds for the birds – I'm connected with birds.'

Bishal's bird was the crow – it connected him to Garuda, the mount of Vishu. He said he felt no trauma when he meditated there: his mind became free. Spirits guided him. That was a few years ago, and now Bishal was in a better place. He worked as a manager at a pizza takeaway and in his spare time sold hippie-style clothes that he bought over from Nepal. He spoke reverently of friends – true yogis – who had successfully transcended their physical form and departed their bodies. He hadn't managed that yet – he was still learning. He was 'on the path' but felt something was about to change.

'People are awakening. People are trying to find out why we are here, what is our purpose. Right now they're keeping us in nine-to-five jobs: telling us to just buy a car, buy a house, make lots of money. But it's not about that. The time is coming.'

Bishal would not be staying for sunrise as he had to help Rajkumar move house in the morning. But he made me promise that, when dawn came, I would take off my shoes.

After the two left, the reign of darkness faltered – a violet sky sharpened against the silhouettes of the sarsen stones. Suddenly you could make out faces and imagine that (in some small way) tribes had assembled once again at the temple on the plain. There were pagans draped in foliage, wearing antlers, cosplaying horned gods. There were teenagers pulling an all-nighter, fired up on cans of Monster. Panpipes played under the flag of the Indigenous People of the Andes, men in blue turbans read from little books and a Welshman carried a dragon flag and a didgeridoo. Among these pilgrims you could read lifetimes: the toddlers who slept soundly under blankets in wheelbarrows; the gap-year girls lured here by dubious hippie boyfriends; couples who would ditch the hemp clothes and ponchos by freshers' week and break up by Christmas – but who might one day reflect on the midsummer of their lives from an office desk. And there were long-termers – whose crisp tattoos had grown vague and blue with the renewal of skin cells and the accumulation of so many solstices. Most interesting were the first-timers: the curious folk who had come on a whim to this place they knew from *Time Team*. They did not quite know what to expect but found themselves fired by the frenzy of drums, found a place where the year was turning, the rules were bending, where a lid had lifted on the weirdness and wonder of England. They peered inside. They could not take their eyes away.

It might by now seem late in the day to touch on the contemporary historical interpretations of Stonehenge: that the Neolithic temple started taking form around 3000 BC: that it may have been a temple of the dead, a counterpart to the temple of the living that stood at nearby Woodhenge. That it seemed possible Neolithic pilgrims made ritual journeys between the two sites, and around the wider sacred landscape of the plain. That the smaller stones – the bluestones – were quarried from the Preseli Hills of west Wales (where it was speculated that they had formed a separate stone circle) and that the mighty sarsens were quite possibly lugged down the Avon valley along which I had walked, setting the ground quaking as they went. Either carried by humankind or perhaps borne by glaciers (the latter was a minority view these days), these stones had come on a pilgrimage of their own to the plain.

Nothing stopped pilgrims lugging their own weighty interpretations here. This time I had my own. Over the course of just over a year I had climbed cliffs and mountains, walked city streets and tidal foreshores, followed rivers, railway lines and slept in a sea cave. My abiding memory of writing this book is of islands: the true islands of Iona and St Herbert's, the sometimes-island of Lindisfarne, the once-island of Glastonbury Tor, the island peak of Skirrid, where persecuted pilgrims sought sanctuary. The islanded hills of the Ridgeway not far from here, by now marooned in pre-dawn mist. The island of that shed in the sea. Consecrated by water, stone or contours, all these islands lay in orbit of a greater holy island, or else were set within it. The free festival had been an island of freedom in the United Kingdom. Its ghost could still be sensed that night – a submerged presence, within the stones where security guards seemed reluctant to step.

In building Stonehenge, those Neolithic masons had created an island in the sea of the plain, had, in the simplest terms, set a place apart. Theirs was an act recognized and honoured by the solstice-goers today. Those prehistoric builders, it seemed to me, had succumbed to a universal instinct – that mystery and magic required a permanent home beyond the lonely claustrophobia of the human mind. A physical location to which people might travel, where a community might gather to collectively consider the business of existence. Here they might share their burdens, make their load lighter for the return journey. Twentieth- and twenty-first-century pilgrims had come to Stonehenge, heaping new meanings, adding new ballast to this ancient site. Be they archaeologists, tourists, festival-goers or pilgrims – ancient or modern – the stones would be nothing but for the people who continually came here, who knotted their journeys to this place, who renewed its power with their presence. It was true of so many other places I had been.

Morning came not as a thunderbolt beam of light but a slow, diffuse and dreamy dawning: a sun-gilded mist. The drums stilled for a moment. I felt some of that light inside. And since I had stood on that causeway at Lindisfarne, I had come to see my home country in another light. Throughout my long journey I had encountered many people who said we were on the cusp of a great awakening, a new golden age. Some of them seemed deluded, dubious or daft, but in that short moment of communion between earth and sky, feeling the grass between my toes and sun on my face, I could not have disagreed with any of them.

It was said often that pilgrimage itself was entering a new golden age – that hundreds of thousands of people were now walking the path to Santiago, and binding their journeys with meanings. I too had wanted to walk that great Iberian path: I was someone who perceived wonder in those faraway places. The pandemic meant our country had been briefly cut off from the world, but now – in an age of global instability, when carbon emissions were wreaking damage on our planet – more of us would need to find our Jerusalem in our own backyard. To travel deeper, not further: to break through the crust of the familiar to find the fantastical. To feel something seismic beneath our feet, as I had done those midsummer days walking the plain.

And, if such a golden age was to come to Great Britain, what would also be needed was disobedience. A disobedience like the young man with sky-blue eyes who had a radical plan for Stonehenge. The disobedience of people like Tudor Pole, Hope Patten and others – who invited ire and mockery in daring to re-enchant this island. A disobedience to voices of reason and rationality – to sense there were mysteries that the mind could not solve, but which the beat of footsteps might. The disobedience of any pilgrim who stepped over the cordons, detoured from the official footpath – who followed an unmarked trail down to that great, echoing sea cave.

The thunder of the seven drums resumed. Eventually, the sun climbed higher, revealing people with grey, exhausted faces. The light flattened, and the moment had passed. Soon after someone started packing down the cheese toastie van. An Eddie Stobart truck boomed past on the A303. I also felt exhausted. I lay against a stone at the edge of the circle, and fell into a half-sleep, dimly registering the conversations of people coming and going.

'Is there a Greggs in Amesbury?'

'Top trick is, if you don't want Old Bill to see you haven't got a tax disc, just pop the bonnet up when they pull you over.'

'They said a minute here feels like a millennium and a millennium like a minute … load of bollocks if you ask me!'

'Now the stones are in a perfect circle. Tell me: how could the builders have done this, if they hadn't seen it from HIGH ABOVE? Now do you see what I'm saying?'

'Is Portia coming? I think maybe her phone died. What about the other guys from Hackney Wick?'

'Wahnsinnig. Was für ein Land ist …?'

[A man who sounded like he was talking about a fuse box] 'Try not to step there my love – that's where the power is strongest.'

'Can I bum a cig?'

'Om Mani Padme Om.'

'I just want to …'

'Shantih, Shantih.'

'I just want to stay in this field forever and ever and ever and I want to …'

'Excuse me.'

'EXCUSE ME, SIR.'

It was by now just gone half-past eight. A man in a hi-vis tabard was standing over me. He politely explained they had just 20 minutes to clear the site and would I mind making for the exit now please.

So I did as I was told.

Acknowledgements

My thanks and love to everyone who read all or part of this book in advance of publication, among them: Sam Birkin, Sean Bradbury, Flora Drury, Jessica Elgot, Ed Pulford, Peter Puxon, Bethan Smith, Stephen Smith and Dave Wilkinson. My thanks too to the editors who have encouraged my writing over the last decade, too many to name, but foremost among them: Amanda Canning, Duncan Craig, Liz Edwards, Peter Grunert, Tom Hall, Christa Larwood, Tom Robbins, Erin Riley, Orla Thomas and Rochelle Venables. Gratitude to my wonderful agent, Lisette Verhagen for having the faith, and likewise to editors Tomasz Hoskins, Fahmida Ahmed and Mathew Taylor at Bloomsbury Continuum.

The British Pilgrimage Trust website is an outstanding resource for anyone looking to undertake a modern pilgrimage (britishpilgrimage.org) – sincere thanks to Dawn Champion for conversations both on the road and during the writing of this book, and also to Guy Hayward. Thanks to Dr Anne Bailey for her perspectives on pilgrimage and reading list recommendations.

I owe the greatest thanks to Hannah, who offered both encouragement and the wisests of edits during a summer of writing. Without her this book would not have been written. This book is dedicated to her, Felix and Margot. It is also dedicated to Almaas, my oldest and best walking friend, and the rest of the wanderers too.

Notes

2. A CAVE

1 Charles Darwin, *The Works of Charles Darwin*, vol. 29 (New York: NYU Press, 2010), p. 129.
2 William Buckland, letter from William Buckland to Mary Talbot, 31 December 1822, quoted in Marianne Sommer, *Bones and Ochre: The Curious Afterlife of the Red Lady of Paviland* (Cambridge, MA: Harvard University Press 2008), p. 61.
3 William Buckland, *Reliquiae Diluvianae* (London: John Murray, 1823), p. 85.
4 William Jones of Usk, *Gods Warning to His People of England*, Early English Books Online, 2011.
5 Stephen Moss, 'The Secrets of Paviland Cave', *The Guardian* (25 April 2011).

3. A RIDGE

1 Henry Shukman 'Hiking History: England's Ancient Ridgeway Trail', *New York Times* (29 October 2009).
2 Richard Jefferies, *Wild Life in a Southern County* (Boston, MA: Roberts Brothers, 1879), p. 51.
3 Edward Thomas, *The Icknield Way* (London: Constable, 1929), p. 250.
4 Kenneth Grahame, *The Wind in the Willows* (London: The Reprint Society, 1954), p. 165.
5 Kenneth Grahame, *Pagan Papers* (London: Elkin Mathews and John Lane, 1894), p. 2.

6 Paul Newman, *Lost Gods of Albion* (Stroud: Sutton Publishing, 1997), p. 7.

7 Paul Newman, *Lost Gods of Albion*, p. 2.

8 'Wulf Ingessunu and Woden's Folk: How a 1980s TV Series Inspired a Racist Cult', radicalbritain.blogspot.com, 13 June 2014.

9 Clive Henry, 'The Swords of Wayland: From Family Television to Fascist Mythos', https://www.radicalrightanalysis.com, 20 January 2022.

10 John Aubrey, *Monumenta Britannica, or A Miscellany of British Antiquities*, vol. 1 (London, 1693).

4. AN ISLAND

1 Thomas Owen Clancy and Gilbert Markus, *Iona: The Earliest Poetry of a Celtic Monastery* (Edinburgh: Edinburgh University Press 1995), p. 147.

2 William Maxwell, *Iona and the Ionians* (Glasgow: Thomas Murray and Son, 1857), p. 35.

3 Adomnan, *Life of St Columba*, trans. Richard Sharpe (London: Penguin Classics 1995), Chapter 5.

4 Fiona Macleod, *Iona* (Edinburgh: Floris Books 1982), p. 34.

5 Fiona Macleod, *Iona*, p. 13.

6 Fiona Macleod, *Iona*, p. 26.

6. A ROAD

1 Hilaire Belloc, *The Old Road* (London: Constable, 1910), p. 2.

2 Hilaire Belloc, *The Old Road*, p. 2.

7. A MOUNTAIN

1 Hannah Cowell Roberts, 'Re-Examining Welsh Catholicism, *c.* 1660–1700', PhD thesis, Swansea University, 2014, p. 155.

2 Fred Hando, *Hando's Gwent* (Llanfoist: Blorenge Books, 1987), p. 87.

3 Sir John Trevor, *An Abstract of Several Examinations Taken upon Oath in the Counties of Monmouth and Hereford* (London: John Gain, 1680), p. 14.

8. A WELL

1   Geoffrey Ashe, *King Arthur's Avalon* (Cheltenham: The History Press, 2013), p. 2.
2   Signed statement from Wellesley Tudor Pole, 22 February 1907, quoted in Patrick Benham, *The Avalonians* (Glastonbury: Gothic Image, 1993), p. 60.
3   Gerry Fenge, *The Two Worlds of Wellesley Tudor Pole* (Everett, WA: Starseed Publications, 2011), ebook location 3926.
4   Quoted in Albert Bigelow Paine, *Mark Twain: A Biography*, vol. 3, part 2, *1907–1910* (Project Gutenberg, 2004), eBook #2987.
5   *Daily Express* (26 July 1907).
6   *Chalice Well: The Story of a Living Sanctuary* (Glastonbury: Chalice Well Press 2009), p. 123.

11. A STADIUM

1   Lee Grimsditch, 'Most ECHO Readers Say They Won't Be Backing England on Sunday', *Liverpool Echo* (10 July 2021).
2   *Catholic Pictorial* (23 April 1989).

12. THE STONES

1   Penny Rimbaud, *Shibboleth: A Bit of My Revolting Life* (London: Exitstencil Press, 2021), p. 59.
2   Penny Rimbaud, *Shibboleth: A Bit of My Revolting Life*, p. 149.
3   *The Times* (13 August 1974).
4   Penny Rimbaud, *Shibboleth: A Bit of My Revolting Life*, p. 155.
5   Andy Worthington, *Stonehenge: Celebration and Subversion* (Nottingham: Alternative Albion, 2004), p. 89.
6   Andy Worthington, *Stonehenge: Celebration and Subversion*, p. 139.

Index